CREATING NEW EDUCATIONAL
COMMUNITIES

CREATING NEW EDUCATIONAL COMMUNITIES

*Ninety-fourth Yearbook of the
National Society for the Study of Education*

PART I

Edited by

JEANNIE OAKES AND KAREN HUNTER QUARTZ

Editor for the Society
KENNETH J. REHAGE

19  95

Distributed by THE UNIVERSITY OF CHICAGO PRESS • CHICAGO, ILLINOIS

The National Society for the Study of Education

Founded in 1901 as successor to the National Herbart Society, the National Society for the Study of Education has provided a means by which the results of serious study of educational issues could become a basis for informed discussion of those issues. The Society's two-volume yearbooks, now in their ninety-fourth year of publication, reflect the thoughtful attention given to a wide range of educational problems during those years. In 1971 the Society inaugurated a series of substantial publications on Contemporary Educational Issues to supplement the yearbooks. Each year the Society's publications contain contributions to the literature of education from more than a hundred scholars and practitioners who are doing significant work in their respective fields.

An elected Board of Directors selects the subjects with which volumes in the yearbook series are to deal and appoints committees to oversee the preparation of manuscripts. A special committee created by the Board performs similar functions for the series on Contemporary Educational Issues.

The Society's publications are distributed each year without charge to members in the United States, Canada, and elsewhere throughout the world. The Society welcomes as members all individuals who desire to receive its publications. Information about current dues may be found in the back pages of this volume.

This volume, *Creating New Educational Communities*, is Part I of the Ninety-fourth Yearbook of the Society. Part II, published at the same time, is entitled *Changing Populations/Changing Schools*.

A listing of the Society's publications still available for purchase may be found in the back pages of this volume.

Library of Congress Catalog Number: 94-069015
ISSN: 0077-5762

Published 1995 by
THE NATIONAL SOCIETY FOR THE STUDY OF EDUCATION

5835 Kimbark Avenue, Chicago, Illinois 60637

First Printing
Printed in the United States of America

Acknowledgments

The National Society for the Study of Education is indebted to all whose efforts have made it possible to bring out this volume. Readers will recognize at once that these authors are no strangers to schools and classrooms. Moreover, the work upon which they report here demonstrates a commitment to the concept that genuine reform takes place in settings where students and teachers work together to "create new educational communities."

We are especially grateful to Jeannie Oakes and Karen Hunter Quartz, co-editors of the Yearbook, for planning the volume so as to include reports on ongoing projects in several parts of the United States and for inviting contributions from authors whose accounts of their work will surely be helpful to others. In spite of their own busy schedules, Dr. Oakes and Dr. Quartz have put into this enterprise the incredible amounts of time and effort needed to bring the work to completion on schedule.

Professor Margaret Early of the University of Florida at Gainesville has devoted many hours to reading manuscripts for this volume and to preparing penetrating commentaries on each chapter. The Society is greatly in her debt for her invaluable contribution to the editing of this Yearbook.

Robert Mehler, assistant in the NSSE office, has prepared the name index.

NSSE is proud to add this volume to its distinguished series of Yearbooks.

KENNETH J. REHAGE
Editor for the Society

Table of Contents

Section One
Introduction and Overview

CHAPTER

Section Two
New Educational Communities

Section Three
Implications for Research and Policy

Section One
INTRODUCTION AND OVERVIEW

CHAPTER I

Normative, Technical, and Political Dimensions of Creating New Educational Communities

JEANNIE OAKES

A century ago, in a period of school reform as energetic as the one we now inhabit, Charles Eliot, president of Harvard University and author of one of that era's most important reform documents, reflected, "It is a curious fact that we Americans habitually underestimate the capacity of pupils at almost every stage of education from the primary school through the university. . . . It seems to me probable that the proportion of grammar school children incapable of pursuing geometry, algebra, and a foreign language would turn out to be much smaller than we now imagine."[1] Eliot's confidence reverberates in the Committee of Ten recommendations in 1893 for reorganizing American high schools. His optimism was not to prevail, however. National and local norms and politics of the turn of the century drove schooling far from Eliot's vision of highly rigorous, academic schooling for all students.

By 1925, other reformers had transformed the purpose, character, and organization of elementary and secondary schools. What was in 1890 a rather haphazard assortment of mostly ungraded "common" primary schools and a handful of secondary schools serving a small and privileged segment of the nation's youth became by the late 1920s bureaucratic mass institutions characterized by such organizational strategies as distinct school "subjects," age grading, ability grouping, and curriculum differentiation and tracking.

Jeannie Oakes is Professor of Curriculum and Education Policy, Graduate School of Education, University of California at Los Angeles.

The set of school reforms proposed by Eliot at the turn of the century made sense to most policymakers and educators, given the social and political circumstances of the time. The quite staggering influx of Southern and Eastern European immigrants, changes in the nation's economic base and industrial structure (accompanied by the shift from a largely rural to an increasingly urban society), and the Topsy-like growth of public secondary schools as mass institutions worked together to render nineteenth-century schooling inefficient and inadequate to meet the demands of modern life. The social ideas and movements that permeated these three decades—scientific management and industrial efficiency; social Darwinism; the intelligence quotient (IQ); the Americanization of immigrants; the psychology of adolescence; and an apparent shift in the popular conception of a democratic education—shaped the cultures and structures of the newly reformed schools.

School reform was viewed as both necessary and desirable if secondary schooling was to be relevant to its new twentieth-century constituency—a school population increasingly diverse in ability, social class, and ethnic background. The need for transformation was bluntly articulated as early as 1909 by Ellwood Cubberley: "Our city schools will soon be forced to give up the exceedingly democratic idea that all are equal, and our society devoid of classes . . . and to begin a specialization of educational effort along many lines in an attempt to adapt the school to the needs of these many classes."[2] In a somewhat gentler version, this view was cemented as conventional wisdom in 1918 with the publication of *Cardinal Principles of Secondary Education.* That report argued for the modern comprehensive high school with clearly differentiated programs of studies for students of different abilities, declaring that "education in a democracy should develop in each individual the knowledge, interests, ideals, habits, and powers whereby he will find his place and use that place to shape both himself and society toward ever nobler ends."[3]

Clearly, the cultures and structures of reformed elementary and secondary schools at the turn of the century embodied norms giving great significance to individual and group differences in intelligence, as well as norms of equality and the schools' obligation to serve democracy by providing practical, useful studies to the masses of less capable students. Schools were expected to provide lower-class immigrant children, who were considered of lower intelligence and diminished moral capacity, with specific and direct training for responsible citizenship and work: what Finney in 1929 called "followership for the duller intellects."[4] This reform direction was considered both as an instrument for securing economic growth and social stability and as an ethically commendable response to the growing demand for secondary education.

Nevertheless, these reforms also reflected the political struggle for wealth, status, and power in a rapidly changing society with a rapidly increasing demand for universal access to a high school education. Bureaucratic, differentiated schools provided white and wealthy parents a means to transfer the privilege of access to their children (by way of school credentials) in the merit-based, modern industrial society, at the same time that they trained others with technical skills and socialized them with the work habits and attitudes such as proper deportment, punctuality, willingness to be supervised and managed, which were required if they were to "fit in" as factory workers.[5]

Turn-of-the-century school reform, then, was a compromise, an accommodation to the complex interactions between concepts of democratic schooling and perceptions of social differentiation from wider ideological, social, and economic contexts. An important effect was to channel poor children—children who were not "smart"—into subordinated school curricula which would lead to subordinate economic and political roles and to restricted social mobility. This compromise—the battle that Charles Eliot lost—has shaped schooling throughout the twentieth century.

Charles Eliot Redux

More than one hundred years later, impressive numbers of education researchers, reformers, and practitioners have returned to Charles Eliot's unabashedly optimistic view of U.S. students' intellectual capacity, and the conviction that schools can and must be places where *all* children, not just a few, can be "smart." While most assertions that "all children can learn" may be little more than current window dressing for the same old beliefs and practices, a growing number of researchers, educators, and policymakers across the nation are taking quite seriously a radical new view of children's intellectual capacity. In addition to critiquing conventional school practices, these educators are mounting efforts to create new learning communities where all children can be smart.

These promising democratic reform projects share a commitment to comprehensive reform, recognizing that changes in any one aspect of schooling such as curricula or assessment must be accompanied by other changes in school and classroom. Most of these projects aim simultaneously at developing integrated curricula, more varied pedagogy, multidimensional assessment strategies, heterogeneous grouping, and more flexible use of time, space, and staffing. These strategies are viewed as a comprehensive reform bundle rather than as a reform menu from which schools pick or choose. Many projects effect a reorganization of learning environments in schools-within-schools or interdisciplinary teams, and they expand learning opportunities outside the classroom and beyond the school day. Techniques for involving parents and community members are also central to many of these new learning communities, combining home, school, and community-based learning to provide students with an integrated core of knowledge as well as social support.

The comprehensive and mutually supportive sets of "technical" changes being mounted by the research-into-practice reforms described in the chapters in this volume challenge the traditional norms and political relations that govern school activities and bolster conventional school cultures. Educators and researchers participating in these end-of-the-twentieth-century reforms are subjecting to greater scrutiny beliefs and practices that have seemed rational and democratic for nearly a hundred years. For example, they are raising serious questions about the ways schools respond differently to children who are judged according to conventional criteria to be bright, average, or dull. School practices such as ability grouping, remedial and compensatory programs, and curriculum tracking, conventionally considered appropriate responses to individual differences in intellectual ability, are being scrutinized for how they create insupportable inequalities in students' access to curriculum content, learning experiences, and qualified teachers, with children who are thought to be less able simply getting fewer of the rich experiences likely to help them develop and learn. While few if any of the current crop of reformers think that all children should be expected to do and learn exactly the same things at school, the driving force in these projects is increasing the engagement and learning of both the most and least successful students over what has previously been thought possible.

Members of the new learning communities described here appear to be working toward a more integrative approach to knowledge and learning, more cooperative forms of social interaction, and a more just distribution of resources and authority. Moreover, they are seeking broad community support for their efforts.

Why Now?

Are these 1990s reforms any more likely than Eliot's turn-of-the-century proposals to take hold and reshape the culture and structure of schools in the next decade? Much about our current social and economic turmoil mirrors quite clearly the upheaval of a century ago. To be sure, current patterns of immigration from Latin America and Southeast Asia raise renewed fear about the demise of our national language and culture, as well as xenophobic conceptions of the abilities of these newcomers. Concerns about crime and degradation in big cities press educators toward social control in schools rather than intellectual pursuits, just as at the beginning of this century. Moreover, as at that time, today's economic insecurity and unsettling shifts in the nature and organization of work in the United States add a sense of urgency about socializing and training newcomers, as well as other "underprepared" groups, to participate in the highly sophisticated technological work of the future.

Not only do the reforms face these daunting social conditions; they also face the normative and political legacy of the turn of the century that is embedded in the cultures of most contemporary schools. These normative and political cultures are clearly antithetical to the changes these projects seek.

Current school practice remains grounded in faulty conceptions that intelligence is global (for example, a single entity that can be measured by an IQ test), that it is fixed quite early (either before birth or soon thereafter), and that learning is primarily the accumulation of a linear sequence of knowledge and skills. Also important are historically rooted beliefs about individual and group differences in intelligence and learning. These conceptions play out in school as educators interpret the skills and knowledge that educationally and economically privileged parents pass on to their children as innate intelligence—interpretations that guide decisions about the learning opportunities afforded to different students. The fact that learning capacity seems to be unevenly distributed among groups—with disadvantaged minorities exhibiting less—appears to schools to be beyond their control. Thus, schools typically conclude that the disproportionate assignment of low-income and minority students to special remedial programs consisting of deadeningly repetitive skill-and-drill curricula is an appropriate, if regrettable, response. Even more troubling, these interpretations are reinforced by ostensibly objective standardized tests, which not only fail to measure different forms of intelligence, but are also biased toward the knowledge and skills that advantaged students learn at home.

Moreover, the factory-like, industrial-age structure of schools remains solidly intact, with teachers isolated in assembly-line classrooms performing their specialized piece of the work. Rigid school calendars and classroom hours wedded to units of school credit standardize students' learning time. The notion of scientific management—that complicated production tasks can be made more efficient when divided into hierarchical levels and specialized categories—persists in schools, even as it loses credibility in industry.

Perhaps most pernicious, old power structures remain. Conventional school practices are sustained, in part, by the political interests of constituents—interests that are shaped by the norms mentioned above. The pressure placed on educators by savvy parents who want their children enrolled in the "best" classes is just one manifestation of these interests. White and wealthy parents seem as able as ever to use the structure and practice of schooling to advantage their own children. Special academic magnet schools, separate programs for gifted and talented students, and Advanced Placement courses typically provide contemporary enclaves for advantaged (mostly white) students in public schools. In a competitive system that offers only a small percentage of students slots in the "best" classes, these parents have few options but to push to have their children better educated than others. Efforts to tamper with these programs in the name of reform run headlong into vehement resistance from individual parents and organized advocacy groups. Within classrooms, efforts to have students work cooperatively in small learning communities are targeted as exploitation of bright students on behalf of the less able.

This political pressure reflects a competitive, individualistic attitude toward the purpose of schooling, but in racially mixed schools it takes on another dimension. Although not all politically efficacious parents are white, in most schools white parents, especially middle-class white parents, better understand the inequalities in the school's structure and feel more confident that the school will respond positively to their pressure. Because all schools need political support, not only for funding and physical resources but also for credibility, policies that provide advantages to more privileged students, even if they result in racial segregation within desegregated schools, are often exchanged for the political credit that more advantaged and involved parents bring to a school. The politics of privilege have reined in more than a few educators and policymakers who have sought reform.

Yet despite these structural and cultural similarities between the current education reform environment and that of a hundred years ago, there are grounds for optimism for today's reform efforts. Times are very different now, as well. Perhaps most striking, the long-standing platitude that "all children can learn" has been given new meaning by recent theory and evidence about intelligence and cognition. This scholarship argues compellingly against conventional notions of intelligence as fixed and unidimensional, and of learning as the process of receiving knowledge transmitted by others. To the contrary, psychologists now view intellectual capacity as developmental and multidimensional, and learning as a process of constructing meaning.[6] This new view argues from a solid base of theory and empirical evidence that all children can be far "smarter" than conventional definitions and measures of intelligence seem to allow. It provides considerable support to reformers' optimism that, given the right opportunity and support, nearly every child is capable of achieving every worthwhile educational goal, regardless of gender, regardless of skin tone, and regardless of their scores on outmoded measures of intellectual ability. Importantly, because this new knowledge largely discredits the types of tests schools use to assess students' "ability"—that is, their "potential"—this work also helps many educators to shake the lingering suspicion that minority students are not as intelligent as whites because they tend to score less well.

Consequently, the success of these new learning communities is likely to depend not only on the cleverness of the new techniques they employ, but also on the extent to which they use this new scholarship to ground a fundamental rethinking of long-standing educational beliefs and values. If they are to succeed in sustaining and spreading such reforms, educators and researchers attempting to build commitment for these projects must confront head on obsolete conceptions of intelligence and tackle the deep-seated racist and class-biased attitudes and prejudices these conceptions support. Educators, policymakers, and parents as well, must come to view intellectual ability as primarily a *social construction*, like racial and gender biases, rather than as a genetic inheritance. For as long as the *capacity to learn* is understood, for all practical purposes, as unalterable, and the range in capacity among school children is perceived as great, reforms based on the notion that all children can learn will not seem sensible.

Additionally, for reforms such as those discussed in this volume to make sense, educators will need to consider the shortcomings of the deeply ingrained value of bureaucratic efficiency when applied to schooling. For example, does the practice of teaching distinct school subjects in regularly scheduled chunks of time over 180 days really define a meaningful increment of learning? Does the well-established practice of having one teacher alone in a classroom of thirty students provide the most educationally effective combination of adults and children? Is the sorting of students into separate classes and providing them with differentiated curricula really the best way to accommodate differences among them?

Finally, reformers are beginning to face the fact that Americans value competition and individualism over cooperation and the common good and that these values further bolster and legitimize norms which imply that "good" education is a scarce commodity available only to a few. Reformers must also confront directly the fact that, although American public education might have been intended originally to promote community interests by preparing children for participation in democratic governance, the emphasis during the twentieth century has been on what individual students can "get out" of schooling in terms of income, power, or status.

The move away from the dominant ethic of bureaucracy and competitive individualism and toward more democratic values of support, diversity, and community is most possible within a political climate of shared responsibility and trust. Projects aiming to create new learning communities, therefore, attend to establishing new political relations among teachers, administrators, parents, students, and community members. This implies acts that are explicitly political in nature such as granting permission, taking risks, redistributing power, and forming coalitions. Implementing democratic reforms may also require that competing interests, such as advocates for the gifted, for the disadvantaged, and for minorities, create a collective advocacy for schools that serve all children well. Building such coalitions among these divergent constituencies (and maintaining political credit) probably means that schools undergoing reform guarantee that their new technologies will create educational opportunities that are *at least* as rich and rigorous as those previously enjoyed by a few. But it also requires confronting likely opposition to a system that takes away the *comparative* advantages enjoyed and effectively used (both in school and beyond) by children whose parents are privileged.

Central to a more equitable distribution of schooling opportunities is a more equitable distribution among all educational stakeholders of the power to make educational decisions. This political thrust attempts not to take power away from those parents who now enjoy it, but rather to develop power among those parents and community members who are currently without it. The hoped-for political process that would result promises to be more inclusive and balanced, reflecting a new norm that schools and classrooms should be participatory and caring communities for all their members. Effecting this new distribution of power, however, is a political process that requires astute political leadership by educators.

Efforts to create democratic learning communities where all children can be smart, then, launch a critical and unsettling rethinking of the most common and fundamental educational beliefs and values. They also require a fundamental realignment of political interests. Such rethinking and realignment challenges not only the efficacy, but also the moral rightness of entrenched views of what schools are for, how schooling should be conducted, and who should have access to what types of learning experiences. That is an incredibly tall order for school reform. Yet without these fundamental changes in the culture of schooling, these reforms seem likely to repeat the usual cycle of superficial changes wherein new techniques are merely co-opted to fit the existing norms and politics of schooling. If that happens, the modern day Eliots who have contributed to this volume will have lost again.

New Educational Communities

Our purpose, then, in assembling this collection of essays is to address the technical, normative, and political dimensions of creating learning communities where all children can be smart. It brings together recent theory, research, practice, and policy analysis from those deeply involved in better understanding what creating, defending, and sustaining such schools in North America might entail. In the essays that follow, researchers actively involved in school reform efforts combine their insights with those of practitioners to discuss (1) how they challenge deeply held norms and political relations within the context of comprehensive technical reform, (2) what they take to be evidence that such changes are actually occurring and having their intended impact, and (3) how they hope to sustain these reforms as "regularities" of the school culture. These highly visible reform efforts, therefore, receive a new perspective as their advocates and researchers go beyond the predominantly technical language of research on school reform to recognize as important the beliefs, values, relationships, and power allocations required to create learning communities where all children can be smart.

In chapter 2, Elizabeth G. Cohen, Diane Kepner, and Patricia Swanson discuss the Program for Complex Instruction—a "multiability" approach to curriculum and instruction that engages heterogeneous learners in high-level social studies tasks. Cohen and her colleagues provide a provocative discussion of how cultural beliefs about intelligence, race, and social class undergird the problem of status hierarchies in classrooms. They show how the dominant belief system surrounding "smartness" or intelligence shapes students' expectations of their peers' competence and incompetence when working in small groups and, as a consequence, determines the extent to which students participate and learn. They also make clear that, just as students' beliefs about their peers' levels of "smartness" need to be challenged, so too do teachers' beliefs about their students' abilities. They describe the dynamics of changing students' and teachers' expectations about "smartness" with a "multiability" curriculum. Cohen and her colleagues argue, "If the curriculum only requires reading, writing, and computing, then it is not possible to talk about multiple abilities and to find intellectual abilities on which each low-status student will excel." They illustrate how, when teachers use new strategies for reaching low-status students and those students perform well, these strategies bring about a shift in the way students' capacities are judged.

In chapter 3, Kris Gutierrez and Brenda Meyer describe efforts in Los Angeles to create communities of effective practice for language-minority students. They describe promising approaches to writing instruction in classrooms enrolling language-minority Latino children, highlighting the use of "responsive/collaborative scripts" that alter teachers' and students' roles in classroom learning. These classroom contexts allow students to function both as novices and as experts, assisting one another to develop literacy skills. These efforts stem from beliefs and values quite contrary to conventional assumptions about language arts teaching. In communities of effective practice, literacy for Latino immigrant students is grounded in an understanding of the relationship between language development and the context in which it occurs, including the socially constructed contexts of schools and classrooms. In other words, this new approach embod-ies the belief that, if literacy instruction is based on an understanding of the nature of language development, which is socially constructed and contextually influenced, then all children will become literate. Gutierrez and Meyer describe how difficult classroom transformation of this sort is, and they argue that it requires "fundamental changes in the social relationships" in schools and classrooms, and between schools and their communities.

In chapter 4, Mary Catherine Swanson, Hugh Mehan, and Lea Hubbard describe the AVID project based in San Diego. AVID places previously low-achieving, minority students in college preparatory classes in senior high schools throughout the county. During an elec-tive which meets each day, the project also provides these students with the support and study skills necessary to succeed in these chal-lenging academic classes. In their essay, Swanson and her colleagues outline the normative and political bases for the program, as well as the operational strategies that contribute to AVID's success in prepar-ing underrepresented students for college: (1) markers of group iden-tity and opportunities for group solidarity; (2) explicit socialization in the hidden curriculum; (3) teacher advocacy and sponsorship; and (4) formation of voluntary associations. At the same time as AVID focuses on providing a demanding academic program and a system of supports for a targeted group of low-achieving students, Swanson and her col-leagues argue that only when low achievement is considered a school-wide problem will high schools become learning communities in which all children can be smart.

In chapter 5, Robert E. Slavin and Nancy A. Madden assert that it is difficult, if not impossible, to create schools and classrooms where all children can be smart if some students are very poor readers. Moreover, they argue that reading failure is "fundamentally pre-ventable." Their prevention strategy, Success for All, is a comprehen-sive program of classroom organization, curriculum, and pedagogy in the early elementary grades. Success for All, by its very name, suggests that no child will fall behind, and its comprehensive approach—including reading tutors, a structured reading program, eight-week reading assessments, preschool and kindergarten, family support team, program facilitator, teachers and teacher training, special education, and advisory committee—stresses prevention and immediate, inten-sive intervention when trouble arises. With comprehensive approaches to reform such as this one, Slavin and Madden argue, children can become "skillful, strategic, and joyful readers." Achieving this, "heterogeneity among students could be celebrated, . . . a resource rather than a problem. Then we could truly create schools that would work for all students."

My colleagues Gretchen Guiton, Jennifer Gong, Karen Quartz, Martin Lipton, Julie Balisok, and I explore *Turning Points* in chapter 6, a national effort spearheaded by the Carnegie Corporation of New York to engage states and schools together in reforming education in the middle grades. *Turning Points* brings ideas about how schools should be made developmentally appropriate for young adolescents, and, at the same time, become inclusive and socially just communities where even the most disadvantaged students excel. The eight principles that guide the reform effort simultaneously challenge classroom practice, school organization, governance arrangements, and relationships between schools and communities.

Ann Lieberman, Beverly Falk, and Leslie Alexander in chapter 7 focus on the role of leaders in six elementary schools that are members of the Center for Collaborative Education, an affiliate of the Coalition of Essential Schools, in District 4 of New York City Schools. All six schools are learner-centered and are philosophically rooted in progressivism. They view teachers as facilitators and their professional development as a process of collegial dialogue and reflection. The role of leader is redefined as a "teacher-director" and the entire school culture as a democratic school community. The authors explore the formation of leadership values, particularly how leaders can develop and sustain norms that support learner-centeredness within an inquiring, democratic community. The political dimensions involved in balancing tensions are also discussed, especially in terms of how teacher-directors in these schools balance competing challenges and commitments from both outside and inside the school community.

Thomas Edison Middle School, described in chapter 8 by Gene Chasin and Henry Levin, embodies the principles of the Accelerated Schools movement, wherein educators, staff, and parents engage in inquiry-based "internal transformation of the school culture" in schools serving at-risk children. This schoolwide inquiry begins with "taking stock" of the school and proceeds as "cadres" of faculty, staff, and parents investigate solutions to recognized school and classroom problems. Chasin and Levin describe the change process as stemming from the same principles as those that are to guide student learning in Accelerated Schools: "The overall training approach is based upon a constructivist model in which it is assumed that humans learn most effectively when they actively construct their own understanding of phenomena rather than being passive recipients of someone else's understanding." Throughout, the school's inquiry process is guided by a set of agreed-upon principles: shared focus on bringing all students into the mainstream; local school responsibility for educational processes and outcomes; and building on the strengths of students, their parents, and the faculty and staff of the school. While the Accelerated School model has been used more often by elementary schools, Chasin and Levin use the example of Edison to demonstrate the process at the middle school.

In chapter 9, Adria Steinberg and Larry Rosenstock reflect on CityWorks, a project aimed at redefining vocational education and its purpose in high schools. CityWorks focuses on community development and integrated academic and vocational curricula in which students can be smart with both their hands and their minds. Steinberg and Rosenstock argue that two conditions are central to bringing about a radical redefinition of vocational education that challenges the assumptions or norms upon which prior practice has been based. First, teachers need time to meet, plan, and collaborate on projects. Second, it is important to be open about change and invite the scrutiny of others; this openness pushes participants to describe the program well, which in turn convinces stakeholders of the inevitability of change. Like many of the authors in this volume, Steinberg and Rosenstock argue that because teachers are not "empty vessels into which the current wisdom can be poured," it is important "to respect and make room for them as thinkers as well as doers."

Project Spectrum and the New City School are described by Mara Krechevsky, Thomas Hoerr, and Howard Gardner in chapter 10 as illustrative of Project Zero's reform efforts—projects grounded in Gardner's theory of multiple intelligences. The chapter contrasts Project Spectrum, a laboratory-based effort to reconstruct teaching and assessment, with New City, a field-based experiment to implement the theory of multiple intelligences throughout an urban elementary school. Both efforts draw on the new conception of intelligence to "offer a variety of stimulating, hands-on materials and experiences drawn from the nonschool world that will engage children and encourage their investigation." These two efforts also share common principles about teaching, learning, and assessment; yet, each of these efforts is different in ways that are appropriate to their context. The authors conclude: "From the many other 'lab' and 'field' experiences of MI that we have witnessed in the past few years, we can assert that these other stories would be as complex and in many ways as different from one another as the two accounts chronicled here."

In chapter 11, Paul Heckman, Christine Confer, and Jean Peacock describe the Educational and Community Change (ECC) Project which brings together researchers, teachers, students, parents, and other community members with the common goal of "reinventing" urban elementary schools and their neighborhoods. The ECC project is based on three propositions: (1) democratic norms will best promote reinvention; (2) educational development is furthered when adults and children make substantive changes in their schools and communities; and (3) educational advancement is achieved and interconnections between school and community are developed best when the local educational ecology serves as the axis for change. These propositions guide the project's work toward simultaneous school and community development (expanded learning opportunities, parent and community involvement, and decentralized governance) structured through interdisciplinary, thematic, "real" curricula. Heckman and his colleagues provide examples of changes that illustrate vividly the dynamics of normative and political reform, including the development of teaching and learning about trash—a reform idea that emerged from collaborative dialogue about "real work" and made its way into the classroom, the community, and finally into a city council meeting covered by the media.

In chapter 12, Patricia Wasley, Sherry King, and Christine Louth describe a little discussed aspect of Theodore Sizer's Coalition for Essential Schools—a reform effort aimed at transforming high schools into democratic, academically challenging learning communities. The authors describe how the process of collaborative inquiry among researchers and practitioners is used in the Coalition to promote normative and technical shifts in school practice. Targeting a critical incident of feeding back a "snapshot" to one school, the researcher (Wasley), the school's principal (King), and a teacher (Louth) each recount how the inquiry process challenges deeply ingrained norms of teacher autonomy and researcher detachment. They argue that only when the adults at a school are engaged in using *their own* minds well is it likely that they will create schools in which students use their minds well. Collaborative critical inquiry among adults is essential, not simply as a promising change strategy per se, but also because it matches the content of the curricular changes being sought in this reform. Like many of the authors in this volume, Wasley and her colleagues demonstrate quite poignantly that reforms aimed at creating schools where "all children can be smart" require change processes that depart dramatically from approaches to implementation that merely substitute one technology for another.

The last section of this volume offers two perspectives on the efficacy and promise of these reform efforts. Kati Haycock first looks at the implications of schoolwide reform for national policy, arguing that categorical programs such as Chapter 1 must be radically reformulated if they are to promote such efforts as those described in this volume. Then Karen Quartz examines the promise of these reform projects for transforming the ways schools approach change, arguing that sustaining such radical changes depends upon fostering new norms to guide reform enterprises—norms that reflect the concern of a new culture for transformative reform rather than the concern of the dominant culture for stabilizing reform.

NOTES

1. Charles W. Eliot, "Shortening and Enriching the Grammar School Course," in *Charles W. Eliot and Popular Education*, edited by Edward A. Krug (New York: Teachers College Press, 1961), pp. 52-53. Eliot was chair of the National Education Association's Committee of Ten on Secondary Studies that issued its report on the reform of secondary education in 1893.

2. Ellwood P. Cubberley, *Changing Conceptualizations of Education* (New York: Houghton Mifflin, 1909), pp. 18-19.

3. National Education Association, Commission for the Reorganization of Secondary Education, *Cardinal Principles of Secondary Education* (Washington, DC: National Education Association, 1918).

4. Ross L. Finney, *A Sociological Philosophy of Education* (New York: Macmillan, 1929), p. 387.

5. Among historians there is little disagreement about the sequence of events that led to curriculum differentiation in twentieth-century high schools. There is, however, considerable diversity in historians' interpretation of why and how these events came about and in their assessment of the consequences for schools and students. See Jeannie Oakes, Adam Gamoran, and Reba Page, "Curriculum Differentiation: Opportunities, Outcomes, and Meanings," in *Handbook of Research on Curriculum*, edited by Philip W. Jackson (New York: Macmillan, 1992).

6. For examples of work that argues compellingly that intelligence is multifaceted and developmental and that learning is a complex process of constructing meaning, see Howard Gardner, *Frames of Mind: The Theory of Multiple Intelligences* (New York: Basic Books, 1983) and chapter 10 of this volume. See also, Robert J. Sternberg, *Beyond IQ: A Triarchic Theory of Human Intelligence* (New York: Cambridge University Press, 1984) and idem, *Applied Intelligence* (Boston: Harcourt Brace Jovanovich, 1986).

Section Two
NEW EDUCATIONAL COMMUNITIES

CHAPTER **II**

Dismantling Status Hierarchies in Heterogeneous Classrooms

ELIZABETH G. COHEN, DIANE KEPNER,
AND PATRICIA SWANSON

"Oh, she never knows anything. I'm not going to ask her what to do." "He's really smart—he reads so beautifully." "She is just the best student—so verbal and smart; there isn't anything she doesn't do very well on." "That kid is clueless—just not too swift." "She's so quiet and does her work so carefully—I wish I had more like her." "Like most children who can't speak English well, he has trouble with abstractions."

How many of us have heard statements very much like these? How many of us have said something similar? How many of us have used in our research the same assumptions about student intelligence?

We should not be surprised to recognize ourselves in these statements because the underlying ideas are found all around us. These statements reveal beliefs that are deeply embedded in Western culture—beliefs about the nature of what it is to be "smart" and about what are valid indicators of "smartness" in students.

These same beliefs constitute a major barrier to educational reform. A key part of this belief system is the assumption that intelligence is unidimensional and that there is only one way to be intelligent.

Elizabeth G. Cohen is Professor of Education and Sociology in the School of Education at Stanford University, where she is also the Director of the Program for Complex Instruction. Diane Kepner is also connected with the Program for Complex Instruction in the School of Education at Stanford University. Patricia Swanson is Assistant Professor of Education at California State University—Stanislaus at Turlock, California.

Thus it makes sense to talk about people in terms of their placement along a continuum of "smartness." Furthermore, where a person stands on this dimension predicts competence on an infinite set of intellectual tasks.

These beliefs about the nature of intelligence are linked to status orders that form within the classroom. High-status students are believed by their teachers and peers to be very intelligent; low-status students are seen to be intellectually incompetent. In this chapter we will discuss the problem of status hierarchies in the classroom. We will describe the sources of status differences and how these differences relate to the beliefs we have described. We will present evidence of the consequences of status hierarchies for participation and learning. As part of the work of the Program for Complex Instruction at Stanford University, we have developed several ways to modify these problems of status differences so that many more students are successful in the classroom. These will be described here. Finally, we discuss the challenges of implementing what has been learned from research and development in schools and classrooms.

The three authors of this chapter have worked closely together as part of the Program for Complex Instruction. Complex instruction is a set of curricular and instructional strategies designed for heterogeneous classrooms. The teaching objectives are conceptual and stress higher-order thinking. Students use each other as resources in cooperative groups, working on demanding, open-ended tasks requiring a wide range of intellectual abilities and skills. The three authors bring different perspectives to the topic of dismantling status hierarchies. One is the perspective of the classroom teacher who has had practical experience in treating problems of dominance and nonparticipation arising from status orders. A second perspective is that of a staff developer who has worked with teachers while they mastered the underlying concepts and the treatments presented here. Still a third perspective is that of the researcher and program developer who has seen the work on dismantling status hierarchies develop from academic theories, through laboratory and classroom experiments, to practical and widely disseminated strategies for teachers. There is not a clear-cut division of labor here, for each of us has played more than one of these roles.

Status Hierarchies in the Classroom

Classrooms are public places. Evaluations that teachers make are not private; students eagerly compare their written performances and make their own evaluations of each other's public performances. Thus, in most classrooms, the perceptions of where one stands on a single dimension of academic ability is generally agreed-upon knowledge.

This ranking on perceived academic ability becomes an academic status order. Those seen as "smart" are expected to be good at all school tasks. Those seen as "not smart" are expected to be incompetent at all school tasks. We are not just talking about expectations of teachers, but expectations for competence that students hold for each other and for themselves.

Once general expectations for competence and incompetence have been formed, the stage is set for self-fulfilling prophecies. Those students who are generally expected to be competent will participate more and learn more on school tasks requiring student interaction. Similarly, those students for whom there are general expectations for incompetence will talk less and therefore learn less when they work together with other students in a group.

THE TEACHER'S PERSPECTIVE OF A STATUS PROBLEM

Diane Kepner recalls a challenging student from her teaching experience:

Roberto entered my seventh grade core class from the bilingual program at the end of the first quarter. The bilingual teacher said that his English skills were good enough for him to be out of her program. She said that he still had some problems with reading and writing at grade level, but that his general comprehension was adequate. He was quiet, pleasant, and well-behaved but he did absolutely no work and by mid-term he was failing in both English and social studies. None of my usual interventions was successful and Roberto was rapidly becoming invisible to me and to the rest of the class.

During our complex instruction unit on poetry, Roberto sat with a lively group who were studying sound and rhythm. They were reading William Carlos Williams's poem *The Dance* and looking at a painting by Breughel. They were to discuss the sense of motion in the poem and how it was created; to identify the words that mimicked the sounds of the instruments which they could also see in the painting; and to explore the mood created by the different sounds and rhythm. Then they were to choose from several other pictures and create lines of poetry that would bring out the sound and rhythm of the activities in the picture they chose.

Kristy, Latoya, and Jason sat with their desks close together and huddled over the cards with the pictures and the poem. Roberto's desk was apart from the rest and he leaned back in it away from the group. He watched them intently, played with his pencil, and from time to time gazed curiously around the room. When I reminded them that everyone had to be included in the activity, they were quick to tell me that Roberto didn't really understand what was going on and that he never wanted to say anything anyway. Roberto's only reply was a smile and a shrug. In my best directive manner I told Roberto to pull his desk up with the rest and to pay attention; I then commanded the others to include him in their discussion. They obeyed me perfunctorily, but the situation didn't really change.

THEORY AND RESEARCH

According to status characteristic theory,[1] Roberto fails to participate and others in his group fail to listen to his ideas when he does try to participate because he is a low-status student in the classroom. He is not expected to be smart. He may be low on several different kinds of status orders in that classroom. His failure in the class is probably public knowledge so that he is undoubtedly seen as a poor student in social studies; he may be a social isolate and thus low on peer status; as a relative newcomer to the country, while he communicates proficiently in English, he may still have a generally low social status based on his ethnicity and accent.

Each of these different kinds of status represents a rank order of social perceptions in which it is generally agreed that it is better to be high than be low. Clearly, it is better to be seen as a good student than a poor student. It is better to be perceived as popular than friendless. And finally it is better to be an Anglo than an immigrant from Mexico who speaks with an accent.

Associated with being high and low status is a set of expectations for competence for a wide variety of intellectual tasks. When the teacher gives a collective task such as creating lines of poetry that would bring out sound and rhythm, these expectations for competence become activated. Group members use these expectations to decide how good everyone will be at the new task. Roberto was not expected to contribute; the others explicitly stated that he did not understand and did not want to say anything anyway. Roberto accepted this state of affairs by sitting apart from the group and by playing with his pencil. He spoke very little, and in the end Roberto had no influence over the final product of the group. As a result, the net effect of the group's interaction on this creative and rich new task was to confirm preconceptions concerning Roberto's incompetence.

Considerable research evidence shows that expectations based on differences in status have the power to spread to new tasks, even when the skills called for in the new task *have nothing to do with the original differences in status*.[2] If students perceive there is only one general ability that is relevant to school tasks, then they will use cues they have on how good a student a person is to estimate his or her ability on all tasks.

Academic status is the most powerful status characteristic in determining what happens within small groups because it is seen as the most relevant to school tasks. Grades, teachers' evaluations, ability to read out loud in the reading circle—all these act as cues to where classmates stand on the academic status order.

However, peer status based on being frequently chosen as a friend or being seen as very popular is also a source of inequality in small groups. Peer status is closely related to the status characteristic of "attractiveness."[3] Using a combined measure of peer status and academic status, Cohen has found that those children in grades two through four who have more friends and those seen to be better in mathematics and science are significantly more active in groups working on open-ended discovery problems.[4] Similarly, Cohen and Lotan find that, among middle school students in social studies classes using complex instruction, those seen as better at the subject and those who are viewed as popular are more active in groups carrying out role plays, building models, composing songs and other nontraditional academic activities.[5]

Laboratory studies have shown that race and ethnicity are also status characteristics that will affect interaction on a game task; whites and Anglos were more active and influential than African-Americans,[6] and were also more active than Mexican-Americans who looked different.[7] Although girls are less active and influential than boys in cooperative groups of adolescents, gender does not appear to act as a status characteristic in the early elementary years.[8]

In a study of nineteen social studies classrooms in the middle school, Cohen and Lotan found that race/ethnicity and gender only had an effect among students who were low on academic and peer status.[9] If a girl or a minority student were a good student or popular, then gender or minority status (African-American or Mexican-American) did not have any impact on rate of participation in small groups. If girls or minority students were not popular or were not seen as good students, then they interacted less frequently than boys or white or Asian students who were equally low in popularity and academic standing.

CONSEQUENCES OF STATUS HIERARCHIES IN THE CLASSROOM

Educators might not worry about these status hierarchies in the classroom if they did not have consequences for learning. In complex instruction, we have repeatedly found that those who interact more learn more.[10] These findings are consistent at both the elementary and middle school level.[11]

There are other worrisome consequences of status hierarchies. ◆ School reformers who are concerned with equity have advocated doing away with tracking and ability grouping. In addition, they have widely recommended the use of cooperative learning as a major way to work with the heterogeneous classrooms that result from these structural reforms. However, if status hierarchies within small groups based on perceived ability simply substitute for the former status hierarchies based on track or ability group, we will have merely exchanged one form of inequity for another. Instead of students finding out the special talents and skills of classmates whom they do not know well, they will simply confirm their overall judgment of how competent or incompetent other students are. Unless school reformers find some way to deal with status hierarchies and the underlying set of cultural beliefs, the idea of creating schools where "all children can be smart" will be merely lip service to the ideal of equity.

Modifying Status Hierarchies

Using status characteristic theory we have derived several treatments designed to modify the effects of expectations based on status characteristics that operate in the classroom. These treatments have been evaluated for effectiveness in producing equal-status interaction in the classroom. By way of illustration of how these treatments work, let us return to Diane Kepner's report on Roberto to see what can be done to treat the status problems she observed.

ROBERTO'S TEACHER INTERVENES

In social studies I would usually spend two or three weeks building a general background for a particular period of history and then do one of the intensive complex instruction investigations centering around a significant key idea. In our study of feudal Japan, this investigation focused on the theme of social stratification in medieval Japanese society.

In my orientation to the lesson I reminded students that their examination of this topic would require many different ways of being smart. They would need to use visual/spatial abilities to understand diagrams, graphs, pictures, and drawings and to create the details for the models, charts, and posters they would make. Analytical reasoning abilities would be essential in pulling out important information from the stories and eye-witness accounts that they would read. Creativity would be needed in creating skits, fashion shows, models, and posters to represent their findings. I stressed that while no one would be good at all of these abilities, everyone would be good at some of them.

Tina, Joey, and Roberto were to examine a series of pictures and diagrams and were then to design and build a Japanese castle town that reflected the feudal hierarchy. As I watched, Joey immediately took command and Tina became second lieutenant. Together they completely shut out Roberto. He wasn't even allowed to pick up the materials. Tina fetched whatever Joey needed and then stood watching him work. There was no discussion, no investigation. I stepped into the group and reminded them to work together. I pointed out that Roberto had become very good at analyzing a task and making a plan. I suggested that they listen to him because he often paid attention to details that the rest of us easily overlook. Then I left the group to work and observed them from a distance.

Roberto tried to make some suggestions about where different groups of people lived and how they contributed to the defense of the town. He remembered that there was always a small hidden door for emergencies at one side of the castle, but he was still ignored. Their castle ended up more European than Japanese. It was obviously a walled castle but there were no details and nothing was done about the surrounding town. After their presentation, I pointed out that some of the things they were missing were the very details that Roberto had tried to suggest and that it was too bad that the group had not taken advantage of his contributions. I repeated what I had said about his organizational skills and his attention to details. Roberto beamed and nodded.

From this point on in the school year, Roberto gradually became a more active participant in every aspect of the class. Recognition of his abilities enabled him to enter into other classroom activities as a legitimate member. While he did not become a really good student, he was no longer failing. His success and participation in group work made him willing to attempt more traditional kinds of work as well.

The following fall, Roberto stopped by to say hello and to tell me about his new classes. Then, rather casually, he asked if they would be doing any of that 'group stuff' this year in eighth grade. When I replied that they would, he nodded and said, 'that's good,' rewarding me with one last smile as he went out the door.

ANALYSIS OF THE TEACHER'S INTERVENTIONS

The first thing to note about this vignette is the fact that the students are engaged in a set of rich multiple-ability tasks. This is a classroom using complex instruction in which each group is given a different task, each of which reflects the central concept of social stratification in feudal Japan. The tasks call upon the students for a much wider range of abilities and talents than conventional school work. For example, students are asked to create skits and fashion shows, build models, and create charts and posters. Multiple-ability tasks enable a much wider range of students to make important contributions; they set the stage for challenging the assumption that there is only one way to be smart.

The kinds of intelligence called upon in such curricula are more like those used by adults in real-life problem solving. Reading and writing skills are still required for each individual, but they are integrated with solving intrinsically interesting problems and completing group products.

The second thing to note is that in introducing the set of tasks to the class the teacher was using a multiple-ability treatment for status problems. She specifically described the different ways to be smart such as understanding diagrams, analyzing eye-witness accounts, and being creative in developing skits. When she discussed all the different skills and abilities that would be necessary, she was breaking up the implicit assumption that only one kind of "smartness" would be important for these new tasks. When she explicitly said, "No one will be good at all these abilities; everyone will be good at some of these abilities," she was directly attacking both general expectations for competence and the belief that intelligence is unidimensional. In place of these beliefs, she substituted the idea that each person undertaking these challenging new tasks can be expected to be good at some aspects and not so good at others. She was not saying that conventional academic skills do not count; she merely said that these are only some of the many abilities that are relevant to the task.

If she is successful in changing the way the students look at their upcoming work, each individual (including Roberto) will have a mixed set of expectations for competence. High-status students will no longer believe that they have all the abilities and low-status students will believe that they have some of the relevant abilities. Other people in Roberto's group will hopefully realize that, even though he is not fluent in English, there are a variety of ways in which he can make important intellectual contributions to the task.

The description of Tina, Joey, and Roberto's group suggests that the multiple ability treatment was not by itself sufficient to modify the low expectations held for Roberto. He still was not even allowed to handle the materials.

The third thing to note in this vignette is the teacher's use of a second status treatment, "Assigning Competence of Low-Status Students."

Through careful observation of Roberto in other group situations, she had seen that he was very good at analyzing a task, at noting important details, and at making a plan. She watched this group long enough to see that they proceeded to building a model without any overall strategy. She specifically told the group that Roberto was very competent at making plans based on an analysis of the task. She suggested that the group listen to him because he often has important ideas to contribute. Joey and Tina were not observably responsive to this intervention. In the wrap-up, the group presented a walled castle minus the details that Roberto tried to suggest; and it is precisely these details that would have made the castle authentically Japanese. The teacher pointed this out to the whole class, repeating her assessment of Roberto's specific strengths for this task.

Assigning competence to low-status students works because, theoretically, the teacher's evaluations are likely to be believed by other students. By the time the teacher publicly states that Roberto is competent on a valued ability for the second time, Roberto and the others in the group are likely to believe her.

Note that she did not gush over Roberto, nor did she say something very general like "Roberto did a great job." She was specific and matter of fact in pointing out the particular intellectual skill that Roberto possessed. She made sure she was telling the truth by virtue of her previous, careful observations of this student.

By making his skill relevant to the success of the group, she created new expectations for Roberto's competence. These new expectations for competence combine with the old low expectations, and the result should be a significant improvement in expectations for Roberto on this task. However, the intervention did not appear to work immediately for the feudal castle task. It was after the teacher reassigned competence to Roberto in front of the whole class that things began to change. His recognized competence in contributing important details on this task resulted in markedly raised expectations on subsequent tasks. Thus on the next group task, he started out from a different place than the day before. As the teacher reported, he became more active thereby providing the teacher with still more opportunities to point out the value of his contributions. Because the new expectations for Roberto's competence were modifying the old negative expectations, the groups began to acknowledge his contribution. He, in turn, began to put out more effort, not only during cooperative learning but on his regular homework and class assignments.

EVIDENCE FOR EFFECTIVENESS OF TREATMENTS

Cohen and Lotan find that the more frequently teachers use these two treatments in complex instruction classrooms, the higher is the rate of participation of low-status students. In addition, in classrooms where teachers use these treatments more frequently there is no over-all evidence of status hierarchies, that is, there is no relationship between a person's status and how frequently he or she participates.[12]

The Challenge of Bringing about Change

We have acquired extensive experience in working with these treatments in heterogeneous classrooms throughout California, in Arizona, and in Israel. We have learned that implementing these changes in classrooms represents a considerable challenge even when teachers are interested and highly motivated to bring about opportunities for low-status students in their classrooms. In the following sections, we would like to discuss this challenge from the several perspectives of the teacher, the staff developer, and the program developer.

CHALLENGES FOR THE TEACHER

Patricia Swanson reflects on Maria, a low-status child in her mixed fourth-fifth grade classroom:

Maria was the forgotten student in my class. Quiet and well-behaved, she was a consummate survivor who slipped through all the cracks. It took me three months to discover she could not read, and another two to have her tested and sent to special education classes for reading. When asked to identify low-status students in my class, I had little difficulty coming up with Maria—once I remembered she was there.

I remember that year well. A Stanford doctoral student was filming my students in order to help me recognize and treat status problems. I was committed to this course of action. An idealistic bilingual teacher, working in a class characterized by linguistic and academic diversity, I wanted *all* of my students to learn.

My class was completing a series of cooperative science activities centered around the theme of light. Maria's group was constructing a color wheel, a device made with a circle of heavy paper or cardboard and a rubber band. Students paint different color wedges on the circular paper, insert a rubber band through a small hole in the center of their "wheel" and tightly twist the rubber band. Theoretically, when they pull on opposite ends of the rubber band, the color wheel spins. The purpose of the activity, of course, is for students to observe what happens to the different colors as the wheel spins.

I remember feeling harassed that day. The camera's eye followed me relentlessly as I moved about the class. Two of my seven groups were struggling, one with a cooperation problem and the other was clearly confused by the directions for their task. Maria's group looked like the least of my problems. Most of the students had made their color wheels and were trying them out. With a sigh of relief I took a moment to ask the group what new colors they expected to create. While the other students eagerly called out their predictions, Maria was silent. She was the only student still working on her color wheel. I suggested that the group test their predictions, observed a few more moments, and moved on to the next group.

That afternoon I watched the tape of Maria's group. At first I didn't see it. Then it became all too obvious. No one in the group could make their color wheel spin. The paper I had given them for the project was too thin and light. Rather than spinning, the color wheels flopped uselessly side to side. I watched myself on the tape, oblivious to the problem, asking questions and reminding students to test their predictions with their color wheels. Only when prompted to look more closely did I notice Maria, directly in front of me, carefully pasting circles of paper, one on top of another, to her color wheel. When she was satisfied with the thickness of the wheel, she twisted the rubber band tightly and sent her color wheel spinning. I watched myself look through her, turn, and walk away.

In my mind's eye I see that tape again and again. It haunts me. I ask myself how I could have missed so much. And how, when I was so committed to treating status problems, could I have ignored Maria and what she was doing?

It is not a simple matter for a teacher to treat status problems in the classroom, even when she intellectually understands and philosophically embraces the concepts. Putting that knowledge into practice requires a series of changes in perceptions that can be difficult to achieve and may take considerable time to acquire. Recognizing that a quiet, well-behaved student such as Maria is not just shy but is actually excluded by the others because of her low status is such a perceptual shift.

Yet clearly it can be equally difficult to perceive the varying ways in which students are smart. We are limited by our own experiences and assumptions. The classroom is at all times a busy, dynamic place and this is intensified whenever there is group work, especially so when all of the groups are working on different tasks. The system must be working well in order for the teacher to have the opportunity to observe individual students. In this environment it is easy for our preconceptions and conditioned expectations to override our idealistic commitments. We see what we are looking for and what we expect to see. If we are looking for evidence of whether or not the students have followed the directions, made their color wheels, and can predict how colors combine, then we will not see the kind of intellectual ability Maria displayed. Recognition can be very difficult when contributions come from unexpected sources and are outside the performance of the rest of the group.

While recognition is the most difficult challenge teachers must overcome, it is not the final one. Assuming that the teacher recognizes status problems, observes a low-status student's intellectual contribution, and is eager to do a multiple-ability treatment and assign competence, then what does she say? We teachers are generally masters of language. It is one of our most powerful tools within the classroom, and we feel awkward and uncomfortable when we must talk about something that we have not really mastered. It is not easy to learn these new perceptions and the new language all at once. Like our students, we teachers often hesitate to attempt new behaviors at which we are not already sure we will be good.

THE CHALLENGE FOR THE STAFF DEVELOPER

Teachers are well aware that unequal participation is the most persistent and troubling dilemma in cooperative groupwork. Those who are ready to tackle this problem are often the teachers who choose to work with us; they are eager for strategies to combat the problem. For some of these teachers, it is an ideological issue related to their desire for equity. For others, it is an issue of professional growth: the status treatments represent a practical strategy to address the persistent problem of unequal classroom participation. The challenge for the staff developer lies not in capturing interest and commitment of teachers who come to us but in developing sufficient understanding of the theory and the treatments to allow for practical application in the classroom.

In our experience we have encountered very few teachers who reject the concept of status. If they do, it is unlikely that they would implement the status treatments. Most teachers accept the concept, although there is considerable variation in the extent to which they can apply it initially to common classroom situations.

The first challenge in introducing status problems is confronting our cultural predisposition to regard all behavior as the result of individual motivation or capacity. Status orders are a group phenomena. To understand and recognize status problems, teachers must learn to use a sociological lens—to monitor group interaction, not just individual behavior. In a study of preservice education, teachers who explained unequal participation in the group solely in terms of individual personality traits had more difficulty mastering the implementation of status treatments than those who viewed student behavior, at least in part, as a group phenomenon.[13]

The multiple-abilities treatment poses exceptional challenges for staff developers. Some teachers are ideologically opposed to telling students that no one has all the necessary abilities. One teacher stated, "It's a personal value. . . ." Another explained, "A good student prides himself or herself in having mastered all of the necessary abilities."[14]

When teachers feel strongly that some of their students are so gifted that they could do virtually any multiple-ability task well, it is difficult to help them modify the basic status order. The class will continue to believe that high-status students are the most able and high-status students will continue to believe that they have little reason to listen to other group members.

Other teachers have difficulty believing that their low-status students could ever compete intellectually with the more academically able students. In their multiple-abilities treatment they say, "No one is good at all the abilities but everyone is good at *something*." "Something," unfortunately, does not imply an intellectual ability and does little to change anyone's expectations for competence of the low-status student.

The second challenge lies in providing the follow-up support for the treatment of assigning competence. Teachers need opportunities to observe their low-status students and assistance in recognizing their unique abilities. As we noted in the previous section, it is not only hard to see the intellectual contributions of these students, it is difficult to label and describe their abilities.

Classroom observation and feedback are the keys to successful implementation. Prior to implementation, teachers learn how to use our classroom observation instruments. We observe each teacher at least nine times during the school year and summarize our observations on graphs showing both student behavior and types of teacher interaction such as using status treatments. Using the graphs as an objective starting point, we meet with teachers as many as three times during the first year. This process is an open-ended exchange of information and expertise designed to enable teachers to translate the theoretical concepts they have learned into classroom practice. The number of feedbacks teachers receive is directly related to the quality of their implementation and the frequency with which they use the status treatments.[15]

In addition to observation and feedback, good implementation rests on teachers' understanding of the theory.[16] It is this combination of understanding and classroom support that enables teachers to dismantle status hierarchies.

THE CHALLENGE FOR THE PROGRAM DEVELOPER

Multiple-ability curricula are an essential condition for successful status treatments. If the curriculum requires only reading, writing, and computing, then it is not possible to talk about multiple abilities and to find intellectual abilities on which each low-status student will excel.

Design of such multiple-ability curricula is not easily done unless the curriculum developer has a deep understanding of both the concepts of the subject matter and the concept of multiple abilities. If each of the activities is to deepen the understanding of the central concept in a different way, the curriculum developer must be both analytic and imaginative.

Despite all the difficulties of creating suitable curricula, these materials have proved to be a powerful tool for change. An attractive, well-designed curriculum that will excite and interest the students is one of the most effective tools for the adoption, implementation, and institutionalization of changes in a school. Teachers are extraordinarily receptive to a curriculum with proven effectiveness. They will be willing to undergo lengthy staff development to learn how to manage instruction and to make sure that all students in their classroom have access to this new curriculum.

The challenge faced by teachers in this new approach cannot be faced alone. Teachers require organizational support from the principal and from other teachers, working on a collegial basis. Our model of school reform is based on changes in classroom instruction and moves outward from the classroom to the structural changes necessary to provide adequate support for teachers. However, it is also true that if principals and department chairs provide the resources that permit teachers to collaborate and the organizational imperative for change, consistent and high-quality implementation of complex instruction is much more likely.

To return to where this chapter began, what does the program developer do about the general cultural beliefs that act as a barrier to reform? In order to analyze tasks in terms of specific abilities that will be required, the approach we have used requires as a first step a new view of human intellectual ability as multidimensional. This is also a different view of what it means to be "smart." Beyond this specific change in beliefs, measures of other related beliefs concerning the limitations of individual intellectual ability are uncorrelated with a teacher's mastery of status treatments.[17]

Once teachers have a good conceptual understanding of how and why to carry out status treatments, they are ready for the second stage in which students exhibit very new and different abilities in the radically changed setting of complex instruction. When working with a multiple ability curriculum and with the new strategies of talking about multiple abilities and observing how low-status students are successful with these abilities, teachers are surprised and pleased to discover the many intellectual abilities their students possess. Thus the situation itself helps to bring about the necessary shift in the way students are viewed. By producing a new situation in which all students can contribute, it becomes possible for "all children to be smart."

NOTES

1. Joseph P. Berger, Bernard P. Cohen and Morris Zelditch, Jr., "Status Characteristics and Expectation States," in *Sociological Theories in Progress*, edited by Joseph Berger and Morris Zelditch, Jr., vol. 1 (Boston: Houghton Mifflin, 1966), pp. 29-46; Joseph Berger, Bernard P. Cohen, and Morris Zelditch, Jr., "Status Characteristics and Social Interaction," *American Sociological Review* 37 (1972): 241-255.

2. Susan J. Rosenholtz, "Treating Problems of Academic Status," in *Status, Rewards, and Influence*, edited by Joseph Berger and Morris Zelditch, Jr. (San Francisco: Jossey-Bass, 1985); David E. Hoffman, "Students' Expectations and Performance in a Simulation Game" (Ph.D. diss., Stanford University, 1973); Julie S. Tammivaara, "The Effects of Task Structure on Beliefs about Competence and Participation in Small Groups," *Sociology of Education* 55 (1982): 212-222.

3. Murray Webster, Jr. and James Driskell, "Beauty as Status," *American Journal of Sociology* 89 (1983): 140-165.

4. Elizabeth G. Cohen, "Talking and Working Together: Status Interaction and Learning," in *Instructional Groups in the Classroom: Organization and Processes*, edited by Penelope Peterson, Louise C. Wilkinson, and Maureen Hallinan (Orlando, Fla: Academic Press, 1984), pp. 171-188.

5. Elizabeth G. Cohen and Rachel Lotan, "Creating Equal-Status Interaction in Heterogeneous Classrooms," in *Understanding Diversity in Education: An International Perspective*, edited by Rachel Ben-Ari and Yisrael Rich (forthcoming).

6. Elizabeth G. Cohen, "Interracial Interaction Disability," *Human Relations* 25 (1972): 9-24.

7. Susan J. Rosenholtz and Elizabeth G. Cohen, "Activating Ethnic Status," in *Status, Rewards, and Influence*, edited by Joseph Berger and Morris Zelditch, Jr. (San Francisco: Jossey-Bass, 1985), pp. 445-470.

8. Marlaine E. Lockheed, Abigail Harris, and William P. Nemcef, "Sex and Social Influence: Does Sex Function as a Status Characteristic in Mixed-Sex Groups of Children?" *Journal of Educational Psychology* 75 (1983): 877; Anita Leal, "Sex Inequities in Classroom Interaction: An Evaluation of an Intervention" (Ph.D. diss., Stanford University, 1985).

9. Cohen and Lotan, "Creating Equal Status Interaction in Heterogeneous Classrooms."

10. Elizabeth G. Cohen, "Expectations States and Interracial Interaction in School Settings," *Annual Review of Sociology* 8 (1982): 109-235; Elizabeth G. Cohen, Rachel Lotan, and Chaub Leechor, "Can Classrooms Learn?" *Sociology of Education* 62 (1989): 79-54.

11. Cohen and Lotan, "Creating Equal Status Interaction in Heterogeneous Classrooms."

12. Ibid.

13. Patricia Swanson, "Linking Theory to Practice: Strategies for Preservice Education" (Ph.D. diss., Stanford University, 1993).

14. Ibid.

15. Nancy Ellis, "Collaborative Interaction and Logistical Support for Teacher Change" (Ph.D. diss., Stanford University, 1987).

16. Rachel A. Lotan, "Understanding the Theories: Training Teachers for Implementation of Complex Instructional Technology" (Ph.D. diss., Stanford University, 1985); Swanson, "Linking Theory to Practice."

17. Swanson, "Linking Theory to Practice."

CHAPTER III

Creating Communities of Effective Practice:
Building Literacy for Language Minority Students

KRIS D. GUTIERREZ AND BRENDA MEYER

Many children are talking, but it is not noisy in the classroom because these first graders are helping one another write in their journals and assisting each other with their talk. They are seated in groups of three or four students, though they are free to move about as needed. The students write, read their writing, seek assistance from their peers, and assist one another. They may, and frequently do, spell words for one another, but they also read their own and others' stories, make suggestions, and help each other to write increasingly elaborated prose. The children are free to choose their own topic and to share story ideas. The teacher walks around, listening to the sentences and stories they have written and asking questions to stimulate writing. She writes in their journals, responding to or questioning something in the text that is confusing, but more often she just talks with them about their writing. The goal, to become a community of writers, underlies the activity, but the means to this end are achieved in as many ways as there are students in the room. There is more than one teacher here, and everyone is considered literate.

This classroom has not always operated in this way. Ten years ago when the teacher walked into her first classroom, she dutifully placed the students in three groups reflecting her perception of their ability. Everyday she provided three or four sentences for them to copy, meticulously correcting their letter formation, and relentlessly drilling the children on letter sounds and new vocabulary. The well-prepared students finished all these assignments with ease while the less-prepared students constantly struggled. Moreover, these less-prepared students became quickly bored with the simplistic material they read

Kris D. Gutierrez is Assistant Professor in the Department of Education, University of California at Los Angeles. Brenda Meyer is a doctoral candidate in the Graduate School of Education, University of California at Los Angeles.

and wrote and the cloak of low expectation that continuously surrounded them.

The Transition from a Teaching to a Learning Community

Gradually the classroom began to change, and with it, the literacy learning that occurred. This classroom began to emerge as a community of effective practice. This transformation pervaded all subject areas and was the result first, of the teacher's prolonged observation of students in various learning situations and second, of an expanding theoretical teaching framework based on research, theory, reflection, and collaboration. Systematic observation of her students affirmed that independent work only served to stratify the learning opportunities available to individual students. The teacher began to rely less on a methodologically oriented curriculum in which direct and explicit instruction of language skills is the normative practice. She began to examine her own assumptions about how children learn best and about which classroom conditions seem to enhance literacy learning for all children. Informed by theory and reflective practice, the teacher began revising her teaching strategies, basing them on an apprenticeship and interactive model of learning. Within this new framework, the classroom included literacy activities that encouraged full participation and peer assistance. In this way, the teacher moved from a focus on "teaching" to a focus on "learning" in which literacy learning, the specific concern of this chapter, began to be scaffolded by the participants in this classroom community through the talk and interaction between the teacher and students and among the students themselves. The teacher also began to talk and interact with administrators, peers, parents, and researchers who collaborated in her construction of new ways of teaching and learning. She became an apprentice as she simultaneously constructed apprenticeship opportunities for her students.

The effectiveness of an apprenticeship framework is supported by sociohistorical and sociocultural theories and cross-cultural language socialization theories that suggest very interactive contexts for learning in which student talk, assisted learning, and building on students' knowledge and beliefs are salient features of classroom instruction. These theories provide an alternative to traditional learning situations where independent performance is valued and prior knowledge and experience are dismissed. Recent educational reforms aimed at literacy instruction have attempted to redirect attention toward the processes involved in literacy acquisition and away from an emphasis on the development of discrete reading and writing skills. But despite the soundness of these suggested literacy practices, reform-oriented educational strategies in and of themselves are seldom sufficient to generate change because no instructional activity can be separated from its larger setting for learning. While some state frameworks, like the *California Language Arts Framework*, present an excellent discussion for reenvisioning language arts instruction, our studies have shown that teachers are having tremendous difficulty creating contexts for learning that are consistent with the frameworks and the new knowledge base of how children learn, and in particular how they learn literacy.

Several studies of reform-oriented literacy instruction have examined how teachers and students constructed a classroom community of learners and, further, how such communities positively influence the teaching and learning of literacy among elementary and middle school immigrant Latino and other ethnically diverse students.[1] Additional studies have inquired into the nature of teaching and learning in specific classrooms, the role of interaction in literacy instruction, the role of ethnicity in classroom interaction, and the kinds of activities, classroom settings, and assistance that help to create reflective teachers and effective practice.[2] Ultimately, these studies were concerned with how communities of effective practice are created for both teachers and students.

An outcome of these larger research projects is a process model for rethinking and transforming teacher preparation and, thus, literacy instruction for elementary and middle school students. It is a situated model and, therefore, must be reconstructed across contexts and communities; it cannot simply be imposed. This process model is culturally sensitive and accounts for the multiple ways participants co-construct contexts and activities and use language.

An Orienting Framework

Traditional literacy instruction has assumed that before learning to read or write students must first be taught the alphabet, letter formation, letter/sound relationships, and syntax. More important, while such teaching was usually done in a group setting, the students practiced their learning independently. Older students who continued to struggle with these skills and concepts repeated basic writing exercises and read simple sentences over and over again, yet failed to progress. In addition, the literacy experience these children possessed was neither strengthened nor respected by such activities. Consequently, the students who were unable to move beyond the most fundamental components of the literacy process were denied access to other and richer elements of the reading and writing curriculum.

Instruction in communities of effective practice, in contrast, assumes that literacy emerges in interactive learning activities where all participants are given opportunities to teach and learn. Interactive literacy activities are often observed in natural, informal settings, such as when a parent reads a bedtime story.[3] Language development also emerges in informal, interactive activities. Studies of language development and socialization in everyday situations illustrate how tightly bound language and culture are. Through interaction, caregivers generate and refine oral language skill; they also provide the young learner with essential knowledge of his or her culture.[4] Furthermore, in informal settings where language development and socialization occur, a great deal of importance is placed on those experiences the learner brings to the setting.

In informal settings, learning has been likened to apprenticeship in which an expert, generally an adult, guides a child from the level of novice toward independent performance.[5] Soviet psychologist Lev Vygotsky identified the "zone of proximal development" (ZPD) in collaborative learning.[6] The ZPD defines the distance between what a child can do alone and what she can do with assistance. Traditional learning models begin with exposure to a new concept, such as a teacher directing a group lesson, and move toward independent performance, often called "seatwork" in a classroom setting. The notion of a ZPD, on the other hand, allows for implementation of a curriculum of potential that necessarily incorporates expert assistance in the learning process. Through guided assistance, the child moves to independence. In this way instruction or guided practice precedes developmental level. Assistance within a community of effective practice has been characterized in several ways including "guided participation" and "scaffolding."[7]

Despite the large number of children present in classrooms and their inclination to talk, interactive activities have frequently been absent, as research identifying typical instructional discourse patterns has verified.[8] The expectation in most classrooms is that specific skills will be mastered and to do so requires quiet, independent work styles with virtually no regard for the learner's prior knowledge. Typically, in teacher/student interaction, the teacher *initiates* interaction by asking a question, generates a single *response*, and *evaluates* the response. This pattern constitutes a teaching "script" which has been labeled recitation. In recitation, it is therefore common to find the teacher frequently controlling all aspects of interaction and discussion. Thus the recitation script is not only a pattern of discourse; it can also be a very restricted form of teaching in which the teacher defines what counts as learning, who gets to learn, and how. Yet, the importance of interaction in learning and the benefits in educational settings are well established.

Recitation Instruction and Linguistically Diverse Children

Many of the classrooms we studied were teacher-centered classrooms in which children had few opportunities to demonstrate or use the literacy skills they possessed. As the following classroom interaction illustrates, recitation instruction often does not build on the children's existing literacy and linguistic knowledge. Instead, literacy instruction for many bicultural students is characterized by contexts for learning in which the teacher's knowledge is privileged and students have limited opportunities to weave their linguistic, sociocultural, and academic knowledge into the fabric of the curriculum. In such contexts, as Freire has suggested, teachers confuse the authority of knowledge with their own professional authority[9] and employ a pedagogy of correctness in which integrating students' ways of knowing and being is antithetical to traditional notions of teaching and learning.

RECITATION INSTRUCTION: GETTING THE RIGHT ANSWER[10]

T = Teacher
R = Rudy
M = Marla
A = Alvaro
C = Cristina
E = Elena
S = Students

01   T: Does anyone know what this word is?
02   ((The teacher holds up a card with the word
03   rhinoceros written on it.))
04   Would you raise your hand if you know what this word is?
05   If you can't see it then you need to scoot down a
06   little bit so you can see better. Rudy – oh you can see

07   it.
08 R: Yeah.
09 T: Oh, ok. If you think you know what the word is – you
10   know, sweetheart – I can't call on you because you're
11   not following my directions. Juan – you're not following
12   the direction of where you're suppose to be.
13 M: She doesn't want you by the chair.
14 T: Marla, Marla, Marla. I can take care of him myself
15   thank you. You need to move over here now. Move up to
16   the group now and sit the right way. Do not touch the
17   chair again. Alvaro . . .
18 A: Ri no ser os
19   ((The student pronounces the word rhinoceros as it would
20   read in Spanish and does so with a pronounced Spanish
21   accent.))
22 T: Really close – not quite. Really close. He has the
23   right sound in there.
24 A: ((He attempts the pronunciation again.))
25 T: I had to look up the spelling because I wasn't sure, but
26   this is the right way, so . . . Rudy.
27 R: Rinosarus
28 M: Brontosaurus
29 T: Close – I like how Rudy raised his hand. What do you
30   think Cristina?
31 C: Rhinoceros ((with a heavy Spanish accent))
32 T: We call it – el mismo en español – es posible, pero (   )
33   ((the same in Spanish . . . it is possible but))
34   What do you think? There's one in the room I think.
35 E: ((Speaking very slowly)) Rinoseros
36 T: Oh – you're so close. I think I should say it . . .
37 S: ((Many students are attempting to pronounce rhinoceros at
38   once.))
39 T: [If I tell you this is where the accent goes
40 S: [((The students attempt to pronounce the word.))
41 T: Do you want to try it?
42 S: [rhinoceros
43 T: At least in English that's how we say it. Does anyone
44   know what this is, a rhinoceros?
45   ((Marla eagerly waves her hand and gasps with excitement
46   as she volunteers to answer the question.))
47   Ok, Marla, ok. Put your hands on your head please.
48   I'm glad so many people want to tell me the answer, but
49   it's hard with this many kids in the room – so we really
50   have to take our turns. Ok – Take your hands off your

51   heads and listen. Does anybody know what a rhinoceros
52   is? Anything about it at all? What is a rhinoceros?
53   Marla, did you know what it was? Do you want to share it
54   now? ((Marla shakes her head no.))
55   Cristina?

The teacher proceeds to call on students in an attempt to get the correct definition of rhinoceros. The children categorize it as a "fish mammal" and a dinosaur. The teacher then writes the word "rhinoceros" on the board for the students. Marla quickly raises her hand to share what she knows about the spelling of rhinoceros.

56   M: Ms. Lee – it's not spelled like that. It's not
57   spelled like that . . .
58   T: [Yeah it is – I looked it up
59   M: But in that book it doesn't have the C on it.
60   T: It just has rhino, yeah, that's right. It's easier to
61   say rhino.
62   M: [I can read it. I can read it.
63   T: [It's my turn to talk. I'll take the questions at the
64   end of the story.
65   ((Marla puts her head down, her eyes looking
66   down toward her chest.))

In recitation interaction, exemplified by this teacher's talk, the rich social, cultural, and linguistic mosaic is replaced by literacy instruction in which "correctness"—that is, getting *the* right answer—and "doing being student"[11] become the foci of literacy instruction. In such contexts for learning in which socializing students to particular social roles and interactional patterns is the goal of instruction, the teacher consistently determines the content of instruction: who talks, when, for how long, and for what purpose. Consequently, students rarely actively co-construct the context, as well as the written and oral texts. In short, they are provided few occasions to participate in and use the very discourse they are expected to appropriate.

Although recitation instruction is prevalent in many classrooms and thus affects what and how learning occurs for all participants, it appears to have particular consequences if it is the only pattern of talk and interaction in classrooms with language minority students. For example, Gutierrez found that the pervasiveness of the recitation script in literacy learning activities resulted in tightly bound, teacher-managed instructional events that significantly limited the production of both the oral and written texts of second and third grade students who had recently shifted from Spanish to English language instruction.[12] In nearly half of the seven second and third grade combination classrooms studied, students were provided few opportunities to interact regularly about oral and written text, to use elaborated language, and consequently to appropriate the linguistic and social knowledge needed for successful classroom membership.[13]

Even when used to implement more reform-minded writing process activities, the use of recitation resulted in static and highly structured contexts in which children had few occasions to produce elaborated written or oral language, to build on each other's talk, and to generate relevant ideas based on personal experiences and knowledge. Thus, in these classrooms, children had limited opportunities to resolve the tensions created by their transition into a new discourse community—a community with a different set of norms, expectations, and actions.

Co-constructing Communities of Effective Practice

In recent ethnographic studies of the effects of writing process instruction on Latino children and of the social contexts of literacy instruction for Latino students,[14] a very different context for literacy learning was observed in several classrooms. In these more interactive contexts for learning, the use of a "responsive/collaborative script" transformed the nature of participation and created new, as well as more, opportunities for students to function as apprentices and as experts in the literacy learning process.[15] Responsive/collaborative classrooms have been labeled "child-centered," "authentic," "democratic," and "empowering."[16] While these terms may indeed be appropriate descriptions of these classrooms, they do not specifically account for the ways activities that foster certain kinds of literacy learning are organized and sustained.

Analysis of the activities in responsive/collaborative classrooms and the interaction and talk during those activities revealed that these particular literacy contexts were characterized by more symmetrical relationships between students and teacher. Unlike classrooms in which recitation was the predominant script, the social relationships between teachers and students were significantly transformed even though the teacher still framed and facilitated the activity. In particular, students had regular opportunities to co-manage the classroom talk, to raise related subtopics, to ask questions about and elaborate on or incorporate other participants' talk without relying on the teacher as knowledge and language broker. Thus, in these particular interactive contexts, students were socialized through the language and interactional patterns of the classroom into new communities of discourse and practice. Simultaneously they built upon their own literacy practices and skills; language socialization thus was bidirectional.

The transformation of the roles of both teacher and student, however, had even more significant consequences. The traditional participation structures of literacy activities in which students are the receptors of information, responding to teacher questions with brief correct answers, were transformed into communities in which students could be both experts and novices. Central to this learning community was the student novice's direct engagement and increased participation in joint activity.[17] Of particular importance to literacy development was the fact that language use within and about the activity allowed students opportunities to be both "socialized to use language and socialized through language."[18] As in other communities of effective practice, acquiring linguistic and sociocultural knowledge resulted from legitimate participation in communicative practices, not from talk about the structure and forms of language.[19]

In communities of effective practice, student novices with varying levels of expertise were full participants in both whole-class and small-group literacy activities in which they could assume legitimate and multiple roles of reader, writer, listener, critic, storyteller, and teacher. Of particular importance, however, was that students were first socialized through guided observation and participation in whole-class activities that required contributions to both the talk and the task. In these activities, students could function with varying degrees of participation as they were apprenticed into fuller and broader levels of participation. Small-group activities, then, provided opportunities for students to interact in ways they had observed and had taken part in as participants in the larger group setting.

Thus these apprenticeship activities accommodated the changing roles students assumed as they moved through the various zones of development. Through joint activity with more expert others and through social interaction with other members of the community, the children had access to skills, content, patterns of language and interaction to which they would not otherwise be exposed. Students' continual movement from observation to guided participation as a way of learning assisted their language development and provided access to all the rules and means of being a successful member of the classroom community.

Membership in Communities as Effective Practice

The construction and assumption of varying roles crucial to the development of communities of effective practice may be found in both whole-class and in peer-directed, small-group interaction. The following examples demonstrate how students assist each other's language development and understanding of content. What distinguishes these particular examples from other small-group activity is that students in these classrooms had been socialized into participating as full contributors to the shaping and carrying out of learning activities.

RESPONSIVE/COLLABORATIVE INSTRUCTION:
STUDENTS AS MEANING SEEKERS

In the first example, a group of seventh and eighth grade Latino students in an integrated social studies/literature activity share their individual responses to an assignment in which they were asked to compare issues of prejudice and racism in *Roll of Thunder, Hear My Cry*[20] to present-day social conditions. Throughout the excerpt students negotiated both text features and meaning in order to come to some shared understanding of both the task and the content of the task. In particular, students sought both information and clarification from one another, as they collaborated on reconstructing their texts. Nancy begins by reading her text to the rest of the group.

N = Nancy
M = Mary
E = Elsa
R = Richard
T = Teacher

01 N: O.K. ((begins reading)) The Nightmen in the book
02   *Roll of Thunder, Hear My Cry* were a group of white,
03   prejudiced men who burned black people's houses
04   down because the black people disappointed the
05   nightmen. They wouldn't just take revenge by burning
06   down black people's houses, but sometimes when they
07   could, they harm the black people in another way than
08   just shooting them. In our community we do have people
09   to fear like burglars, rapists, kidnappers, child

10   abusers, etc. But in the 1990's there is no protection
11   as there was in the past. The black people handled
12   their situation by playing it safe, and made sure not
13   to upset the white people – the white people?
14   What does we "cope" mean? What is "cooope?"
15   M: Like . . .
16   N: It – it asks "How do you cope?"
17   E: Cope. How do you handle it?
18   N: How do we handle it? We already put that here. We
19   have no protection.
20   E: Okay.
21   M: Yeah – but how do you handle it? They have no
22   protection, but what does that me=
23   E: =Okay, okay . . .
24   M: That's good. ((Applauds))
25   N: Oh, we handle it by locking our doors.
26   M: Okay, my turn.
27   E: Wait a minute.
28   E: Wait – wait – wait – wait ((writes)) By having more
29   policemen, things like that . . .
30   ((The teacher observes the group's progress and moves
31   to the next group. Nancy adds the following to her text,
32   "We cope by playing it safe also. Like at night locking
33   our doors at night, closing the windows, having more
34   protection."))

In this particular interaction, students had opportunities to ask clarifying questions (Lines 14, 16-18). One student, Nancy, did not fully understand the assignment which asked students to also write about how they thought people "coped" with today's social problems. In the course of listening to one another's texts, students revised and/or extended their own texts as Nancy did (Line 32-34) and assisted one another (Elsa, Line 28-29). As students were provided regular opportunities to collaborate, they began to demonstrate that they valued the ideas and writing of their peers (Line 24). In this particular activity, as in other responsive/collaborative activities, students co-managed the discourse and co-constructed the activity. Although the teacher is often present as a facilitator in an activity, in this event she functioned at the margins of the activity and only entered when students needed certain kinds of assistance. It is important to note that students had been provided frequent occasions to interact and function as communities of learners; indeed, the socialization into this literate community had been an ongoing and gradual process.

WHEN PEERS CO-CONSTRUCT TEXT

As illustrated in the next excerpt, students continued to share their texts and through discussion began to co-construct both oral and written text. Mary began by reading her text about the Nightmen in which she defined today's new Nightmen as men in gangs.

```
37   M:   O.K. ((begins reading)) The Nightmen were some –
38        white men who made a little group and in the night they
39        would go out and do things to black people and to their
40        properties. I think that our Nightmen are gangs. That's
41        what people are mostly afraid of in our society. That's
42        what disturbs our town and kills people from other gangs.
43        The only difference between Nightmen and gangs – is that
44        with the Nightmen there isn't – er uh – another group=
45   N:   There isn't another what?
46   M:   [Group]
47   E:   [Group]
48   M:   =There isn't another group of people to fight back.
49        Gangs are a big thing here. They have rumbles to
50        fight over – territory just as the Nightmen want the
51        blacks out of their land.
52   N:   That's good. I wanna copy. ((She focuses on her text.))
53   E:   Lemme see. ((She looks at M's text.)) Well – you know
54        what? We forgot about something. You know what?
55        There is still prejudice against – um . . .
56   M:   Blacks.
57   E:   Um – blacks and everything. The Ku Klux Klan . . .
58   R:   And South Africa.
59   E:   The Ku Klux Klan, tambien, is still . . .
60   R:   They showed it on the news.
61   E:   And the skin heads . . .
62   M:   Oh yeah. ((Mary begins writing))
```

Again, student talk was focused on the activity and students were able to facilitate their own participation in this literacy activity by assisting and building on one another's oral and written texts. After Mary read her text, Elsa suggested an addition to the text, a discussion of prejudice (Lines 53-55). Prompted by Elsa's suggestion, Mary, Richard, and Elsa herself (Lines 56, 61) further co-constructed the text and assisted Mary in the revision of her own text (Line 62). The activity continued as Elsa read her text about the wild and ruthless Nightmen who believed they were superior to blacks. Elsa's reading did not provoke any interaction; instead, Richard immediately read his text after Mary, who allocated turns, called on him.

68   M: Richard.
69   R: ((Reads)) The Nightmen in this day and age are drug
70   users and gang members. They are in the street at
71   night terrifying you. They are not liked by anyone
72   except themselves. Nightmen in their time, were
73   feared because they beat up people and terrorized
74   them.
75   M: They didn't just beat 'em up. They killed 'em
76   N: Hey – what did you put – like – the Nightmen felt
77   superior to the blacks – right? So what do you
78   – like – see they felt superior to the blacks and
79   what else?
80   M: All the white men, not just the Nightmen.
81   E: Um – but, I'm going to write – what other Nightmen
82   are there? So I could write more of it.
83   ((She writes in the margin and lists other
84   analogies.))
85   N: Hey, they felt superior to the blacks and what –
86   what else?
87   M: ((to Elsa)) We're not gonna rewrite this are we?
88   E: Yes we are.
89   N: What else? Like – why did they harm them?
90   M: 'Cuz they were black and they wanted their land.
91   N: What? They felt superior to the blacks – um . . . The=
92   E: =And they accused them of lots of crimes they didn't
93   commit.
94   N: And – accused – them – of – things. ((She talks
95   aloud while writing.))
96   E: What other Nightmen are there?

Richard's peers responded immediately with suggestions for revising his text. In line 75, for example, Mary pointed out that blacks were not only terrorized by the Nightmen; in fact, they were killed by them. Nancy then questioned Elsa's incorporation of the notion of superiority among the Nightmen (Line 76-79). Mary, however, clarifies Elsa's assertion that only the Nightmen felt superior to blacks (Line 80). In fact, she stated, all white men felt that way. As students assisted Richard, however, Elsa focused on her own text and asked a question that would allow her to write more of her own text (Lines 81-82). After a very brief exchange between Mary and Elsa, Nancy brought the group back on task (Line 89). Nancy then incorporated their suggestions into her text (Line 94).

Language use and interaction were salient features of the activity. It was only through such interaction and continual guided practice that these students co-constructed text and assisted one another in clarifying their own thoughts and intentions as writers. These particular kinds of extended interactions with and around text proved to be central to the literacy development of these Latino students. Moreover, these co-managed activities were often more productive than teacher-led classroom activities.[21]

In the course of participating in this activity, students were allowed to assume multiple roles of reader, writer, critic, critical listener, and scribe. In this way, students with varying levels of expertise were provided occasions to be apprenticed into full participation and thus take on all the roles expected of a successful member of this particular community. Richard, for example, was able to participate, even peripherally, in an activity that required varying levels of participation and performance. Through face-to-face interaction with his peers, Richard began the socialization process of becoming a writer and active participant. Likewise, the students were provided opportunities to build on their own understandings of the book they had read and the texts they had written and to examine their own sociocultural contexts outside school. In doing so, students did not just explore social studies content and literature; they participated in activities that required them to use literacy skills and historical knowledge to collaborate on their own constructions of text.

Assisting Emergent Writers: Assuming Multiple Roles

In an investigation of small-group interaction, first grade children of diverse economic and ethnic backgrounds, demonstrated the ability to participate effectively as part of a group as they completed a journal writing activity.[22] For these children, effective participation featured text production, the assumption of more than one role in this process, and peer assistance.

Kathy, a first grader whose abilities by traditional performance measures fall into the average range in most academic subjects, has been engaged in journal writing on a daily basis throughout a school year. She is able to generate complete if not lengthy narratives. She writes on a variety of self-selected subjects, assists others during group interaction, and, like many of the students observed, is extremely focused on generating text. The following exchange between Kathy and Michelle, which occurred during one journal-writing session, illustrates how these students assume the various roles of writer, reader, and critic as they discuss Kathy's text.

ROLE ASSUMPTION DURING TEXT REVISION

M = Michelle
K = Kathy

```
01  M:  My mom –
02      I mean mommy.
03      My mommy is my best friend.
04  K:  ((Writing)) And . . .
05  M:  Your mom's your best friend?
06      She's your *mom*.
07      How can she be your best friend?
```

Michelle began by assuming the role of reader as she read from Kathy's journal (Lines 1-3). This allowed her to take on the role of critic as she raises an issue extremely significant to the intent of Kathy's story. Kathy did not respond directly to Michelle's question. Instead, she returned to her journal and added the following, which she read aloud:

```
08  K:  My mom.
09      My mommy is my best friend and my dad –
10      daddy –
```

Kathy had begun to extend her notion of friendship to include not only her mother, but her father as well, based on Michelle's critique (Line 11). However, before she can complete this thought (her finished text reads "and my daddy is too") she was interrupted on an editing point by Michelle:

```
11  M:  That's not daddy.
12  K:  Uh huh.
13      What's that?
14      A "A."
15      This is a O.
16  M:  Hey!
17      Look it, look it, look it, look it . . .
18      What's *that* then?
19  K:  Mom
```

Reader Michelle suggests that Kathy has not correctly spelled "daddy" (line 11). Kathy argues that there is a difference in vowel sound in the words "mom" and "daddy" (lines 14-15), and, furthermore, that she had used the correct letter in each case. After defending her spelling choice, she was then able to silently reread and reevaluate her own story. When she was satisfied with what she had written, she enlisted Michelle as content critic of her finalized piece (lines 20-23):

20 K: Does this make sense?
21   Does this make sense Michelle?
22   ((Reading)) My mom –
23   She is my best friend and my daddy is too.

This exchange illustrates how students both offered assistance to each other and assumed the roles of writer, reader, and critic. These students had been given the opportunity to interact while acquiring literacy skills and it has led to a revision of Kathy's text that is slight (but significant for emergent writers). Michelle questioned the main point of Kathy's story and, though Kathy did not verbally defend this point, it ultimately changed the direction of her story. Kathy, though, later constructed a reasonable oral defense of her spelling of "daddy" pointing out the differences in vowels found in the words "mom" and "dad." Kathy has demonstrated that she was both a writer and a reader, that she was able to incorporate criticism and revise her text, and that she could logically defend an editing point with no change to the text.

Although text revision is rarely observed in emergent writers, these writers were able to focus on editing and assistance that resulted in more conventional text. From these records it is clear that these students consistently concerned themselves with spelling. Nearly all of them had a keen awareness of the difference between their spelling inventions, which they utilized frequently, and conventional spelling. They often sought or offered advice on spelling, and were much more willing to edit their spelling and punctuation than they were to revise content. With guided practice and opportunities to interact with and assist each other, however, they will begin to deal with simpler issues of content as they become more mature writers and readers.

In the following example, Tanya has written "Beauty N the beast." Her group, led by Joseph, assisted her in her spelling of "and," which, as she eventually realized, made her text much clearer. Joseph pointed to Tanya's journal, which he has been reading silently.

GROUP-ASSISTED TEXT REVISION

```
01  J:   How come you writed – beauty and the beast?
02       And that's not the way you write –
03       And that's not the way you write AND.
04       You write AND this way.
05  T:   N
06  J:   [Aaaa
07  S:   [A N D
08  J:   N D
09       That's the way you spell it.
10  T:   N
11       That's a regular N.
```

At first Tanya did not realize that her text was unclear. She had written what she had heard, and because she and the others were able to read her text, she was satisfied (lines 10-11).

However, Joseph's persistence and the other group member's support later helped Tanya to understand her error and improve her text. Through example, they explained the difference between the words "in" and "and," and how incorrect usage, regardless of the spelling, was causing confusion (lines 12-14, 20-24).

```
12  J:   Like you wanna spell beauty in the beast?
13  S:   Beauty in ((She laughs.))
14       Nope . . .
15  J:   That's not the – A.
16  B:   (You happy?)
17       Put a A then a D.
18       Put a D here and put a A right here.
19       That's how you spell and.
20       Not in the beast.
21  S:   In the beast. ((She laughs again.))
22  B:   Beauty and the . . .
23       And the . . .
```

Based on the assistance of her group, Tanya did eventually change her text. However, it is important to realize that Tanya came to this decision only after her group challenged and assisted her. Furthermore, it was her own decision to make the change. It was not necessary or desirable for the teacher to instruct her to make the change, though the end result would have been the same. However, direct instruction may not have resulted in the depth of understanding demonstrated by Tanya and the other group members. Whether the assistance is direct and specific, as in the last example, or indirect and provocative, as in the previous two examples, these students are engaging in meaningful, literacy-centered interaction as a community.

Implications for Educational Change

The problems of schooling are not, at their most fundamental level, pedagogical. Above all, they have to do with the ways in which institutions and communities of adults reproduce themselves. Rather than viewing learning as simply replicating the performances of others or acquiring knowledge transmitted in instruction, we suggest that learning occurs through active participation in a classroom in which the focus of the curriculum is learning, not teaching.[23]

Transforming the nature of the teaching and learning of literacy, however, is a long and complex process, even for experienced, committed, and knowledgeable teachers such as those participating in these studies. The recent emergence of very different kinds of classrooms, like the responsive/collaborative classrooms identified in this chapter, suggests that the construction of communities of effective practice in schools is possible if there is a radical transformation in the organization of the school and the classroom contexts for learning. Thus, creating school and classroom communities where all children can be smart, like those observed in our responsive/collaborative classrooms, requires fundamental changes in the social relationships in the schools, in the classrooms, as well as between schools and communities. In these new communities, teachers, students, administrators, and parents are provided regular occasions for apprenticeship, guided and meaningful practice, and full participation in learning communities composed of peers. There are spaces and places for everyone to participate in learning communities in which the "funds of knowledge" of both the community and the larger social and academic community are integrated.[24]

In short, the school communities are transformed so that they reflect newer understandings of how children learn, of what counts as knowing and teaching, of what constitutes being smart. Such changes require substantive changes in the beliefs of school and community about teaching and learning that inform the continued construction of teacher-led instruction in which children have limited opportunities to build on their own definitions and uses of literacy and to participate in new discourse communities in the school and classroom.

Normative practices evident in communities of effective practice where all children can be smart include opportunities for all students to assume multiple roles in learning activities and to have regular access to participation in a variety of contexts for learning in which different and multiple patterns of talk, interaction, and assistance are used. In these contexts, varying levels of expertise are both tolerated and exploited so that novices are assisted by more expert others, including peers. In such apprenticeship forms of learning experts can also benefit in that they too are still developing breadth and depth of skill and understanding as they participate with peers. These new relationships among peers are scaffolded by teachers who assume very different roles in the learning process.[25] These teachers become authorities but they relinquish authoritarian roles in which teachers are at the center of the curriculum.

Similarly, teachers assume roles of authority as they participate in meaningful decision-making activities about how schools and classrooms should work. Schools that limit teacher's participation in the co-construction of school and classroom life will also reflect minimal transformation in the ways teachers imagine education for the twenty-first century. In particular, the construction of contexts for learning in which few children can be smart, as well as literate in two languages, is perpetuated by isolating teachers from their peers and from context where talk and collaboration are a part of everyday classroom life. These organizational structures perpetuate the construction of "teaching" communities where neither teacher nor student flourishes. Instead, when schools and classrooms function as communities of effective practice, the zones of possibility for developing successful instruction for biliterate students are significantly increased.

Creating communities of effective practice, then, requires rethinking our understanding of how learning occurs and how the contexts for learning influence what is learned, as well as who has access to learning and doing. These are critical steps in redefining who counts and what counts not only in schools but also in the larger communities. Thus, in these communities, the target of instruction is both learning and social justice.

Notes

1. These studies have been funded by grants from the University of California, Linguistic Minority Research Institute, the National Council of Teachers of English, and the Academic Senate of the University of California, Los Angeles.

2. Kris D. Gutierrez, "A Comparison of Instructional Contexts in Writing Process Classrooms with Latino Children," *Education and Urban Society* 24, no. 2 (1992): 244-262;

idem, "How Talk, Context, and Script Shape Contexts for Learning to Write: A Cross Case Comparison of Journal Sharing," *Linguistics and Education* 5, nos. 3, 4 (1993): pp. 335-365.

3. Shirley Brice Heath, "What No Bedtime Story Means: Narrative Skills at Home and School," *Language in Society* 11 (1982): 49-76.

4. Elinor Ochs and Bambi Schieffelin, "Language Acquisition and Socialization: Three Developmental Stories," in *Culture Theory*, edited by Richard A. Schweder and Robert A. Levine (Cambridge: Cambridge University Press, 1984), pp. 276-320.

5. Barbara Rogoff, *Apprenticeship in Thinking* (New York: Oxford University Press, 1990).

6. Lev S. Vygotsky, *Thought and Language* (Cambridge, MA: MIT Press, 1962); idem, *Mind in Society: The Development of Higher Psychological Processes* (Cambridge, MA: Harvard University Press, 1978).

7. Rogoff, *Apprenticeship in Thinking*; David J. Wood, Jerome S. Bruner, and Gail Ross, "The Role of Tutoring in Problem Solving," *Journal of Child Psychology and Psychiatry* 17, no. 2 (1976): 89-100.

8. Courtney B. Cazden, *Classroom Discourse: The Language of Teaching and Learning* (Portsmouth, NH: Heinemann, 1988); Gutierrez, "A Comparison of Instructional Contexts in Writing Process Classrooms with Latino Children"; Hugh Mehan, *Learning Lessons: Social Organization in the Classroom* (Cambridge, MA: Harvard University Press, 1979).

9. Paulo Freire, *Pedagogy of the Oppressed* (Harmonsworth: Penguin, 1970).

10. Throughout this chapter the discourse samples utilize conventional punctuation wherever possible to facilitate reading. The content of the samples has not been altered. Symbols used are based on the system developed by Gail Jefferson, "Transcript Notation," *Structures of Social Action: Studies in Conversation Analysis*, edited by J. Maxwell Atkinson and John Heritage (Cambridge: Cambridge University Press, 1984). The following symbols appear:

–   short untimed pause
(( )) descriptions of accompanying events
( ) transcriptionist uncertainty or, if empty, inaudible speech
[paired with another bracket, overlapping speech
=   paired with another equal sign indicates no pause between utterances.

11. Sylvia Scribner and Michael Cole, *The Psychology of Literacy* (Cambridge: Cambridge University Press, 1986).

12. Kris D. Gutierrez, "Scripts, Counterscripts, and Multiple Scripts" (Paper presented at the Annual Meeting of the American Educational Research Association, Atlanta, Georgia, 1993).

13. Gutierrez, "How Talk, Context, and Script Shape Contexts for Learning to Write"; idem, "A Comparison of Instructional Contexts in Writing Process Classrooms with Latino Children"; Kris D. Gutierrez and Joanne Larson, "Language Borders: Recitation as Hegemonic Discourse," *International Journal of Educational Reform* 1, no. 1 (1994): 22-36.

14. Gutierrez, "The Effects of Writing Process Instruction on Latino Children" (Paper presented at the Annual Meeting of the American Educational Research Association, Chicago, Illinois, 1991); Gutierrez, "The Social Contexts of Literacy Instruction for Latino Children" (Paper presented at the Annual Meeting of the American Educational Research Association, San Francisco, California, 1992).

15. Gutierrez, "A Comparison of Instructional Contexts in Writing Process Classrooms with Latino Children"; idem, "How Talk, Context, and Script Shape Contexts for Learning to Write."

16. Paulo Freire and Donaldo Macedo, *Literacy: Reading the Word and the World* (South Hadley, MA: Bergin and Garvey, 1987); Henry Giroux, "Literacy and the Pedagogy of Voice and Political Empowerment," *Educational Theory* 38, no. 1 (1988): 61-75; Yetta M. Goodman and Kenneth S. Goodman, "Vygotsky in a Whole Language Perspective," in *Vygotsky and Education: Instructional Implications and Applications of Sociohistorical Psychology*, edited by Luis C. Moll (Cambridge: Cambridge University Press, 1990), 223-250.

17. Jean Lave and Etienne Wenger, *Situated Learning: Legitimate Peripheral Participation* (Cambridge: Cambridge University Press, 1991).

18. Elinor Ochs, *Culture and Language Development* (Cambridge: Cambridge University Press, 1988).

19. Lave and Wenger, *Situated Learning*.

20. Mildred D. Taylor, *Roll of Thunder, Hear My Cry* (New York: Dial Press, 1976).

21. William Saunders, "The Influence of Three Different School Contexts on the Writing and Learning of Four Seventh Graders" (Ph.D. diss., University of California, Los Angeles, 1993).

22. Brenda Meyer, "Peer Influence on a Writing Task: A Sociocognitive Perspective" (Paper presented at the Conference on Education, Democracy, and Economy: Contradictions, Changes, and Mutual Influences, Graduate School of Education, University of California, Los Angeles, May, 1993).

23. Lave and Wenger, *Situated Learning*, p. 100.

24. Luis Moll and James Greenberg, "Creating Zones of Possibilities: Combining Social Context for Instruction," in *Vygotsky and Education*, edited by Luis Moll (Cambridge: Cambridge University Press, 1990), pp. 319-348.

25. Rogoff, *Apprenticeship in Thinking*.

CHAPTER IV

The AVID Classroom: Academic and Social Support for Low-Achieving Students

MARY CATHERINE SWANSON, HUGH MEHAN, AND LEA HUBBARD

Josefina came to San Diego from Tijuana, Mexico, when she was in the eighth grade. She spoke no English and recalls spending an entire year in classes learning how to pronounce in English the days of the week and the time on a clock. When she asked for a book, the teacher refused because "Mexican girls all have babies before they graduate from high school." Josefina read her first book in Spanish when she was thirteen; it was *Don Quixote*.

In high school, Josefina was recruited into the AVID program. She was placed in college-preparation classes and received support to succeed in these rigorous courses in her AVID elective class. Josefina graduated from Clairemont High School with a B+ average in advanced level classes and enrolled in San Diego State University. She will graduate next year with her degree in English. Today she not only reads novels in English; she is also writing one.

Josefina is one of 6,000 AVID students in San Diego County and 5,500 AVID students across the nation who are proving that hopeful futures (including college attendance) are possible for students from minorities that are presently underrepresented in postsecondary education. According to the California Department of Education, 60 percent of the jobs in California in the 1990s require a baccalaureate degree.[1] Although 1.8 million students in our K-12 classrooms are African-American or Latino, fewer than 1,500 of these students graduate from our public colleges and universities each year. Therefore we must do

---

Mary Catherine Swanson, who is with the San Diego County Office of Education, is the author of the first part of this chapter where she writes about AVID, a highly successful program that places previously low-achieving students in college preparatory classes. Hugh Mehan and Lea Hubbard, both of the Department of Sociology, University of California (San Diego), are the authors of the second part of the chapter where they describe the social processes and institutional practices that have contributed to the success of the AVID program.

more to prepare African-American and Latino students for college or they will be shut out of the workforce in the twenty-first century.

AVID: The Inception and Development of an Untracking Program

AVID stands for Advancement Via Individual Determination. The word comes from the Latin *avidus*, "eager for knowledge." AVID's purpose is (1) to increase college attendance among African-American, Alaskan/Native American, Latino, and low-income students who are most underrepresented in postsecondary education, and (2) to restructure secondary school teaching methodologies to allow college preparatory curricula to be accessible to all students.

RAISING STUDENT EXPECTATIONS AND ACHIEVEMENT

The impetus for AVID was the impact that court-ordered desegregation in the San Diego Unified School District had on Clairemont High School in 1980. At that time I was Chair of the English Department at Clairemont, which was providing a traditional enriched curriculum to a homogeneous middle class student population, 80 percent of whom enrolled in college. In 1980, a new high school drew away our most affluent students, and 500 low-income Latino and African-American students were bused into our school.

I planned the AVID program as a response to this change. In order to prepare students from minority backgrounds that are underrepresented in postsecondary institutions for admission to four-year colleges, I had to consider carefully the power structure and political ramifications of my actions on the school and district.

My first course of action involved the principal. I told him that I would prepare a group of ethnically diverse students who were academically underprepared for enrollment in four-year colleges where they would succeed. Because he was retiring at the end of the school year and would not have to face the faculty and administrators who undoubtedly opposed such an unrealistic idea, he gave me the "go-ahead." I then contacted the head of student outreach at the University of California at San Diego (UCSD) for help; he agreed to provide tutors for the program, whom I supported with grant funds. The tutors worked three class hours per week, two hours of which were devoted to direct instruction in writing which I conducted.

For the first AVID class I recruited thirty ethnically and culturally diverse students who were not in college preparatory classes and had grade point averages in the 1.5 to 2.5 range. They agreed to enroll in college preparatory classes and to do homework regularly in exchange for an elective class that was to provide them with academic and motivational support.

The new Clairemont principal asked me if I was staying or going to the new high school. I told him it depended upon his support of AVID. He pledged his support. I stayed.

School began with thirty AVID students placed into rigorous courses for which they did not have the prerequisites. Instead of physical science, they took biology; instead of consumer mathematics, they took algebra; they all enrolled in advanced English, foreign language classes, physical education—and the AVID elective class.

The faculty was skeptical regarding the plan, but I think they were willing to allow it because they wished to teach advanced classes and needed the enrollment (which AVID could provide), and they did not want to invest the time to oppose the "crazy teacher" and her students. Truthfully, few teachers believed that the AVID students would be successful and many thought the bused-in students should be enrolled in remedial classes.

Not infrequently I received notes from colleagues such as "this student is your responsibility; he does not belong in this school, much less in my college preparatory class." I quit eating lunch in the faculty cafeteria because the talk around the lunch table was constantly focused on the troubles the bused students caused, e.g., "these students" were ruining "our" school. The teachers did not want to recognize that schools are to serve students and that teachers must accept students as they are when they come to school.

On the first day of the elective class, the AVID students received binders filled with notetaking paper and forms for record keeping. I asked them to take notes using the Cornell system (in which students jot detailed notes in a wide right-hand margin and questions in a narrow left-hand column) in all their academic classes. In the elective course, we developed subject-specific study groups based on the students' questions which they developed from their Cornell notes as homework. We insisted that the tutors implement an *inquiry method* in which they helped the AVID students clarify thought based on their questions rather than giving them answers. We did not want the AVID class to become a glorified study hall or a place where students did homework.

Because AVID students were such active notetakers, academic teachers began to view them as serious learners. Honors students began to ask them about their notetaking techniques. As an English teacher, I knew the value of using writing as a tool of learning; therefore, I encouraged the students to keep learning logs and practice "quick writes" to clarify thought. Because the purpose of much of our writing was to gain an understanding of concepts rather than to publish, students were encouraged to write and speak in a nonthreatening atmosphere, using their "thinking language." In other words, students' language was recognized as a legitimate form of expression, and their communication of ideas was not interrupted by insistence on "correctness."

Often a student would leave my class saying, "I am so tired. I have never tried to express myself for so long in English." They could not sit passively in class, and the insistence on class participation allowed them to improve their language skills very rapidly. They began to live out two AVID maxims, the first adapted from E. M. Forster: "How do I know what I think until I see what I write or hear what I say?"[2] The second one was adapted from Reigstad and McAndrew: "It is better for a student to be a partner in learning at a teacher's side for five minutes than a disciple at his or her feet for five months."[3]

AVID students, tutors, and I melded almost as family. We knew when a student was in trouble academically, or emotionally, or both. We learned about child abuse, drug abuse, gang activity—lessons rarely revealed to English literature or calculus teachers—and we helped sort through students' problems.

GAINING FACULTY SUPPORT FOR IMPROVING CURRICULUM AND INSTRUCTION

Our progress was not always smooth. Just before winter break of the first year, some students were accused of cheating by the science department chair because most had received "A" or "B" grades on a biology midterm examination. The science chair and I spoke individually with each student. All shared their notebooks filled with study notes; some cried at the accusations. The science teacher realized her incredible mistake and told the faculty about the wonderful AVID students. The incident fostered camaraderie among the group, and led us to develop a plan.

First, we sent a letter to all faculty explaining the students' goals. Second, we invited the faculty to visit the AVID class. About ten teachers with AVID students in their classes came, and they saw students gathered in circles of seven to ten, with a college tutor, notebooks open, talking in an organized and animated manner and challenging one another to formulate questions developed as a response to homework. They saw the names and assignments of each student posted, a system we used to determine our study groups. Faculty were surprised by the open discussion of their own assignments. AVID students did not sit in classes anonymously, and the teachers could no longer teach anonymously.

We were now ready to take the next step. If I was to insure that a group of students who normally slip through the cracks of the educational system obtained the best education our school had to offer, then I could no longer ignore inequities in teaching quality.

AVID has at times been described as a subversive activity, and perhaps it is. When AVID students were having difficulty in learning concepts in classes such as algebra or biology, I worked with those teachers. So that the teachers would not feel threatened, I always placed blame with the students, e.g., "the AVID students are having difficulty with . . . ." I proposed sending college tutors into their classrooms to take lecture notes so tutors could work more effectively with the students. Teachers agreed. When teachers perceived that an expert was observing their lessons, they taught more effectively. Before long the tutors developed a good working relationship with the teachers. The tutors and I developed mini lessons for teachers, and the tutors demonstrated them in classes. For example, while the teacher was taking roll, the tutor would ask the students to do a three to four minute "quick write" focusing on the day's lesson. At the end of the time, the tutor randomly selected some students to read their quick writes aloud. The teacher now had insight into the students' understandings so that subsequent work could be focused on students' needs. The tutor also assigned extra credit for quick writes, showing the teacher that writing could be used for learning without having to "grade papers."

By the spring semester, the AVID students wished to have discussions with teachers regarding learning strategies. I invited the faculty to problem-solving sessions. The principal and twenty teachers listened to the students' candid assessments of what facilitated and what inhibited their learning. For example, science teachers often showed films filled with complicated vocabulary which explained complex concepts and then immediately quizzed the students on the film. AVID students with limited English skills said they had difficulty working this quickly, but if they could take notes and discuss their notes collaboratively before an exam, they had much better access to the information. The teachers listened and accommodated the students' needs. The topics in these bi-weekly meetings included effective teaching strategies, the inadvisability of using "watered down texts" for AVID students, and the validity of placement exams required for honors courses. Teachers shared successful strategies. Many began to use writing in subject area classes. Almost all started to use collaborative groups.

In 1982 this group worked with UCSD faculty members to prepare a body of writing lessons employing the "writing process" in discourse modes addressing all subjects. Through the work of Charles Cooper, Director of Writing Programs at UCSD, these lessons were incorporated in the California Assessment Program.

In the first few years of AVID, we had made significant progress. The students proved that they could be successful. The thirty original AVID students, many of them taking honors classes, graduated from Clairemont with a cumulative grade point average of 3.2. All entered college, twenty-eight going to four-year colleges and two to community colleges. They received more than $50,000 in scholarships and loans. By the end of their freshman year, those attending UCSD and San Diego State University had a cumulative grade point average of 2.46.

By 1984 (the first year AVID students graduated) the increase (over 1983) in Clairemont's scores on the Comprehensive Test of Basic Skills (CTBS) was higher than the districtwide increase by 46.6 percent in total language and by 35 percent in total mathematics. That year, Clairemont became one of the three top feeder schools to UCSD and ranked fourth of seventeen comprehensive district high schools in the number of graduates enrolled in full-time postsecondary education.[4]

We were also somewhat successful in achieving our second goal—changing and improving teaching practices. The Clairemont faculty was delighted that after twenty-five years, it was actually discussing student learning and implementing the writing process, inquiry methods, and collaborative groups.

Developing and Replicating AVID

In 1986, under the auspices of California Assembly Bill 232.1, I was asked to move to the San Diego County Office of Education to disseminate AVID. AVID had attracted attention not only because it fostered success among underrepresented students but also because the CTBS scores at Clairemont had improved so dramatically.

Currently more than 115 middle-level and senior high schools within San Diego County and more than 200 secondary schools in 58 districts outside San Diego County are implementing the program. In addition, nineteen schools in the State of Kentucky and ten U.S. Department of Defense Dependents Schools are replicating AVID.

In order to expand AVID, and to move from a highly personal program at a single school to one which exists as an integral part of many schools, I needed to accomplish a number of tasks: (1) convince school officials to recognize the serious academic gap between "majority" and underrepresented students; (2) identify an outstanding teacher to work as the AVID elective lead teacher at each school and recruit an interdisciplinary site team to carry out the program; (3) add AVID elective classes to the master schedule while allaying the fears of existing elective teachers that their programs would be threatened; (4) find money to pay for tutors; (5) create a staff development process for administrators, counselors, teachers, and tutors; (6) develop coordinated school site plans. I discuss each of these tasks briefly.

Recognizing the issue. Many schools deny reality. They do not realize that underrepresented students are not performing at the upper limits of their academic potential. I have found it helpful to employ statistics generated by the school district or the state to point out the gap between "majority" and "minority" students. District and state reports are useful in making this case because they are written by outside agencies and do not single out individual teachers. Their impersonality helps make a personal case. For example, "School Performance Reports" indicate students' enrollment in rigorous course work. The "California Postsecondary Education Reports" show, by ethnicity, how many students graduate from high school and where they enroll in college. The "California Basic Education System" reports indicate, by ethnicity, how many high school students take and how many complete college preparatory courses. Such reports are invaluable in bringing staff to a realistic view of their schools.

Selecting the AVID lead teacher. Appropriate selection of the AVID lead teacher is absolutely critical to developing a strong program. Experience has taught us that the teacher needs to be academically strong and to understand "academic press" in order to prepare students adequately. The teacher must be a coach to the students, working with every aspect of the student's life that affects academic performance. The teacher must be a respected instructional leader who can lead colleagues to teach more effectively. Finally, he or she must have enough experience in the educational system to know how to manipulate it so that students receive the best education possible. These teachers must assume a new role—hiring and training paraprofessionals to work in classrooms. Many AVID teachers become fund-raisers to cope with the plight of inadequate funding, or expert field trip coordinators and parent facilitators (teachers who work closely with parents). Every campus has one such teacher. Most are carrying heavy loads of extra responsibilities. But these are the very professionals who can implement a successful program.

Adding AVID classes to the master schedule. With colleges and universities increasing entry requirements, students' schedules in high school are crowded. Adding an extra elective to the program is not easy. Some schools have needed to lengthen the school day; others have offered electives as independent study courses. Teachers of other elective courses often feel threatened by AVID because students may drop one of their classes to enroll in AVID. This dilemma is usually solved by allowing students to make the choice of whether they wish to enroll in AVID or another elective class.

Funding tutors. Most schools have little extra money to pay for AVID tutors, but funds from several categorical programs, including Chapter 1, Chapter 2, and the California School Improvement Program, have been used. Although all of these programs have strong constituencies among the faculty, school sites need to set priorities and combine programs in order to fund AVID. We have found that as soon as schools have success with AVID, school boards are willing to commit general funds to it.

Developing staff development models. We now know that AVID cannot rely on "one shot" workshops. Ongoing staff development and support is needed in order to achieve our program's goals. When new schools adopt AVID, they commit to sending a team of faculty, consisting of the principal, the head counselor, the AVID teacher, and instructional leaders from English, foreign language, history, science, and mathematics to a one-week AVID Summer Institute. While at the institute, the team examines data about its school, develops a vision statement about its school, and outlines the steps needed to actualize that vision. Participants also learn to use writing to learn, inquiry, and collaboration methods. Because the institute is residential, teachers have to learn more about each other, professionally and personally. Although beliefs may not change in one week, actions may. Teachers return to the institute the following year to coach other teachers within their academic departments to spread the methodologies throughout the school.

The Summer institute is reinforced by monthly workshops for AVID lead teachers, semiannual site team meetings, and semiannual site visitations by County Office AVID staff. Additionally, quarterly tutor and parent workshops are conducted, and feeder school and postsecondary liaisons are established.

Developing a cohesive educational plan. Finally, most schools have numerous site plans, many with disparate ideas and goals. AVID seeks to amalgamate the plans into a cohesive overall plan which guides the school toward goals which provide an excellent education for *all* students.

The Processes Responsible for AVID's Success

Mary Catherine Swanson's intuitions about the success of AVID are borne out by our research. In 1990 and 1991, 253 students who had participated in the AVID untracking experiment for three years graduated from fourteen high schools in the San Diego City Schools (SDCS) system. We interviewed 144 of these students. Of that number, seventy-two (50 percent) reported attending four-year colleges, sixty (42 percent) reported attending two-year or junior colleges, and the remaining twelve students (8 percent) said they were working or doing other things.[5] The 50 percent four-year college enrollment rate for students who have been "untracked" compares favorably with the San Diego City Schools' average of 37 percent[6] and the national average of 39 percent.[7]

The college enrollment rates for the 1992 graduating class are not quite as good, but they are still impressive when compared to local and national averages. When we interviewed them in 1993, 46 percent of 105 students who graduated from AVID in 1992 said that they were enrolled in four-year colleges, 39 percent said they were enrolled in two-year colleges, and 5 percent said they were working.

This untracking program works evenly across ethnic and socioeconomic lines. AVID students from the two major underrepresented ethnic groups, African-Americans and Latinos, enroll in college in numbers which exceed local and national averages. Of the Latino students from the classes of 1990, 1991, and 1992 who participated in AVID for three years, 43 percent enrolled in four-year colleges. This figure compares favorably to the San Diego City Schools' average (25 percent) for Latino students not in AVID and the national average of 29 percent. African-American students who participated in AVID for three years from 1990 to 1992 also enrolled in college at rates higher than the local and national averages. Fifty-four percent of African-American students in AVID in 1990-1991 and 58 percent of the class of 1992 enrolled in four-year colleges, compared to 38 percent of the non-AVID African-American students in the San Diego City Schools and the national average of 33 percent.

AVID students who come from the lowest income strata (parents' median income below $19,999) enroll in four-year colleges in proportions equal to or higher than the proportion of AVID students who come from higher income strata (parents' median income between $20,000 and $65,000). AVID students who come from families in which parents have less than a college education enroll in four-year colleges more than AVID students who come from families who have a college education.

On the basis of interviews with 144 graduates of the program and with 150 students who are currently in the program at Monrovia, Saratoga, Pimlico, and Churchill High Schools (fictitious names for the schools) and observations in these four schools, we are uncovering the social processes and institutional practices which contribute to AVID's success.

Isolation of group members and public markers of group identity. In order to transform raw recruits into fighting men, the military isolates them from potentially conflicting social forces. Religious orders and gangs operate in a similar manner, shielding their recruits from competing interests and groups.[8] AVID has adopted this principle, selecting promising students and isolating them in special classes which meet once a day, every day of the school year. Instead of going to shop or drivers' education for their elective class period, they go to the AVID room, a classroom identified by signs and banners. Students often return to the AVID room at lunch time or after school to do homework or socialize, actions which further mark their distinctive group membership.

AVID students·are given special notebooks, emblazoned with the AVID logo, in which they take AVID-style class notes. These notebooks signal their membership in this special group. Some schools have designed distinctive ribbons and badges which AVID students wear on their clothes. Others have adorned their graduation gowns or mortarboards with AVID ribbons. Still other AVID classes publish a newspaper reporting on the accomplishments of AVID students. All of these actions further distinguish AVID students as members of a special group.

Explicit socialization in the hidden curriculum. Once isolated as a group in these classes, AVID students are provided social supports which assist them through the transition from low-track to academic-track status. These "scaffolds"[9] include explicit instruction in the hidden curriculum of the classroom, those often implicit techniques which are key to academic success.

At a minimum, students in all the AVID classrooms we observed were given instruction in note taking and study skills. When a more extensive approach to the hidden curriculum was taken, students were provided explicit instruction in test-taking strategies, including ways to eliminate distracting answers on multiple-choice questions, strategies for approximating answers, and probabilities about the success of guessing. One AVID teacher devoted two successive weeks to SAT preparation, including practice with vocabulary items, administering practice tests, reviewing wrong answers, and teaching strategies for taking tests. This teacher reviewed the kinds of analogies typically found on the SAT with her students so they could practice the kinds of problems they would encounter on their tests. This teacher also sent her students to an expert mathematics teacher for assistance on mathematics test items. She reinforced this teaching by explaining that she was teaching them the same academic tricks found in the expensive Princeton Review SAT preparation class.

While note taking, test taking, and study skills were taught routinely, by far the most striking activity in the four AVID programs we studied involved the college application process. Procedures for filing applications, meeting deadlines for SAT tests, and requesting financial aid and scholarships dominated discussion. At Pimlico High, for instance, students must complete an AVID assignment each week in which students complete writing and/or reading tasks directly related to college. The junior class at Saratoga was given a handout, "Choosing Your College," containing a checklist of information typically found in college catalogs. Students were instructed to fill in the information for that college according to the assigned checklist. This task presumably made them more familiar with college catalogs and helped them choose a college to fit their personal needs.

Teacher advocacy and sponsorship. Another role AVID teachers adopt is that of student advocate. When interviewed, students at the four schools we studied consistently reported that AVID teachers intervene in the academic maze on their behalf. If students are absent, they call them to see why they have been absent, and then check with teachers to insure that they get missing assignments, catch up on their work, and are not penalized for their absence.

The AVID coordinator at Monrovia High School circulated a list with the names of the AVID students to all advanced English teachers. She informed them that the students would be receiving extra help in this subject, but if they were having any problems, she was to be contacted. By this strategy, the burden of failure is shifted away from the student and toward the teacher who must monitor the student's progress.

We observed several episodes of teacher advocacy. During the new "tardy sweep" policy at Saratoga, one of the AVID students was late to a class. The punishment prescribed by the new policy was detention, which meant the AVID student could not make up missing work, including tests. The student was irate and complained to Mrs. Lincoln (AVID coordinator at Saratoga): "I'm just trying to get an education. I just want to learn. They are keeping me from learning, just for being a minute late."

Mrs. Lincoln arranged for the vice principal to hear the student's complaints the very next day. Many students affirmed that no one would have listened to them had they not been AVID students and if Mrs. Lincoln had not acted on their behalf. Clearly, this teacher has adopted an advocacy role that extends beyond traditional teaching duties.

When several students complained to the AVID teacher about their failing mathematics grades, and blamed the teacher for their plight, she spoke with the principal and the teacher on the students' behalf and arranged extra tutoring. Although it was difficult to prove the students' assertion, the AVID coordinator insured that both the academic teacher and the principal knew that the situation was being monitored. She was able to help other AVID students by advising them to take mathematics from a different teacher.

Advocacy on behalf of students is not limited to the academic realm; it extends into and blends with the personal realm as well. The following are typical student comments (by African-American female students at Saratoga) about this dimension of the teacher's role:

The AVID teacher is someone you can talk to. You need to have someone.

The AVID coordinator is someone who takes time to listen to individual needs. She keeps pushing you and reminding you that you can do well.

The AVID coordinator at Saratoga confirmed our impression that her role included duties as a personal advocate. She has intervened in suicide attempts, visited sick students, and called parents if she felt that their child was employed for too many hours or was having difficulty at home.

AVID teachers also mediate the college-going process by taking their students to colleges. Of particular note, the AVID Coordinator at Pimlico takes her students to black colleges and universities in Washington, D.C. and Atlanta each spring. These field trips provide the first opportunity for many students to see a college campus. While there, students visit classes, talk to college students, and stay overnight. The following comment underlines the importance AVID students attach to such trips:

Field trips were great. I didn't even know what a college looked like until Mrs. Lincoln took us. It's like eating a cookie. It really tempts us to eat another one. You've smelled it and seen it and you want to buy it really bad.

Formation of voluntary associations. Special classrooms and badges of distinction are visible markers which define the space for AVID students to develop an academically oriented identity. Within this space, AVID students developed new academically oriented friends, or joined academic friends who were already in AVID.

Several Saratoga students told us that they really did not know anyone in AVID when they joined, but after a few years almost all of their friends were from AVID. These friendships developed because they were together in classes throughout the day and worked together in study groups. Coordinators encouraged these friendships by minimizing competition. The AVID Coordinator at Monrovia High School, for example, told her students that they should think of themselves on "parallel ladders with each other. There should be no competition between students, but rather an opportunity to share notes and to help one another."

Some AVID students joined AVID to be with their friends. Cynthia, a Latina from Monrovia High School, said her friends were already in AVID, and because they were doing well, she wanted to be with them. Now all her friends are in AVID. Thomas, an African-American male at Saratoga, said that he told his two good friends from elementary school that "they had to get into AVID because it would really help with their grades." He even called the mother of one of his friends to convince her that AVID was good for her son. These three boys have remained good friends in AVID and always study together.

Informal activities also help develop academically oriented associations. Students in AVID classrooms often discuss among themselves matters relevant to their adolescence. Students use this period of time to bounce their values and troubles off one another, to test their principles and ideas, and to react to others. In magnet schools where African-American and Latino students are bused in, the AVID classroom may be the only time these students see each other during the school day. In those classes where AVID students from grades 9 through 12 are mixed, the younger students observe older students' behavior and how teachers interact with them.

The longer students are in the program, the more ties seem to intensify. These sentiments were articulated by a Latina who attends Monrovia. AVID provides a different environment for her. "At home they expect me to get married. Here they expect me to go to college." Because of the pressures she receives from home, Maria attributes much of her academic success to the girlfriends she cultivated in AVID. She studies together with her two friends and says:

We chat a lot about college and what we want out of life. Our study group really opens up a lot of issues. Everyone is really motivated to go to college. It really helps to be around others that want to go. It makes you want it more.

We thought the highly visible markers of AVID (the notebooks students are required to carry to classes, the special class periods established for them, the college visits arranged for them, the newspapers they publish) would stigmatize AVID students in the eyes of their peers. But this marking process has had the opposite effect. AVID students reported that their friends who were not in AVID were jealous. They wanted to be in AVID for the camaraderie to be sure, but also because they wanted to take advantage of the resources which AVID made available to its students, such as information about scholarships, college entrance exams, and visits to colleges.

Conclusion: Social Scaffolds Support Academic Placement

The college enrollment record of students who have participated in AVID's untracking program gives us some evidence to support the idea of organizing schools where an academic curriculum is emphasized as an alternative to the prevailing practice of placing underrepresented students in vocational or general education tracks. AVID's special instructional orientation is vital to the success of AVID's untracking program. By emphasizing "writing as a tool for learning," the inquiry method, collaborative learning groups, and intensive staff development, Mary Catherine Swanson makes a convincing case for the importance of the academic portions of her program. Complementing AVID's academic practices and instructional orientation are the social scaffolds supporting student placement. By isolating AVID students in special groups, marking their academic identity, and dispensing academic strategies, AVID is giving students explicit instruction in the implicit, or hidden, curriculum of the school. Included in the hidden curriculum are the special ways of talking, writing, thinking, and acting that are demanded by the school, but seldom discussed openly by the school.

The sons and daughters of middle-income (and upper-middle-income) families routinely gain access to the hidden curriculum via implicit socialization practices at home. But the sons and daughters of low-income parents often do not gain access to this implicit knowledge because their parents have not had direct personal experience with higher education. By exposing AVID students to test-taking and note-taking techniques, by helping them to complete application forms for admission to college and for scholarships, and by taking them to visit college campuses, AVID explicitly teaches low-income students what middle-income students learn implicitly at home. In Bourdieu's terms, AVID gives low-income students some of the cultural capital that economically advantaged parents give to their children at home.[10]

Teachers' sponsorship of students augments this explicit socialization process. The academic life of AVID students in school is supported by dedicated teachers who enter the lives of their students and serve as mediators between them, their high schools, and the college system. By expanding the definition of their teaching role to include the sponsorship of students, AVID coordinators encourage success and help remove impediments to students' academic achievement.

It is a simple fact: students cannot go to college if they do not take the appropriate classes. By insisting that previously underachieving students enroll in college preparatory classes, AVID is increasing the possibility that students from backgrounds which are underrepresented in colleges and universities will have the preparation necessary to enroll in them. But low-achieving students cannot be left to sink or swim in academically demanding classes. Unless untracked students are wrapped in a system of social supports, they will not succeed; and if they fail, then the entire untracking effort may be derailed.

If students do not succeed in untracked programs or collaborative learning groups, then skeptics will have a new round of ammunition to fire at the prospect of low-income and underrepresented students succeeding in academic programs. To meet that criticism, it appears necessary to treat the academic success of low-achieving students as a schoolwide issue, because researchers who have studied educational reform[11] show that educational innovations have the greatest chance of success when significant portions of the school culture are mobilized to support them.

NOTES

1. Bill Honig, "Second to None: Redesigning High Schools," a seminar on the High School Task Force Report, San Diego, CA, 1992.

2. E. M. Forster, *Aspects of the Novel* (New York and London: Harcourt Brace Jovanovich, 1927, 1955).

3. Thomas J. Reigstad and Donald A. McAndrew, *Theory and Research into Practice* (Urbana, IL: National Council of Teachers of English, 1984).

4. Peter Bell, *San Diego City Schools Class of 1984: Six Months after Graduation*, Graduate Follow Up Study (San Diego, CA: San Diego City Schools Research Department, 1984).

5. Hugh Mehan et al., *Tracking Untracking: The Consequences of Placing Low Achieving Students in High Track Classes*, Final Report to the Linguistic Minority Research Institute (La Jolla, CA: Teacher Education Program, University of California at San Diego, 1993).

6. Peter Bell, *San Diego City Schools Class of 1991: The First Year after Graduation*, Graduate Follow Up Study (San Diego, CA: San Diego City Schools, School Services Division, 1993).

7. Deborah J. Carter and Reginald Wilson, *Minorities in Higher Education*, Ninth Annual Status Report (Washington, D.C.: American Council on Education, 1991).

8. Erving Goffman, *Asylums* (New York: Doubleday, 1964); Martin Sánchez Jankowski, *Islands in the Street: Gangs and American Urban Society* (Berkeley, CA: University of California Press, 1991).

9. David Wood, Jerome S. Bruner, and Gail Ross, "The Role of Tutoring in Problem Solving," *Journal of Child Psychology and Psychiatry* 17 (1976): 89-100.

10. Pierre Bourdieu, "The Forms of Capital," in *Handbook of Theory and Research for the Sociology of Education*, edited by John G. Richardson (New York: Greenwood Press, 1986).

11. Seymour Sarason, *The Culture of the School and the Problem of Change* (Boston: Allyn and Bacon, 1982); Larry Cuban, *Teachers and Machines* (New York: Longmans, 1986); Jeannie Oakes, Karen Hunter Quartz, Jennifer Gong, Gretchen Guiton, and Martin Lipton, "Creating Middle Schools: Technical, Normative, and Political Considerations," *Elementary School Journal* 93, no. 5 (May 1993): 461-480.

CHAPTER V

Success for All: Creating Schools and Classrooms Where All Children Can Read

ROBERT E. SLAVIN AND NANCY A. MADDEN

At a community meeting to discuss a plan to eliminate ability grouping in a middle school, a woman stood to speak. "I believe in a good education for all students. I want my daughter to learn to get along with all kinds of kids. I am concerned about what I've heard about the quality of education for kids in the low-ability groups. But my sixth grader and most of her friends are reading far above grade level. She read *Jurassic Park* last summer just for fun. There are other sixth graders, mostly from the _____ school (which serves a high-poverty area), who are reading at the second or third grade level. How can a teacher teach a class with such a wide range of student performance levels?"

Something like this mother's question almost always comes up in any discussion of ability grouping. There are plausible answers; an English teacher might use different versions of the same reading material to allow the poor readers to participate, or put readings on tape, or provide for tutoring, or use cooperative learning, or rely more on teaching than on independent reading.[1] Yet each of these solutions has its own difficulties and none can solve the fundamental problem. As long as there are children reading far below grade level, teaching heterogeneous classes in subjects that depend heavily on reading skill will be difficult. More important, it is impossible to have schools in which "all students can be smart" if some students are very poor readers. Even with the best teaching, the most enlightened school organization, and the most flexible and appropriate assessments, it is hard to see a student who is not reading adequately as successful in school.

Robert E. Slavin is Principal Research Scientist and Director of the Elementary School Program at the Center for Research on Effective Schooling for Disadvantaged Students at Johns Hopkins University, where Nancy A. Madden is also a Principal Research Scientist.

Unfortunately, the problem of poor reading performance is far from rare. According to data from the National Assessment of Education Progress,[2] 20 percent of all eighth graders are reading less well than the average fourth grader. Among African-American eighth graders, 30 percent are reading below the level of the average fourth grader, and among Latino students, 36 percent. These students did not typically fall behind between the fourth and eighth grades. Poor reading performance almost always begins in first grade; it is very unusual, for example, to find a fourth grader failing in reading whose first-grade reading performance was adequate. In a longitudinal study by Connie Juel,[3] 88 percent of students who were poor readers in first grade were still poor readers in fourth grade, scoring more than two grade equivalents lower than their first grade classmates who were good readers.

Clearly, one of the key requirements for schools in which all students can be smart is schools in which all students can read. Yet the problems of poor reading performance among large numbers of children are long-standing and complex. Can schools in fact guarantee that virtually all students will be readers?

At present, there is a growing body of evidence to support the idea that reading failure is fundamentally preventable. Studies of Reading Recovery[4] and of other one-to-one tutoring programs for at-risk first graders[5] show that nearly all first graders can be successful in reading by the end of first grade and that these effects can be detected through the fourth grade. However, to ensure the reading success of all students throughout the elementary grades, especially in schools serving many disadvantaged students, additional comprehensive changes are needed in curriculum, instruction, school organization, and other aspects of the elementary program.

This chapter describes Success for All, a program designed to ensure the reading success of all students in high-poverty schools. The program and the research done to support it are discussed in light of the question, "What would it take to create on a broad scale schools and classrooms in which all children can read?"

Success for All

The Success for All program began in one school in Baltimore in 1987-88. As of Fall, 1994, it is being implemented in 140 schools in 56 districts in 20 states located throughout the United States. The program is adapted to local needs, conditions, and resources, but all sites

share a set of basic principles and procedures. Our basic approach to
designing a program to ensure success for all children began with two
essential principles: *prevention* and *immediate, intensive intervention.*
That is, learning problems must first be prevented by providing children with the best available classroom programs and by engaging their
parents in support of their school success. When learning problems do
appear, corrective interventions must be immediate, intensive, and
minimally disruptive to students' progress in the regular program.
That is, students receive help early on, when their problems are small.
This help is intensive and effective enough to catch students up with
their classmates so that they can profit from their regular classroom
instruction. Instead of letting students fall farther and farther behind
until they need special or remedial education or are retained in grade,
students in Success for All are given whatever help they need to keep
up in the basic skills. The elements of Success for All are described
below.[6]

READING TUTORS

One of the most important elements of the Success for All model
is the use of tutors to support students' success in reading. One-to-one
tutoring is the most effective form of instruction known.[7] The tutors
are certified teachers with experience teaching classes in Chapter 1
programs, special education, and/or primary reading. Tutors work
one-on-one with students who are having difficulties keeping up with
their reading groups. Students are taken from their homeroom classes
by the tutors for twenty-minute sessions during times other than reading or mathematics periods. In general, tutors support students' success in the regular reading curriculum, rather than teaching different
objectives. For example, if the regular reading teacher is working on
stories with long vowels or is teaching comprehension monitoring
strategies, so does the tutor. However, tutors seek to identify learning
deficits and use different strategies to teach the same skills.

During daily ninety-minute reading periods, tutors serve as additional reading teachers to reduce class size for reading. Information on
students' specific deficits and needs pass between reading teachers and
tutors on brief forms, and reading teachers and tutors are given regular
times to meet to coordinate their approaches with individual children.

Initial decisions about reading group placement and need for
tutoring are made based on informal reading inventories given to each
child. After this, reading group placements and tutoring assignments

are made based on eight-week assessments, which include teacher judgments as well as more formal assessments. First graders receive first priority for tutoring, on the assumption that the primary function of the tutors is to help all students be successful in reading the first time, before they become remedial readers.

READING PROGRAM

Students in grades 1 through 3 are regrouped for reading. That is, children are assigned to heterogeneous, age-grouped classes of about twenty-five students most of the day, but during a regular ninety-minute reading period they are regrouped according to reading performance levels into reading classes of fifteen students all at the same level. For example, a 2-1 (second grade, first semester) reading class might contain first, second, and third grade students all reading at the same level.

Regrouping allows teachers to teach the whole reading class without having to break the class into reading groups. This greatly reduces the time needed for seatwork and increases direct instruction time. We do not expect reduction in class size to increase reading achievement by itself,[8] but it does ensure that every reading class will be at only one reading level, eliminating workbooks, dittos, or other follow-up activities which are needed in classes with multiple reading groups. The regrouping is a form of the Joplin Plan, which has been found to increase reading achievement in the elementary grades.[9]

The reading program itself has been designed to take full advantage of having 90 minutes of direct instruction. The reading program emphasizes development of basic language skills and sound and letter recognition skills in kindergarten, and uses an approach based on sound blending and phonics starting in first grade (although kindergarten students who show readiness are accelerated into the first grade program if the school chooses). Students in pre-kindergarten, kindergarten, and first grade experience the Peabody Language Development Kits to help them build language concepts essential to later reading success. The K-1 reading program uses a series of "shared stories," in which part of the story is written in small type and read by the teachers, while part is written in large type and read by students. The student portion uses a phonetically controlled vocabulary. Combining the student and teacher portions makes a book that is interesting, complex, and worth reading. Over time, the student portion grows and the teacher portion diminishes, until the students are reading the entire book. The program emphasizes oral reading to partners as well as to the teacher, instruction in story structure and specific comprehension skills, and integration of reading and writing.

When they reach the primer reading level (usually spring of first grade), students use a form of Cooperative Integrated Reading and Composition (CIRC) with novels or basals. CIRC uses cooperative learning activities built around story structure, prediction, summarization, vocabulary building, decoding practice, writing, and direct instruction in reading comprehension skills. Research on CIRC has found that it significantly increases students' reading comprehension and language skills.[10]

Every eight weeks, reading teachers assess student progress through the reading program. The results of the assessments are used to determine who is to receive tutoring, to suggest other adaptations in students' programs, and to identify students who need other types of assistance, such as family interventions or vision/hearing screening.

OTHER FEATURES OF "SUCCESS FOR ALL" SCHOOLS

Most Success for All schools provide a half-day preschool and/or a full-day kindergarten for all eligible students. The preschool and kindergarten provide a balanced and developmentally appropriate learning experience for young children. The curriculum emphasizes the development and use of language. It provides a balance of academic readiness as well as activities in music, art, and movement. Readiness activities include use of integrated thematic units, Peabody Language Development Kits, and a program called Story Telling and Retelling (STaR) in which students retell stories read by the teachers.

A Family Support Team consisting of any social workers, parent liaisons, counselors, and others who work in the school provides parenting education and works to involve parents in support of their children's success in school. Also, family support staff are called on to provide assistance when there are indications that students are not working up to their full potential because of problems at home. For example, families of students who are not receiving adequate sleep or nutrition, need glasses, are not attending school regularly, or are exhibiting serious behavior problems receive family support assistance. Links with appropriate community service agencies are made to provide as much focused service as possible for parents and children.

A program facilitator works at the school full time to oversee (with the principal) the operation of the Success for All model. The facilitator helps plan the program, helps the principal with scheduling, and visits classes and tutoring sessions frequently to help teachers and tutors with individual problems. The program facilitator may work with individual children having particular difficulties to find successful strategies for teaching them, and then return the children to the tutors or teachers. He or she helps teachers and tutors deal with any behavior problems or other special problems, and coordinates the activities of the Family Support Team with those of the instructional staff.

Every effort is made to deal with students' learning problems within the context of the regular classroom, as supplemented by tutors. Special education resource services are still provided for students assigned to special education in previous years, but no new assignments to resource services are being made for reading problems, on the assumption that tutoring services available to all students will be more appropriate. Self-contained services for seriously handicapped students are maintained for students whose needs cannot be met in the regular class.

A School Improvement Team or an advisory committee composed of the building principal, facilitator, teachers, and parent representatives meets regularly to review the progress of the program and to identify and solve any problems that arise.

Research on Success for All

From the outset, the Success for All project has emphasized rigorous evaluation of the program in comparison to matched local control schools, emphasizing use of individually administered tests of reading. Because of funding limitations, not all Success for All schools are being assessed in this way, but we currently have high-quality assessment data from fifteen schools in seven districts in seven states: Baltimore, Philadelphia, Memphis, Montgomery (AL), Charleston (SC), Ft. Wayne (IN), and Caldwell (ID). Success for All was assessed in three of the districts by Johns Hopkins staff, and in four (using identical measures and procedures) by an independent evaluation group at Memphis State University. The percent of students in poverty in the fifteen schools ranged from 42 percent to 100 percent; in eleven of the schools more than 75 percent of the students were in poverty. Ten of the schools served entirely African-American populations, four had African-American and white students, and one had Cambodian, African-American, and white students.

A common evaluation design, with variations for local circumstances, has been used in all Success for All evaluations. Every Success for All school involved in a formal evaluation is matched with a control school that is similar in poverty level (percent of students qualifying for free lunch), historical achievement level, ethnicity, and other factors. Children in the Success for All schools are then matched on district-administered standardized test scores given in kindergarten or (starting in 1991 in several districts) on Peabody Picture Vocabulary Test (PPVT) scores given by the project in the fall of kindergarten or first grade. In some cases, analyses of covariance rather than individual child matches were used, and while the Key School in Philadelphia was matched with a similar comparison school, individual children could not be matched because limited-English-proficient students are not tested in kindergarten.

The measures used in the 1992 and 1993 evaluations were as follows:

1. Woodcock Reading Mastery Test. Three Woodcock scales (Word Identification, Word Attack, and Passage Comprehension) were individually administered to students by trained testers. Word Identification assesses recognition of common sight words, Word Attack assesses phonetic synthesis skills, and Passage Comprehension assesses comprehension in context.

2. Durrell Analysis of Reading Difficulty. The Durrell Oral Reading scale was also individually administered. It presents a series of graded reading passages which students read aloud, followed by comprehension questions.

Except at the Key school analyses of covariance with pretests as covariates were used to compare raw scores in all evaluations, and separate analyses were conducted for students in general and for students in the lowest 25 percent of their grades. At Key, analyses of variance were used and results were reported separately for Asian (mostly Cambodian) students and for non-Asian students.

Each of the evaluations follows children who began in Success for All in first grade or earlier, in comparison to children who had attended the control school over the same period. Because Success for All is a prevention and early intervention program, students who start in it after first grade are not considered to have received the full treatment (although they are of course served within the schools).[11]

In fourteen of the fifteen schools, Success for All students performed better than their matched controls at every grade level assessed. The one exception was a school in rural Caldwell, Idaho.

This school's first graders performed very well on all tests, but control first graders also did very well.

The results, pooled across measures, schools, and years, for all children who were in the program since first grade, are summarized in figure 1, which shows that Success for All first graders exceeded their control counterparts by an average effect size (ES) of +.58 (that is, 58 percent of a standard deviation). Among students in the lowest 25 percent of their classes, the effects were even larger, averaging an effect size of +1.04. In second and third grades the advantage of Success for All over control students continued to grow, averaging eight months (ES = +.53) by third grade for students in general. For the lowest achievers effect sizes increased to +1.49 by third grade, indicating that low achievers in Success for All were doing better than 93% of their control counterparts.

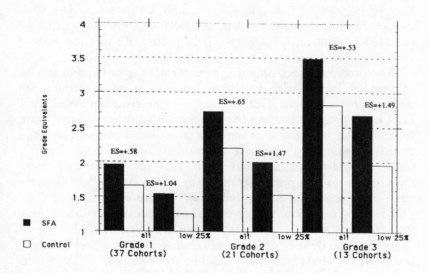

Figure 1. Cumulative mean reading grade equivalents and effect sizes in "Success for All" schools, 1988-1993. (Includes all students in "Success for All" or control schools since first grade (N = 15 school pairs). Schools are in Baltimore, Philadelphia, Charleston [SC], Memphis, Ft. Wayne [IN], Caldwell [ID], and Montgomery [AL]).

In addition to strong and consistent effects on reading, studies of Success for All have found substantial effects on reducing retentions and special education placements and on increasing attendance.[12]

Implementation of Success for All

Research on Success for All shows that the program can substantially increase students' reading achievement, and that these effects can be seen in a variety of circumstances in schools far from our original pilot sites. In recent years, much of our effort has gone into the problem of "scaling up." How can a successful school change model be replicated with integrity and with appropriate adaptations to local needs and circumstances in many schools and districts? How does Success for All typically enter a school, and what happens to it over time as schools incorporate and adapt it? In order to disseminate Success for All, we currently have a staff of twelve full-time trainers, all of whom are experienced teachers and most of whom have been teachers or facilitators in Success for All schools. In addition, we are helping to establish regional training sites at Memphis State University, at the Southwest Regional Laboratory in Southern California, and at Midwestern State University in Texas, and we frequently have staff from experienced Success for All schools help out with training in new schools nearby.

The process of becoming a Success for All school requires buy-in at many levels. Typically, districts or schools contact us for information, and may ultimately ask for an on-site presentation. We have a brief video presentation and many written materials to describe the program. Our staff may then negotiate with district officials about the practicalities of implementing the model: costs, staffing changes, Chapter 1 and special education changes, and so on. Often, presentations will be made at principals' meetings, and a set of principals interested in implementing Success for All will be identified.

The most important part of the "buy-in" process comes next. Our staff will visit schools to explain the program, and after having an opportunity to discuss, debate, and come to consensus, school staffs take a vote by secret ballot. We require a vote of at least 80 percent in favor. By this point the great majority of school staffs vote in excess of 80 percent positive, but the exercise is essential in letting teachers know that they had a free choice to participate from the outset.

When a school has voted to implement Success for All, one of their first important tasks is to designate a school improvement team composed of the principal, staff representatives, parents, and others to help plan next steps. Next, the school must designate a facilitator. This is always an experienced, respected teacher, usually from the school's own staff. We try to impress upon schools the importance of having a facilitator who will be seen as a friend and helper to teachers, not an evaluator or supervisor.

We then schedule training for the facilitator and training for the staff. Training of the facilitator is usually done in Baltimore, and we try to arrange to have new facilitators spend as much time as possible visiting existing Success for All sites and spending time with experienced facilitators to see firsthand what they do.

A schedule of implementation and training is worked out early on. Our objective is to phase in elements of the program gradually, so that each can be successfully incorporated in teachers' routines before the next element is introduced. Some schools will start off with some grades before others (most often, prekindergarten through grade 3 first, then the remaining grades), and schools will generally begin with reading and then add writing/language arts or other elements later. If implementation is to start in September, our initial training will be done over three days in August, although we are finding greater success in many schools that started with some parts of the program in the winter or spring and then used August training just for program elements (such as Beginning Reading) that cannot be started at midyear. Either way, initial training is followed by visits from our project staff, from regional training staff, and/or from teachers or facilitators from nearby schools. Some of these visits are for formal training on such topics as cooperative learning, pacing, classroom management, family support, or additional curricular elements not covered in initial training, but most are primarily intended to assess and strengthen the implementation. In particular, our staff will spend a great deal of time visiting classes, tutoring sessions, family support meetings, school improvement team meetings, and other activities with the building facilitators. Our most important objective in these followup visits is to strengthen the building facilitators, to see what they are doing and give them ideas about how they might solve whatever problems exist. We know that we cannot hope to provide adequate classroom followup from far away; we must rely on the facilitator and the school staff as a whole to do the essential coaching, troubleshooting, and program adaptation necessary for success in implementing any major classroom innovation.

One of the important goals we try to help building facilitators and principals accomplish is to foster collaboration among all staff within Success for All schools. This is done in a number of ways. One is to establish school improvement teams or, if they already exist, to help them work more effectively. Another is to try to schedule common planning times for teachers at a given grade level and to have facilitators meet frequently with grade level teams (including tutors of that grade level). We encourage facilitators not to try to solve everyone's problems, but instead to let teachers solve each other's problems to the maximum extent possible. We strongly encourage peer coaching, and many facilitators will offer to cover a teacher's class so that he or she can visit another teacher for mutual coaching. The facilitator plays a major cheerleading function within the school, helping the whole school staff maintain a vision of success for every child through collaboration, communication, and constant attention to professional growth for all staff. Many teachers in high-poverty schools have come to believe that there are some children they just can't reach. Principals and facilitators play an essential role in combating this belief by communicating the idea that if children fail one way it is the school's responsibility to try another and another until the child succeeds.

Between visits to the schools, our staff is in constant communication with building facilitators and others by telephone. Also, we strongly encourage networking among schools in the same region; some schools have "buddies" on the other side of the country. In some areas building facilitators, principals, and other staff meet and visit each other's schools on a regular basis.

Each spring, we hold a conference in Baltimore for experienced Success for All schools. Nearly all schools at least send a facilitator; some send principals and other staff as well. At these conferences the school staffs present innovations they have made in the program, problems they have had and solutions to those problems, and so on. Many schools bring displays with photographs, videos, and student work samples to show off what they are doing. In addition, our staff presents new developments in curriculum, new manuals, and other updates. The conferences provide a rich opportunity to build networks among the schools and with our staff. Beyond the substantive contribution these networks make in sharing ideas, they also provide critical emotional and intellectual support. Most Success for All schools are located in large districts in which they are a small minority, and getting together with others who have the same concerns and speak the same language is extremely important in maintaining quality implementation over time.

The issue of maintaining an ambitious school change process over long time periods is a central concern for our project. Among our

140 schools are many that have been implementing Success for All for three to six years, yet only three schools have ever dropped out of the program (all because of a change in principal). Others have survived changes in principals, superintendents, facilitators and key staff, major funding cuts, and other threats. The keys to this longevity are the extended contact and follow-up from our staff and the strength of the building facilitators. The facilitators are able to induct new staff into the school's program, and are usually able to convince new principals to continue the program (although change in principal presents the greatest danger to the program as new principals often have their own agenda). As changes take place in the district's central administration, curriculum, Chapter 1, or special education policies, external assistance is often critical; our staff is often able to suggest changes to satisfy new policies or interests, and can help school staffs stand up to pressures within their districts. Our experience is that neither demonstrated effectiveness nor overwhelming staff support nor even local or national visibility guarantees maintenance of innovations over time. There are always pressures to erode the quality of innovative programs, and schools implementing such programs need continuing contact and support from the outside to maintain the integrity of these programs.

The nature of political and normative pressures that often work to undermine Success for All vary from place to place, but there are several worth noting. Perhaps the most important, as mentioned earlier, is the tendency for new administrators to want to do away with programs introduced by their predecessors. In particular, new superintendents, reading supervisors, Chapter 1 directors, and especially principals may find it difficult to support an existing program when they have an agenda of their own.

One form of opposition to Success for All comes from advocates for "pure" forms of whole language. Success for All uses a reading approach that contains a systematic presentation of word attack skills in the context of meaning. This is not a problem with relatively eclectic whole language advocates, but is unacceptable to individuals who are opposed to direct teaching of phonics. This has been a particular problem in districts just making a move to whole language, and is the primary explanation of why one school dropped the program after two successful years.

A moment of great danger for any innovative program is when funds have been deeply cut. Ironically, the direction of change seems more important than the amount of money available; a school whose Chapter 1 allocation was just cut from $200,000 to $100,000 is at much more risk than one that was always limited to $100,000. Contact from our staff is critical at this time. School staffs may have come to believe that certain program elements are essential and that the program cannot continue with less. Our staff is able to suggest adaptations and to assure a school that it can still do an adequate job with less money.

While there are many problems that Success for All schools are likely to encounter, there are some that they rarely meet. While there are always problems with a few ineffective teachers, we find the great majority of teachers in even the highest-poverty schools to be willing and able to implement a comprehensive change program if it is well laid out and if training and follow-up are of good quality. As a rule, elementary teachers believe in children; they entered teaching with idealism and deep concern for helping children grow. Even teachers who appear dispirited and burned out at first can return to the feelings that brought them into teaching if they are given the right tools, resources, supports, and school climate. Obviously, some teachers do a better job than others; some stick to the letter of the program, and some use it as a base from which to soar. Yet, we find very few teachers who are unable or unwilling to adopt the main elements of Success for All.

We also find great support for Success for All from parents. One key program objective is to build positive relationships between the school and parents, which involves many programs to draw parents into schools, home visits, and other activities. We have learned from the schools that parent involvement will be maximized in activities that involve the children, provide food and fun, engage parents in social activities, have a direct connection to their children's success in school, and provide activities for younger or older siblings. If a child's teacher or someone else in the school personally asks parents to attend an activity, chances are excellent that they will. Schools with effective family support teams often have staff look for particular parents to make a personal invitation. For example, we have a program called "Books and Breakfast" in which parents come in with their children to learn ways of reading with them. The teachers demonstrate the reading methods and parents are given books to try out immediately with their own children. They then take the books home to use, and can trade them in later for other books. Coffee and sweet rolls are provided, and sometimes there are door prizes or other fun activities. We often have as many as 70 percent of parents at the relevant grade levels who will show up for Books and Breakfast, in neighborhoods where less than a half dozen parents typically come to PTA meetings. These and many other activities are valuable far beyond their contribution to students' reading. They communicate to parents that the school cares about them and their children and wants to see them in the school. We try to build a good basis with parents so that they will be partners rather than antagonists if any problems should arise with their children later on. Even those parents who never attend school events hear about them from their neighbors and know that the school respects and values parents and is doing its best for their children.

Our experience with high-poverty schools across the country convinces us that there is nothing wrong with children, with parents, or with teachers that would keep any school from successfully implementing a program as comprehensive as Success for All. What is more often lacking is the political will to support long-term, comprehensive change at the school level and to sustain change when it proves to be effective.

Can Success for All Be Replicated?

The demonstration that reading achievement can be substantially accelerated in high-poverty schools is very important. If reading failure, retentions, and special education placements can be markedly improved in such difficult schools, it is logical to assume that reading failure can become a thing of the past in more typical schools. Yet this demonstration would have relatively little practical importance if the Success for All program could not be replicated.

As noted earlier, the Success for All program is currently being implemented in 140 schools in 20 states in all parts of the United States. The level of poverty is relatively high in all these schools, but otherwise the schools vary considerably. Most are urban, but many are rural. Most serve African-American student bodies, but many serve white, Latino, and Asian students and many are integrated. In fact, the program now exists in Spanish and is therefore increasingly being used in bilingual education. One school in San Francisco is working on a Cantonese version of Success for All.

The main limitation on the replicability of Success for All is its cost. The program is expensive, primarily because of the salaries of the facilitator and tutors; yet these costs are almost always met primarily by reallocating dollars already going to the schools rather than seeking additional dollars. Sometimes, school districts will supplement existing funds by $30,000 to $60,000 for materials, training, released time, and so on, but this is 1 to 2 percent of the cost of operating a typical elementary school. In most cases, Success for All is funded by some combination of money from Chapter 1, state compensatory education, special education, and/or funds from settlements in desegregation or finance equity decisions. Facilitators and tutors were usually Chapter 1 "pull-out" teachers previously. Not every school can afford the program, but high-poverty schools (which receive high Chapter 1 allocations) usually can if they are willing to restructure their Chapter 1 programs significantly. Schools where the level of poverty is lower usually need fewer tutors and therefore can often afford less expensive versions of the program.

Another important limitation on the replicability of Success for All is the availability of training and support services. Typically, Success for All schools receive twenty person-days of training and follow-up on site during their first year, with declining numbers of days in subsequent years. Providing this service for large numbers of geographically dispersed schools without sacrificing the quality or integrity of the program is an enormous job. As noted earlier, we currently have a staff of twelve trainers at Johns Hopkins University who work with schools throughout the United States, but as we have expanded we are also finding ways to have local or regional personnel help schools implement the program. First, we are helping to establish regional training sites. The first two of these are at the Southwest Regional Laboratory (SWRL) in Southern California and at Memphis State University. In addition, we are increasingly involving facilitators from experienced sites in training and follow-up in new sites. We are working with state departments of education to help establish state networks for assistance and support among Success for All schools, and we have encouraged local networking among facilitators and other staff.

Conclusion

Success for All is not the only effective school restructuring program, and we could not claim that each of its elements is essential or optimal. Yet it is clear that to ensure the reading success of children in high-poverty schools, some program as comprehensive as Success for All will be needed. Experience with the development, evaluation, and dissemination of this program over a six-year period has taught us that it can be effective under a wide variety of circumstances, and it can be replicated with a high degree of quality and fidelity to the basic principles. If this is the case, then there is no excuse for the continuing failure of so many students in the elementary grades.

If we are to create schools in which all students can be smart, we must first create schools in which all students can read. In schools in which all students can read, the concerns expressed by the mother at the beginning of this chapter will be moot. Reading failure is not the only source of heterogeneity in the upper elementary and secondary grades, but if all students were skillful, strategic, and joyful readers, heterogeneity among students could be celebrated, seen as a resource rather than a problem. Then we could truly create schools that would work for all students.

Portions of this chapter are adapted from Robert E. Slavin, Nancy A. Madden, Nancy L. Karweit, Lawrence J. Dolan, and Barbara A. Wasik, *Success for All: A Relentless Approach to Prevention and Early Intervention in Elementary Schools* (Arlington, VA: Educational Research Service, 1992). Preparation of the chapter was supported by a grant from the Office of Educational Research and Improvement, U.S. Department of Education (No. OERI-R-117-R90002). However, any opinions expressed are those of the authors and do not necessarily represent OERI positions or policies.

NOTES

1. Anne Wheelock, *Crossing the Tracks: How "Untracking" Can Save America's Schools* (New York: New Press, 1992).

2. Judith A. Langer, Arthur N. Applebee, Ina V. S. Mullis, and M. A. Foertsch, *Learning to Read in Our Nation's Schools* (Washington, DC: U.S. Department of Education, 1990).

3. Connie Juel, "Learning to Read and Write: A Longitudinal Study of 54 Children from First through Fourth Grades," *Journal of Educational Psychology* 80 (1988): 437-447.

4. Gay S. Pinnell, Diane E. DeFord, and Carol A. Lyons, *Reading Recovery: Early Intervention for At-Risk First Graders* (Arlington, VA: Educational Research Service, 1988).

5. Barbara Wasik and Robert E. Slavin, "Preventing Early Reading Failure with One-to-One Tutoring: A Review of Five Programs," *Reading Research Quarterly* 28 (1993): 178-200.

6. Robert E. Slavin, Nancy A. Madden, Nancy L. Karweit, Lawrence J. Dolan, and Barbara A. Wasik, *Success for All: A Relentless Approach to Prevention and Early Intervention in Elementary Schools* (Arlington, VA: Educational Research Service, 1992).

7. Wasik and Slavin, "Preventing Early Reading Failure with One-to-One Tutoring."

8. Robert E. Slavin, "School and Classroom Organization in Beginning Reading: Class Size, Aides, and Instructional Grouping," in *Preventing Early School Failure: Research on Effective Strategies*, edited by Robert E. Slavin, Nancy L. Karweit, Barbara A. Wasik, and Nancy A. Madden (Boston: Allyn & Bacon, 1994).

9. Robert E. Slavin, "Ability Grouping and Student Achievement in Elementary Schools: A Best-Evidence Synthesis," *Review of Educational Research* 57 (1987): 347-350.

10. Robert J. Stevens, Nancy A. Madden, Robert E. Slavin, and Anna Marie Farnish, "Cooperative Integrated Reading and Composition: Two Field Experiments," *Reading Research Quarterly* 22 (1987): 433-454.

11. Robert E. Slavin, Nancy A. Madden, Lawrence J. Dolan, Barbara A. Wasik, Steven M. Ross, and Lana J. Smith, " 'Whenever and Wherever We Choose': The Replication of 'Success for All'," *Phi Delta Kappan* 75 (April 1994): 639-647.

12. Slavin et al., *Success for All.*

CHAPTER VI

Teaming: Creating Small Communities of Learners in the Middle Grades

GRETCHEN GUITON, JEANNIE OAKES, JENNIFER GONG,
KAREN HUNTER QUARTZ, MARTIN LIPTON,
AND JULIE BALISOK

In 1989, the Carnegie Task Force on Education of Young Adolescents issued *Turning Points: Preparing American Youth for the 21st Century*, a report acknowledging schools' failure to meet young adolescents' unique educational needs.[1] *Turning Points* argues that with reformed school structures, practices, and relationships, all young adolescents could accomplish far more than they now do. It sets forth a comprehensive agenda for the overhaul of middle grades education and argues that current social and economic conditions make such reforms imperative.

The Carnegie Corporation garnered considerable public attention with the release of *Turning Points*, and it has committed substantial resources to making middle grades reform a reality. Its implementation strategy—the Middle Grade Schools State Policy Initiative (MGSSPI)—includes a continuing series of grants and technical assistance to help states develop an infrastructure for policy development and implementation of middle grades reforms. State education policymakers have enthusiastically embraced the ambitious agenda of *Turning Points* and, with Carnegie's support, fifteen states are currently engaged in this complex set of reforms.

In this chapter, we explore how the recommendations of *Turning Points* diverge from conventional school practices, norms, and politics. Then, we examine the initial reform efforts of twelve schools in four states. Like other authors in this volume, we are researchers and

Gretchen Guiton is an Assistant Professor of Education at the University of Southern California. Jeannie Oakes is Professor of Education at the University of California at Los Angeles, where Jennifer Gong and Karen Hunter Quartz are Research Associates. Julie Balisok is a Research Assistant at the University of Southern California. Martin Lipton is a teacher in the Las Virgenes Schools, Calabasas, California.

practitioners involved with school reform. However, unlike these authors who are themselves engaged in making reform happen, we have come to know these schools through their participation in a five-year study we are conducting as part of the MGSSPI.[2]

Current Practices and Proposed Reforms

Turning Points encompasses eight recommendations that require dramatic change in the roles, beliefs, and power relationships that underlie practice in the middle grades. The recommendations call for:

• Reorganized learning settings with smaller learning environments (for example, schools within schools), teachers teamed across disciplines, and adults and students paired in mentoring relationships.

• A core curriculum that integrates subjects in a thematic curriculum, engages students in problem solving, tests a broad range of thinking skills (rather than simply the retention of facts), pays attention to healthy lifestyles, and involves students in community service.

• Heterogeneous classroom grouping supported by cooperative, small-group learning strategies, flexible scheduling, and expanded learning opportunities beyond the school day.

• Restructured decision making with teams of teachers making decisions about their own classroom budgets, space, curriculum, teaching strategies, and scheduling; and school-based governance committees composed of administrators, teachers, support staff, students, parents, and community representatives to coordinate and integrate school activities and school/community relationships.

• Teachers trained and certified as middle school teachers with expertise in adolescent development, sensitivity to cultural diversity, knowledge about providing guidance to students and families, and skills in collegial work.

• Access to health services through limited screening and treatment on school campuses, referral services to other agencies, and a healthy school environment that includes nutritious food, smoke-free school policies, protection from violence.

• Parent participation in school governance, in regular contacts with their children's teacher teams and mentors, and in learning activities at home and at school.

• Partnerships with community agencies and businesses involving youth service activities, health, and social services.

TECHNICAL REFORMS

Turning Points proposes a comprehensive package of related, inter-dependent practices that require an overall restructuring of middle grades education. These practices bear little resemblance to conventional junior high schools that, for the most part, mimic senior high schools in organization and curricula. Junior high school students traditionally take a set of six or seven quite distinct classes taught by specialist teachers who themselves are divided into discipline-based departments. This "departmentalization" limits teachers' ability to accommodate students' personal and social needs, as they single-handedly manage the large number of students they see. Likewise, departmentalization constrains teachers' opportunities to provide interdisciplinary teaching and increases teacher isolation.[3] Students, who usually change classmates each period of the day as they move from one class to another, also are isolated and often experience academic learning as fragmented and irrelevant. These practices are supported by tracking structures that group students into homogeneous classes and rigid time schedules. The lack of after-school programs that provide extra tutoring and the extensive use of paper and pencil tests that focus almost exclusively on basic facts further limit opportunities for flexible grouping.

Furthermore, many middle grades teachers have been trained to be high school teachers. Few have special certification for teaching in the middle grades or the training to meet students' nonacademic needs. The linkages of schools to parents, community agencies, and businesses are far less extensive than envisioned in *Turning Points*. Clearly, the gap between the vision of what middle grades education ought to be and current practice in most schools serving adolescents is substantial.

NORMATIVE REFORMS

Turning Points also proposes fundamental changes in the norms—the beliefs and values—that currently support traditional practices. It challenges schools to reinvent themselves as inclusive and socially just communities. In addition to having school practices more "in sync" with adolescents' needs, the reform advocates that middle schools become places where educators, students, families, businesses, and social service agencies come together to augment the emotional and physical support students need. Such changes rely on new norms to govern how those in schools relate to one another. Acceptance of the new norms means moving away from individualistic and competitive norms toward communitarian norms that promote close and caring relationships, trust, respect, common purpose, and mutual support.

Turning Points eschews dominant bureaucratic norms of separation and specialization in favor of integration. It moves schools away from the segregation of knowledge in discrete, fragmented bits and demands that educators think differently about the nature of knowledge to be learned in school. The middle grades expert relates learning to students' experiences, takes advantage of adolescents' desire to interact with peers and learn by doing, and blurs traditional boundaries among subject areas and between school and community. Guided by new norms of integration, teachers must see connections between a student's well-being and learning if they are to establish and sustain practices such as interdisciplinary instruction, hands-on learning, and heterogeneous grouping.

Such normative changes are extraordinarily difficult to undertake, given the pervasive and deeply rooted nature of the traditional norms of schooling. For instance, agreement that "working together as a community" is desirable does not necessarily mean that those in schools are ready to abandon norms that work against community. Further, as Hargreaves reminds us, loudly heralded but lightly examined norms can have darker sides.[4] Clearly, *Turning Points* envisions deep normative changes that require collaborative relationships but avoid the pitfalls of parochialism and paternalism that also can characterize community.

POLITICAL REFORMS

The complexity of reform is magnified by the significant changes proposed in roles, relationships, and power allocations in middle schools. *Turning Points* seeks to change the power relationships inherent in individual interactions and interdependencies as individuals attempt to carry out school functions. An unstated, but salient, principle is that changes in the formal authority structure will alter existing power relationships within the school and among the school, the parents, and community groups.

Middle grades schools must explicitly recognize and actively seek new ties with social agencies and more active, intensified roles for parents and for business and community leaders in contrast to traditional school attitudes that view such groups with suspicion and assign them to superficial or supporting roles. The participation of these constituencies engenders new obligations, creates new demands, represents different interests, and thus influences how the school functions.

In addition to changing *who* participates in middle schools, reformers recommend changes in *how* participants function. Different groups have responsibility for deciding different issues (for example, teacher teams decide class schedules), and the decision-making process itself shifts from an authoritarian, win-lose stance to a consensus-building, win-win orientation.

Those states and schools that are undertaking middle grades reform, then, face multiple and complex challenges. They must make dramatic changes both in tangible schooling practices and in the less tangible norms and political arrangements that support them.

Teaming as a Lever for Middle Grades Reform

Although *Turning Points* presents a comprehensive vision, schools implement these reforms according to their understanding of what is needed and what is possible. One school might emphasize creating opportunities for all students and begin by grouping students heterogeneously. Another might start by creating a school governance board in hopes of generating more parent interest. Or, a group of teachers might convince their colleagues to join them in creating an interdisciplinary unit, or initiate a change in their assessment methods. To the degree that *Turning Points* offers a "model" for reform, it suggests that starting any reform will soon lead to, invite, or require other reform activities.

Despite the numerous ways that schools might approach *Turning Points*, all twelve schools in our study experienced a new or renewed interest in teaming. Early on, all schools modified their organizational structure to reduce the number of teachers and peers with whom students would interact each day. The new structures embody the schools' emerging beliefs that (1) a small group of teachers working together could be more effective than teachers working alone; and (2) students benefit from smaller, more stable learning groups. Most schools moved quickly to provide time for team meetings and to shift some responsibilities and decision-making authority to these teams.

Teaming receives this attention in part because it serves as a promising vehicle for implementing a number of the recommendations for reform in the middle grades. For instance, *Turning Points* called for increased teacher control over decision making in the classroom, including decisions about grouping practices, scheduling, and budgeting.

Teams offer a method for shifting decisions from administrators to teachers. Given greater control over instructional decisions, joint planning time, and shared student responsibilities, teaming can provide a forum in which teachers plan together and develop an interdisciplinary curriculum. Because teachers deal with fewer students and parents know a student's core teachers, teaming may reduce the bureaucratic distance between school and parents. Teaming also can increase professional contact and dialogue, reduce isolation, foster joint learning and problem solving, and can thus alter the school culture.[5] Ideally, teaming represents a technical modification that can positively affect normative and political changes as well.

The effort to capture the spirit, as well as the structure, of *Turning Points* through teaming finds considerable support in our work. At one of the twelve schools, a *Turning Points*-like team has functioned as a school within a school for twenty years to provide an alternative, parent-selected, child-oriented program for students from Kindergarten through eighth grade. The culture of the team of teachers of grades 6 through 8 involved in our study exemplifies the technical, normative, and political dimensions of middle grades education that reformers want to establish across the twelve schools.

Currently, the middle grades team consists of two teachers and fifty-plus students.[6] The two teachers have worked together for four years. One teacher is a twenty-year veteran of the program and actively participated in the hiring of the second teacher who had studied the program for her master's thesis and was philosophically in tune with the program. Although the program has evolved over the years, it clearly has been multigraded, interdisciplinary, and individualized, and the team has completely controlled the curriculum and direction of the program including devising their own reporting system. Recently, the program has become increasingly student-directed. These four distinguishing elements closely resemble the curricular and instructional recommendations in *Turning Points*. The curriculum is not defined on a grade basis, but operates on a three-year cycle with a thematic focus that changes constantly because of the student-directed nature of the program. Students generate questions about themselves and the world and as a group select themes, usually three each year, to address jointly. For instance, students identified Origins as a theme and explored the creation of the universe, earth, life on earth and civilization, and individual creation. The same year, they investigated the Self and Adolescence. In a unit called "I Can Make a Difference," they explored local and global concerns and each individual addressed one specific problem. Students define individual and group configurations and responsibilities, and they determine whether there will be a culminating activity for each theme. The teacher gives up responsibility for choosing the theme or determining activities, but tries to balance topics throughout the year and makes sure that students are exposed to different concepts and skills that arise while exploring themes. The program benefits from its multiage and K-8 nature as many students have a clear sense of their role and responsibilities by the time they join the middle grades team. Teachers meet with each student individually once a week, or more frequently depending on the student, to assure that the students are clear about their goals and plans. Students set individual goals to meet their needs. Teachers work together in a totally collaborative relationship that extends to the students. The team leader position rotates every two years, so that there is continuity, but no one teacher becomes viewed as the lead teacher. Likewise, teachers work closely with parents. Although the teachers we spoke with recognized the benefits of having parents choose the program, they felt an ongoing need to communicate with parents who themselves had experienced a traditional education and sometimes felt concerns about their child's preparation for a more conventional high school experience. Students in this program have been successful in the high school, a fact that helps alleviate parental concerns. Nevertheless, the teachers make extra efforts to communicate with parents by sending a newsletter and conferencing with all parents.

Each of the twelve schools is attempting to create similarly well-functioning teams of teachers who take the major responsibility for the students they share. Across the schools, teams have taken on numerous new responsibilities—some focusing on the classroom (for example, scheduling, assigning students to classes, determining discipline and reward structures) and others aimed at schoolwide matters (for example, hiring and representing team members on school improvement and/or governance teams).

Over the three years we have observed them, educators at each of the schools have become increasingly convinced that teaming will lead to the reforms they seek, and, with the support and pressure from their state MGSSPI projects, most have made substantial progress. However, these schools also have found that establishing well-functioning teams requires them to grapple with a number of complex issues. These issues include team formation (Is the move to teaming consensual or coercive? How are teams formed?), stability (Do teams remain intact or change frequently?), and responsibility (What do teams do? How? With what resources?). We now provide some examples of the technical, normative, and political tensions these schools face as they address these issues.

TECHNICAL TENSIONS

Seemingly straightforward, technical changes set off snowballing difficulties as schools encounter new, often unanticipated barriers. Moving teachers to new classrooms so team members may be in close proximity provides an obvious example. Because their classroom is the only professional space over which they have control, teachers often resent being asked to move, even when they support the hoped-for result, so that normative tensions arise. Other difficulties are technical. Schools modeled after high schools often have departmental "wings" or halls that place all science classrooms in a single area. Attempts to cluster teams face this physical barrier, and schools grapple with the choice between splitting the teams or compromising the use of the science facilities.

Scheduling is another technical matter that creates tension. The schedule governs two time-related team resources, joint planning time and flexible instructional time. Without modification of the traditional fifty-minute schedule, teachers cannot meet during the school day to plan interdisciplinary activities, address student concerns, or meet with parents. Neither can they adapt their instruction to longer, integrated lessons. Recognizing the schedule's fundamental role, one principal told us, "the thing to move the building [toward reform] is the schedule—not the program or the student, but the schedule."

Scheduling out-of-class meeting time for teams aids collegiality and supports the change process.[7] At schools that have not structured common planning time into the daily schedule, teachers struggle to find time to meet and carry out their team responsibilities. At one such school where the schedule allows teams to meet only one day a week for a half hour after school, a team leader told us:

Our team finds that it's just not enough time, so we take our Friday free period for our team meeting—and that was a consensus. We all decided we've got to do that. Nobody is happy with that. We also meet more often. For instance, we're meeting another time this week because of meeting a parent. We still don't have as much communication as we'd like to. I know that in some schools, they meet everyday . . . and we were all envious of that school.

Creating joint planning time is difficult, and administrators often need special training or assistance to deal with the logistics of scheduling. Principals often fight difficult battles with district personnel, school boards, and teacher unions to gain additional planning time for teams during the school day. For example, in one district the principal confronted a curriculum director who viewed all time when teachers were not directly involved with students as "down time." Other principals campaigned with their superiors to maintain staffing levels so that teams could remain intact despite reduced enrollments. Scheduling changes frequently required shifts in the number of periods per day ("We had to go to a six-period day.") or complicated schedules that rotated over time. Principals must explain and defend these scheduling gyrations to parents, administrators, and school board members. Moreover, some principals spend several periods in the lunch room each day to release teachers for their team planning.

Even when schools provide joint planning time, other tensions sometimes interfere with reform. At one well-funded school, for example, teachers still viewed being restructured into teams with common planning time as an administrative intrusion on teachers' time. These teachers previously had two planning periods each day, but when the school reorganized, they lost one of the planning periods to homerooms, reading time, mini courses, and team meetings. A few teachers (not all) resented this change enough to protest the reforms that they agreed with philosophically. Some refused to meet as a team except during the officially scheduled time, even when they needed extra time to work together and their individual planning periods coincided. At many schools, setting up the schedule is the "biggest problem initially." And, scheduling problems do not disappear once the schedule is altered.

A related political tension involves the extent to which teachers spend their "own" time on teamwork, whether and how schools compensate them for this time, and whether teachers see themselves or others as determining how they spend their time. For example, one school that provides teachers with both an individual planning period and a common, team planning period each day ran into difficulty around the additional tasks the team leaders perform outside of team planning time. One otherwise reform-minded team leader refused to perform these tasks until the school provided additional compensation for this work. This refusal stemmed in part from the fact that this school system paid its senior high school teachers for extra duties such as an assignment to be an advisor to students. The principal concluded, "individual 'prep' time is untouchable."

At another school that had provided teachers two individual planning periods each day, the principal required that two of these periods each week should be used for team meetings. One teacher complained that teaming reduced her time to develop creative lessons and added another layer of administrative transactions that detracted from curricular planning. She lamented,

I'm known as a very creative teacher throughout the district and I no longer have any time to spend on creating new lessons and doing research. I spend all the time I used to spend on that type of thing on paperwork, coordinating the team, and on content mastery students who now are included in the classroom.

Her principal was not happy with the arrangement either, sensing that teams needed more than two periods a week to address curricular and instructional issues.

This school's experience is not unique. Across the twelve schools, teachers—especially those who take pride in being innovative in the classroom—worry that the added responsibilities of teaming will reduce the time needed to prepare for teaching. Ironically, these teachers often become team leaders. One such teacher told us, "I couldn't do my job and do it well, and we're a faculty that likes to do our jobs and do them well. Most people are feeling that they can't do all these meetings." This teacher resigned the team leader position after a year.

These examples show how seemingly straightforward technical reform can revive deep, if apparently unrelated, grievances. For some teachers, administrative demands on their space and time trigger latent conflicts over control and professionalism, even when teachers strongly support reform. For others, the loss of individual planning time and the addition of team responsibilities pits team meetings that focus on individual students against time that teachers use to plan lessons. These largely technical changes engender new tensions over normative issues—in this case, norms of professionalism and collegiality—and over the politics surrounding control of resources such as time. We find early suggestions in these schools that new structures are added before old norms are abandoned. As in one of the cases above, a teacher may see creative lesson planning as an individual activity not well suited to teamwork. The result is that the team adds to, rather than subsumes, existing tasks.

NORMATIVE TENSIONS

Other aspects of middle grades reform present more obvious normative difficulties. For example, at several schools, the promise of smoother ways to deal with "discipline" has been an impetus for implementing teaming, and all twelve schools shifted responsibility for disciplining students from the administration to the teams. This new responsibility requires considerable new skills of communication and collaboration, and it also raises questions about the legitimate reach of collaboration. Teachers at many of the schools grapple with whether team decisions should rightfully govern teachers' individual practice in their own classroom (for example, classroom rules and consequences for students' infractions). As such, team responsibility for students' behavior exposes normative tensions having to do with values of individualism, competition, and community.

Teachers across the schools welcomed their colleagues' support in dealing with behavior problems. Students, too, seemed to feel quite connected to their teams, partly because their teachers kept tabs on their behavior jointly. Having adults share the responsibility of setting and enforcing limits on students seems to enhance support and a sense of belonging for both. However, not all team interactions around behavior achieve the normative benefits of community called for in *Turning Points*.

In all twelve schools, teams of teachers discipline students during team planning time. These meetings sometimes take on an authoritarian tone, with four or five adults simultaneously asserting their dominance over a young adolescent. A team at one inner-city school has adopted a court room like strategy to instill the importance of "good manners." During one meeting, a young man who talked back to a teacher was summoned and interrogated by the team leader who assumed the role of a "judge" arbitrating between the teacher and the student while other teachers observed the proceeding. It is hard to imagine positive normative outcomes from such practices. The teacher may feel "supported," but the teacher's professional status may be diminished if subjected to arbitration with a preteen. And while the student may have some sense of being treated like an "equal," he could just as easily interpret his experience as being berated in front of five powerful grownups.

We have also sat in as teams confer with parents about a student's behavior. During one of these meetings, teachers reprimanded parents for their daughter's absences and denied their request to take a book so that she could make up missed work at home. Again, while the teachers experienced peer support for their decision, we suspect that the parents felt that they had been "ganged up on."

Most team actions around students' behavior are not so destructive to the close relationships teams strive to establish with students. At another inner-city school, for example, one team assigns two teachers on a rotating basis to address discipline issues. With fewer teachers present, the students appear less overwhelmed and more participatory. In this team, and in others, teachers talk respectfully to students about their work and behavior difficulties and jointly develop solutions.

Even when discipline issues are minor, or when teams have effectively improved discipline, some teachers still feel that discipline is an administrative responsibility. Others see benefits in teachers addressing discipline issues but recognize that it requires new skills. As one teacher told us,

Suddenly you begin to think, "My God, you're going to do this?" I mean be responsible. We'd always had TAs [teacher advisories] before, but we didn't have lunch duty. We weren't responsible for calling parents all the time. These were a lot of new responsibilities being placed on people, and people weren't ready for it.

Still other teams find that members have very different "tolerances," and obtaining agreement among teachers is problematic. Teams have trouble determining when they should enforce rules and when to allow differences to exist between classrooms. For example, some teams debate whether the "tardy rule" should apply to students being in their seats or merely in the room. They grapple with whether to enforce a common standard or leave decisions to the discretion of each teacher. We anticipate that the path to greater normative and programmatic cohesion is through discussions around such seemingly prosaic matters. But, teams undoubtedly deal with these questions best over time and with much reflection.

In addition to tensions between teachers and teams around norms of community, teaming strains the locus of community. Is it the school or the team? For example, at one inner-city school where discipline responsibilities were turned over to the team, the administration interfered with a team's decision to allow students to visit their lockers both before and after lunch. Because team members could not agree among themselves to supervise both locker visits, administrators overruled the prelunch visit fearing that it would delay the lunch period for all students. This decision essentially required the few students who brought their lunch to carry it to class all morning, and left team members angry with the administration.

Clearly, principals are left to balance the needs of the entire school with the needs and internal dynamics of the teams. One strategy principals use is to hold out an exemplary team as a model to motivate other teams. Even without the principal consciously attempting to do this, many schools deal with the phenomena we have come to call the "star team." When one team initially seems to make much greater progress toward reforms, it stands out and can become a target. In one school, a grade-level team jelled much more quickly than did teams at the other two grades. In part because this team attended an extensive summer institute before teaming was introduced, the group quickly developed a team identity, received some positive local press, and provided an example of what a cooperative, working team might look like. Needless to say, other teachers resented the comparison. It took two years of effort for schoolwide relations to mend.

In environments with strong competitive norms, comparison quickly turns to competition. Some schools attempt to use competition to motivate others to implement reforms or to build team identity. This seems to have particularly disastrous effects on schools with two teams per grade and active parent involvement. For example, at one affluent school, a team planned a field trip to a local amusement park to develop team spirit, while the second team at the same grade planned a visit to a local historical site in conjunction with a unit. Children visiting the historical site felt cheated and complained, as did their parents, to teachers and administrators. One teacher on the team that went to the amusement park told us, "The kids [on the historical trip team] and the parents just came unglued. They thought it was unfair and we as a team were attacked for taking them [to the amusement park]." The teams disagreed about the value of the trip to the amusement park and there were hard feelings between the teams. Since then, teams coordinate their field-trips and the school instituted one joint grade-level field-trip each year. As one teacher told us,

We have not tried that [intentional competition] between the teams. Many times we come up with ideas and want to do things. We take off and do it. The other team says, "Well, why do you think you can do that? We didn't know anything about it." So we have gotten to the point now where every time we come up with an idea to do something, we send that idea over to them. Why they're feeling left out, I don't know, except that they do have a hard time communicating with each other because some of them have real conflicts going with each other.

Parents, at another affluent school, select their child's team placement. This is considered especially important since students stay in the same multigrade team, with the same teachers, for three years. Teachers present their curriculum to parents at an open house, and parents are invited to visit and observe all teams. These meetings and visitations are staggered and continue over a period of weeks each spring. Teachers generally find this practice threatening; some feel that their jobs are on the line. One veteran teacher told us that the pressure for change and the community scrutiny altered her identity with the school as a whole and negatively affected schoolwide teacher collaboration:

I don't care about the whole school. I care about my team and what's going on in my classroom, but there isn't enough energy left to care about the whole school. Unfortunately, it's gotten to a point where parents come around and check out the teams and which ones they want. I wish we were more solid here and people knew . . . I mean we're professionals. . . . There needs to be solidarity. Our teams should be more alike. It's divisive. We're a very thoughtful, and were a close faculty, but it's changed. You hear things like, "don't tell the other team because they might want to do it."

Teachers repeatedly say that their team has replaced the school as the center of their work lives. Teachers in previously strong departmentalized schools often missed occasions when subject matter specialists met regularly and coordinated curriculum. Schools with a strong schoolwide teacher community sometimes have difficulty sustaining it. For example, many teachers at one school commented on the loss of "whole school family feeling" since the institution of teaming. They attribute this change to their teams' physical isolation and lack of interaction. Efforts by the principal to staff schoolwide committees with members from different teams seem insufficient to overcome teachers' sense of loss.

More divisive than the cross-team rivalry, and even more pervasive, is the dissension team structures can create between the teachers of elective subjects and those of academic subjects. Nearly everywhere, teams are made up of core academic teachers and, occasionally, specialists such as resource teachers and Chapter 1 teachers. Team meeting time typically occurs when the team's students attend elective classes. Thus, core academic and elective teachers do not share planning periods, even in the few schools that attach elective teachers to core teams. Many elective teachers say they are undervalued, as though they are "someone's coffee break." Most schools establish an elective team such as a team for unified arts, but rarely are elective teachers given common planning time.

Two factors exacerbate the negative impact of this academic/elective division. First, most interdisciplinary teaching that occurred prior to the middle grades initiative in these schools involved some of the elective teachers (for example, in language arts and social studies units that involved art). Second, elective teachers often have the most experience teaching heterogeneous groups and using different approaches. The very structure that permits teaming constrains the access that teams have to colleagues with critically relevant experience. Although this schism is pervasive, none of the twelve schools has addressed it successfully. Most schools address this problem as an interpersonal issue by establishing cross-disciplinary teams for schoolwide functions or, in one school, by assigning "buddies" to do informal sharing. Although administrators and teachers in our schools actively try to reduce the amount of bad feeling, they have trouble finding the resources to alter structural barriers.

Such technical changes in the school's structure affect norms of community. Where individualism prevails, introducing teaming can benefit students and teachers alike by building strong communities, but a strong sense of team community appears to weaken or replace the schoolwide community and either introduce dissension among teams or allow it to surface. Efforts to promote teaming that incorporate norms of competition can strengthen team identity at the expense of the school community. These normative tensions further complicate implementation of reform.

POLITICAL TENSIONS

Teaming is seen as a lever for more comprehensive change, partly because it establishes new roles, relationships, and responsibilities. However, because such changes involve shifts in the nature of participation and decision making, schools face considerable political tension as they implement teaming. Both teaming and the other reforms that teams are expected to trigger are aimed, in part, at increasing teacher participation in decision making. Yet, principals spearheading these reforms exert considerable control over the teaming process. In a number of schools, efforts to increase teachers' power conflicts with administrators' efforts to spur and manage the reform.

In three schools in our study administrators organized the teachers into teams after an extended planning process in which a subgroup of interested teachers investigated middle school issues and recommended changes. At one of these schools teachers volunteered to participate in teaming the first year, with the understanding that the school would move toward schoolwide teaming over a three-year period. Another school began with a voluntary pilot group, with the administration forming teams for the next year. At other schools, administrators set up teams with little advance notice or preparation. At one school, teachers told us, "they sprung teaming on us." Two other schools introduced teaming after much discussion, but with clear directives from their principals. Whether teaming was recommended by the principal or by a representative group of teachers, principals generally felt responsible for gauging the faculty's readiness and implementing changes.

Surprisingly, at these schools teachers rarely wanted to form their own teams, preferring, when given the option, to have principals assign them. Although principals vary in their approaches to forming teams, they often describe the process as "matchmaking" or "getting the chemistry right." Principals list a variety of criteria for team assignments, including teacher certification status (What grade or subject is someone allowed to teach?), thinking styles ("Oh, he's a concrete sequential rather than a concrete random."), discipline styles (traditional or laid-back), and gender ("With all the female-headed households, we try to get one male on each team."). Principals usually solicit teachers' preferences for team membership in terms of their subject and grade level preferences and the names of teachers with whom they cannot work.

Notably, some teachers do choose their own teammates. One school's initial team was formed by a strong teacher in consultation with her peers and the assistant principal. Other teachers indicated their preferences, and teams were formed by the assistant principal. Still other teachers, opposed to teaming, were allowed to work alone, at least for the time being. At another school the principal allowed a group of teachers who had pooled their efforts earlier to provide extra tutoring to students to formalize their collaboration and become a team. Supported by the principal, only this group was allowed to remain intact when teams were formed. Here, and in other schools where "voluntary" teams were formed based on preexisting collegial relations, the team was considered the "star team." This privileged position often strains the relationships of such teams with peers, particularly since "star" status and team cohesiveness often make them seem more desirable to parents than other teams. Most often, however, principals create teams strategically by distributing strong teachers among several teams in order to advance reform evenly across the school. This strategy also creates tension by combining teachers who differ considerably in their philosophy and work style.

The process of selecting team leaders creates further political tension. Teachers often interpret appointment by administrators as an effort to control teams. And, in most schools the principal selects or, at least approves, the leaders' assignment in ways that further his or her agenda. Where the leader position carries financial benefits, principals sometimes use the position as a reward. At one school, the principal told us that he gave a resistant teacher the position to "bring him on board," and when that did not work he assigned a new leader the following year. At this school, too, the principal requires all the leaders to resign periodically, so that he can replace those with whom he is not satisfied.

A lack of stability in teachers' team assignments brings other tensions. One principal moves one or two teachers on each team every year or so. Both the principal and the project coordinator at the school feel that this movement aids the institutionalization of teaming—that is, it keeps teams from becoming too dependent on certain individuals or groups. Reconfiguring teams is a common practice. Most principals tell us they mix teams to maintain or increase the momentum for change schoolwide. At another school, the principal changes team assignments annually, except for the initial voluntary pilot team. Over time, nearly all of our principals have faced the dilemma of maintaining well-functioning teams or breaking them up in order to "share the wealth."

The costs of this strategy are evident in one school where the leader of an outstanding team was moved, most teachers suspected, to help another struggling team. Members of the original team reported their profound sense of loss, as they had been meeting socially on weekends or during the summer. The move also changed the composition of their team, so that members had to go through a bonding process again and had to get accustomed to a new team leader. The benefits of bringing a reform-minded teacher to a new team also has costs for that teacher. At one school, "one bad apple" seemed to undermine the team's ability to carry out interdisciplinary units. One teacher, finding the presence of an active resistor intolerable, requested reassignment the following year under threat of leaving the school.

Principals often shuffle teachers when team members have repeated disagreements. Teachers themselves vie to change teams—either by influencing the principal to move them (for example, a team leader at another school requested that she be moved as soon as word got out that a more desirable team might add a teacher) or by splitting into new configurations (for example, one team planned to divide into two separate teams so that teachers with more similar philosophies could work together). In addition, we see a trend among our schools to reduce team size. One school with nine-member teams decided to double the number of teams. Reducing team membership below the number of core subjects, requires more cross-disciplinary teaching within each team.

Whatever the impetus, shifting team membership brings tension. Most teachers say that it takes two years or more to get "comfortable" with one another, and that teaming cannot influence instruction before this happens. Teachers consistently tell us that personalities are *the* critical factor in making teams work. Teachers nearly uniformly prefer stable teams.

Administrators also exert their power over teams when they judge teams to be slow to reform. A frequent strategy is to manage the way teams use their planning time. Principals use a variety of tactics to control team time. Two principals require teams to turn in minutes documenting their team discussions and decisions. Like a teacher grading papers, one principal writes comments on these minutes, often directing teams to address curriculum and instruction. At another school, the principal was loathe to require minutes the first year of teaming, since he had worked with a principal who had "used them like a sledgehammer." However, he did plan to require team minutes the second year as a means of aiding the writing of proposals for grants, and he told teams that he expected them to plan and execute at least one interdisciplinary unit the first year. In other instances, the district places requirements on the teaming process. One district requires that teachers discuss curricular and instructional issues, and the middle grades coordinator conducts surprise visits to observe team meetings.

Elsewhere administration is more casual. One principal approaches teachers individually, asking them, almost as a personal favor, to spend more time developing interdisciplinary units. Still other principals seem unconcerned about structuring team planning time. Possibly because the teams do not have any meeting time during the school day, one principal leaves the topics covered in meetings completely to the teachers' discretion. Another principal, at a school where team participation is voluntary, plans to provide two planning periods a week for teams, but no comparable time for teachers not involved. While not trying to force resistors (he told us, "I learned if you force them, they push back just as hard"), the principal wants to create conditions for teaming that bring peer pressure. He views "gung-ho" teams as standard setters and practices behaviors like "dropping by" the meetings of questionable teams. Perhaps it is not surprising, given the efforts principals must make to secure planning time for teams, that they feel justified, even responsible, for directing and monitoring its use.

Conclusions

The idea of using teaming to foster schools where all children succeed, as prescribed by *Turning Points*, is well founded. The exemplary team described earlier shows the power of this strategy for creating educational communities for young adolescents. During the three years we have been engaged with these twelve schools, both we and they have become aware that their effort to restructure departmentalized junior high programs into teams has brought definite benefits. With few exceptions, teachers find teaming effective for coordinating students' programs. Teachers feel supported by their colleagues as they interact with students and parents. Parents have better knowledge of their child's teachers, and they are more likely to contact teachers and attend school events. In most schools, students are aware—and even appreciative, in their young adolescent way—of teachers' coordinated efforts on their behalf.

However, restructuring that focuses on workplace modifications does not necessarily impact curricular structures or pedagogical practices.[8] And, as a reform that countervails traditional school structures, teaming runs up against the technical, normative, and political relations that support hierarchical bureaucracy. As school faculties deal with the practicalities of organizing teachers and students into team structures (such as finding time for teams to meet, choosing team leaders to coordinate team functions, and shifting decision-making responsibilities) external factors (such as limited resources, shifts in student enrollment, and staff turnover) impinge on their efforts. Likewise, teaming places new demands on schools and thereby introduces new problems. Some teachers lack the interpersonal skills necessary to function in teams. Role conflicts and a lack of trust complicate shifts in decision-making responsibilities. Teacher turnover makes it difficult to sustain even small successes. The effort requires more time than anyone initially expects. Moreover, teaming is not introduced as a *tabula rasa*; the history and status of previous reform efforts strongly influence the understanding, acceptance, and nature of teaming in each setting. Reform efforts benefit by recognizing the interrelated nature of change and by addressing change on all fronts, which we characterize as the technical, normative, and political dimensions of reform, taking into account the contextual and historical specifics of each school.

Given all of the above, some might be puzzled by our conclusion that the experiences of these twelve schools support teaming. An observation is worth making here. We have documented many technical, normative, and political obstacles that accompany restructuring school faculties into teams. But obstacles are a normal part of school life. Otherwise schools would not be so bent on reform. It is significant that the particular pressures that accompany teaming are the product of efforts to install a practice that, even when imperfectly implemented, still manifests some intrinsic benefits not found in highly individualistic school structures.

The advantages of smaller learning environments and joint planning time do not always or quickly lead to the collegiality and increased professionalism required to support curricular and instructional changes. Nevertheless, attempts to use teams engage educators explicitly with normative and political issues typically avoided in prior reform efforts. This reform effort involves remarkably dedicated and persistent educators. We believe that their progress so far justifies their commitment to restructuring middle grades education in a changing society. It is the combination of widespread, modest early successes in tackling these issues and "existence proofs" such as provided by the exemplary team that lead us to conclude that the extraordinary efforts of these schools and the many others like them, with the strong support of their Carnegie-sponsored state projects, may indeed lead to new educational communities where all young adolescents learn and grow exceedingly well.

Notes

1. Carnegie Council on Adolescent Development, *Turning Points: Preparing American Youth for the 21st Century*, Report of the Task Force on Education of Young Adolescents (New York: The Council, 1989).

2. The qualitative, longitudinal case study research that focuses on twelve schools participating in Carnegie's MGSSPI project is directed by Jeannie Oakes and Gretchen Guiton and is sponsored by the Carnegie Corporation of New York. The results reported here represent preliminary findings based on the schools' first two or three years of involvement in the project. Comments from all twelve principals on earlier drafts of this chapter have been incorporated in the final draft. Our promise of confidentiality prevents us from listing them by name.

3. Joyce L. Epstein and Douglas J. MacIver, *Education in the Middle Grades: National Practices and Trends* (Columbus, Ohio: National Middle School Association, 1990).

4. Andrew Hargreaves, *Changing Teachers, Changing Times* (New York: Teachers College Press, 1994).

5. Gene I. Maeroff, *Team Building for School Change: Equipping Teachers for New Roles* (New York: Teachers College Press, 1993).

6. Until 1991-1992, the middle grades team had included 4th through 8th grades, but it was divided when the rest of the school went to a multigraded team structure. Due to increasing numbers of requests for the program, the 6th to 8th grade team anticipated expansion to three teachers the year after our last visit.

7. Maeroff, *Team Building for School Change*; Michael Fullan, *The New Meaning of Educational Change* (New York: Teachers College Press, 1990); Karen S. Louis and Matthew Miles, *Improving the Urban High School* (New York: Teachers College Press, 1990).

8. Joseph Murphy and Philip Hallinger, *Restructuring Schools: Learning from Ongoing Efforts* (Newbury Park, CA: Corwin, 1993).

CHAPTER VII

A Culture in the Making:
Leadership in Learner-Centered Schools

ANN LIEBERMAN, BEVERLY FALK AND LESLIE ALEXANDER

As current school reform efforts grapple with how to build and transform schools into places where all students can learn in challenging, meaningful, and purposeful ways, many aspects of schooling have been examined and reconsidered. Although leadership has been a subject of much discussion,[1] the conversation has focused predominantly on the traditional role of the principal. Little emphasis has been given to other conceptions of leadership. In this chapter we examine one alternative conception—the teacher-director model in "learner-centered schools." These schools that identify themselves as learner-centered schools because they focus on meeting the needs of learners—both children and adults—in school organization, governance, curriculum, and teaching.

The teacher-director model has been developed in schools that belong to the Center for Collaborative Education (CCE), the New York City affiliate of the Coalition of Essential Schools, a national school reform network that was established in 1985. In this study we look at teacher-directors from six of these New York City public alternative elementary schools (Central Park East I (CPE I), Central Park East II (CPE II), River East, P. S. 234, the Brooklyn New School, and the New Program at P. S. 261. The schools range in age from seven to nineteen years but they share a number of characteristics. Their populations are small (anywhere from two to three hundred students) and they reflect the socioeconomic, racial, and ethnic diversity of New York City. They are organized into heterogeneous, multiage classes and are structured to encourage and enhance collaboration among faculty, students, and students' families. Their classroom environments

Ann Lieberman is Professor of Education and Co-director of the National Center for Restructuring Education, Schools, and Teaching (NCREST) at Teachers College, Columbia University. Beverly Falk, a former teacher-director, is a researcher and educator at NCREST. Leslie Alexander is a founding director of a newly formed learner-centered school in New York City.

feature active involvement of students with materials and experiences, peer interaction, and an interdisciplinary approach to learning. Teachers function as facilitators and supporters of student learning rather than as transmitters of information. Although most of these schools are situated within larger buildings, they are autonomous units led by a teacher (who is paid and licensed as a teacher) rather than by a certified principal.[2]

By exploring the unique characteristics and practices of teacher-directors in these schools, we seek to understand better the significance and possibilities of the leadership role. The following questions have guided our inquiry: How do values of "learner-centeredness" get played out in schools? How do leaders work within their schools to build community? How are norms and structures built and sustained that keep a school focused on students' lives and their learning? What does it take to build commitment and motivate teachers to become an inquiring community? How do leaders think about and act on their own individual interests and concerns while dealing with the collective work of running a school? How do they cope with the distractions of daily problems as they struggle to improve the quality of life and learning in the school?

To find answers to these questions we held individual and group interviews with both the current and past school directors,[3] made a series of observations in their schools, and studied the documents produced by the schools. These research efforts provided us with an opportunity to learn not only about issues of leadership, but also about how these schools were created, and how norms, values, and practices have been maintained through successions of leadership and variations in style.

History and Context

These schools are philosophically rooted in the work of child-centered educators and theorists of the late nineteenth and early twentieth centuries[4] who believed that in order to be observant of children's interests and responsive to their needs schools had to create an environment that encouraged student development and autonomy, that established a pattern of support for continuous progress within a school community, and that was nurtured by a democratic ethic. These ideas were enriched and expanded over the years through the work of educators, researchers, and philosophers such as Caroline Pratt, Jean Piaget, Jerome Bruner, Patricia Carini, Maxine Greene, Lev Vygotsky, Eleanor Duckworth, and Sue Bredekamp.[5] They were first developed and brought to life in the public schools of the United States by Lillian Weber, the founder of the City College Open Corridor/Workshop Center Advisory in New York City in the 1960s and 1970s. The initiative she led was committed to introducing teaching practices and organizational structures that reflected these understandings of child development and learning theory. Weber explains:

[The Workshop Center Advisory] was intended to be facilitating of teachers, to support them in a new teacher role, and to provide beginnings for people to break with the traditional isolation of teacher/teacher, teacher/child, and child/child. The idea was to assist the teacher. The point was not to make someone over, but to be supportive of teachers' strengths in the direction of supporting children. [In the course of this initiative] the advisors continually tested out how things worked or didn't work. Questions evolved. "How do you get a *pattern* of support for children's motion forward given that each child is an individual?" Many questions were raised in the course of addressing this question. These inevitably led to battles on the institutional front.

The "institutional front" to which Weber refers was the national, test-driven, "back to basics" trend of the 1970s which developed during the same period in which the Open Corridor initiative was launched. At this time an emphasis on mastery of basic skills as a prerequisite for higher-order thinking was competing with an emphasis on developing habits of ongoing student inquiry. This was reflected in a proliferation of teacher-proof, sequential, discipline-based curricula which discouraged efforts to get teachers to create their own multidimensional, interdisciplinary studies.

Despite the set-backs to child-centered education caused by this clash with the "back-to-basics" movement,[6] many of the practices that were being forged by Weber and her colleagues have since become commonly acknowledged standards of excellence in contemporary professional practice. Classrooms featuring informal arrangements, active involvement with materials and experiences, an inquiry-based orientation, interage and heterogeneous grouping, and authentic assessment of student work are being promoted and increasingly accepted today as an integral part of the movement for educational reform.[7]

Central Park East—Leadership from Within the Community

A powerful offspring of the Open Corridor/Workshop Center Advisory was the Central Park East Elementary School (CPE) created by Deborah Meier, an original participant in Weber's initiative.[8] A small public elementary school of choice located in New York City's East Harlem neighborhood, CPE was designed to be a whole-school community in which understandings about child development were put into practice throughout the grades. Teachers were viewed and treated in the same way that they were being asked to think about and treat their students. The school's intent was to create a racially and socioeconomically diverse community which would identify each individual's strengths and interests, support each student as a capable learner, and do this in an equitable manner. The original ideas about school structure and governance did not include a formal leadership position since it was thought that all decisions could be made collectively so that everyone could share equally in building the school. All teachers would work directly with the children, thereby allowing classes to be smaller.

Initially emphasizing egalitarian values, staff meetings became the centerpiece for making decisions about the fledgling school. But by the end of the second year, budget cuts, district demands, and frustration with the unwieldy process of trying to make *all* decisions collaboratively resulted in the realization that creating a separate position of "teacher-director" was indeed going to be necessary. Someone was needed to assume responsibility for protecting and nurturing the life of the school by managing the work of the organization, representing the school to the district, pressing to keep the focus of the school on students' needs, and developing growing relationships with parents and families. A role thus evolved that is much like that of the "head teacher" in British, Australian, and New Zealand schools—a leader of and for the teachers who assumes neither a supervisory nor a hierarchical stance. This part of the CPE story reveals a view of leadership growing out of the process of creating and defining a "democratic learning community." The "teacher-director" is "of" the community, an advisor rather than a supervisor, a creator of opportunities to learn rather than an enforcer of the status quo, a keeper and developer of values of student-centered practice rather than a maintainer of the system. These values were deepened and extended over the years, not only at Central Park East Elementary School (which came to be known as CPE I), but at the other small New York City public schools that were inspired by the CPE model.

Core Principles of the CCE Schools

The conditions of each of these schools are unique, yet they share some common principles in which are embodied a set of core values and common assumptions about teaching, learning, and human development. These principles guide practice in the schools. They encourage expression of individual differences and the building of cultures uniquely their own. They also bind the schools together in a larger community which offers them a historical perspective on the continuity of their struggle, support to know and do more, and a moral and material base for the difficult task of changing educational practice.

ALL CHILDREN HAVE THE CAPACITY TO LEARN

There is much talk in school reform circles these days that "all children have the capacity to learn," and this slogan is indeed the philosophical foundation—*the* core principle—on which the CCE schools are built and organized. This belief is evident in school policies and structures which provide equal learning opportunities and resources for all students, regardless of their differing experiences and abilities. Classrooms are heterogeneously grouped to include students who represent a span of ages, a range of racial and socioeconomic backgrounds, and a spectrum of individual strengths and talents (including special education students). Each student is supported to develop at his or her own pace while necessary resources for the realization of each individual's potential are made available to the fullest extent possible.

Differences in abilities are provided for in a number of respectful ways. Students who require special learning supports (in Chapter 1 or Resource Room programs) are not isolated from the classroom or stigmatized by their need. In some schools, students with special needs are provided with a program of enrichment in their classrooms that also allows other interested students to participate. For example, a Resource Room teacher in one particular school often connects her instruction to enjoyable cooking activities and, as a consequence, she is frequently inundated with requests by regular education students to join in her projects.

Many of the schools support students' individual interests by providing opportunities for them to select from a range of different types of classes (classes in dance, art, music, and sport are notable examples). In contrast to many schools where both teachers and curricula are rationed only to those whose academic success is most assured,[9] *all* the students in these schools are given access to high quality teaching and what is referred to as a "thinking curriculum." This is made possible by supporting professional growth opportunities for all teachers.

Stress is placed on how to provide all students with work that challenges them to develop the ability to use their minds well: to think critically and creatively, to engage in deep exploration of ideas and topics, and to acquire the skills and knowledge necessary for future school and life experiences.

At the same time that student differences are addressed in these schools, a conscious effort is being made to develop a common standard of excellence for what and how students learn. This is being accomplished in a variety of ways. One is the development of open-ended assignments that provide entry points for many different kinds of learners and that allow students to participate at a variety of difficulty levels. For example, when studying the New York City harbor, all second/third grade students in one of the schools were engaged in a core set of interdisciplinary experiences. In addition, some students, driven by their interests or their abilities, pursued other areas of study connected to the topic. Some engaged in historical research, some wrote fictional stories that centered around the area of study, some built models of bridges or dioramas of the harbor utilizing a range of materials. No two students produced the same work or came away from the study with exactly the same information. But all were exposed to some basic ideas and information and some general principles of learning and inquiry.

Standards of excellence are encouraged through public demonstrations of students' learning, which expose students to a variety of levels of academic success and a variety of forms in which knowledge can be expressed. In many of the schools, units of study are often concluded by exhibitions or "museums," in which students display and explain their work to their classmates, schoolmates, family members, as well as school faculty. These demonstrations have included not only written reports, but experiments, constructions, puppet shows, videos, musical performances, and art exhibits.

Standards for learning and for assessing outcomes are further developed by providing students with regular opportunities for discussion of their different learning strategies. Such discussions take place at classroom meetings, small group forums, or individual conferences between teachers and students. One director describes how such discussions facilitate learning for the children in her school:

When a math problem is discussed at a classroom meeting, many strategies for learning will often be presented. Sometimes one person's strategy will open up an understanding for another. For example, at one meeting Hugh explained how he does multiplication by engaging in repeated addition. This was the only way that Manuel, who had been having a terrible time grasping the concept, seemed to be able to understand it. Although many of us had tried to help Manuel before, it wasn't until he heard and saw a fellow student's explanation that he was finally able to make the connection.

HONORING DIVERSITY

The schools represented in this study all demonstrate a variety of ways in which they consciously acknowledge and demonstrate a respect for diversity of cultures, language, gender, and socioeconomic background, as well as of various thinking styles, learning rates, academic, social, and physical abilities. One of the directors of the schools speaks about the importance of this particular value: "Diversity is not an add-on, but a way of thinking here."

Support for diverse learning styles and strengths is evident everywhere in these schools. Students are often seen working side by side, utilizing their particular interests and strengths to enrich and extend the work of others as well as to create individual paths of entry into their own particular challenges. Two students involved in an animal research project in a fourth/fifth grade classroom in one of the schools provide a good example of this. Both were deeply engaged in study about cats and were exploring a variety of informational texts. We were informed by the teacher that one of the students was particularly able in reading and writing but inexperienced with and intimidated by visual art forms. The other struggled mightily with the printed form but was extraordinarily artistic and able to express his ideas through painting and drawing. As these two worked together, we saw each contributing to the research process in his area of strength; one provided the written text, the other provided the illustrations. Yet both were involved in analysis and discussion of the content, and both were utilizing research and problem-solving skills. The director of the school explained how they work to develop adaptive teaching: "It's about acknowledging that each [person] has different gifts, strengths, and concerns and then finding a way to utilize them."

In addition to respecting different learning styles, these schools also value cultural diversity. It can be seen throughout the learning environment in the books the children read, the stories they write, the songs they sing, the foods they cook, the trips they take, and the conversations they have. It is apparent in the composition of school staffs, which reflect the diversity of their student populations. (Where this is not the case we were told that recruitment of teachers from diverse cultures and backgrounds is a number one priority.) In addition, opportunities are provided for families to be meaningfully involved in the life of the schools: family histories and cultural traditions are used as the starting point of many classroom studies; ethnic meals and artistic performances are a regular feature of the cultural lives of the schools; and home/school conferences and other forms of communication regularly solicit family languages, traditions, and knowledge about the learner to inform the teaching that takes place in the school. The views and voices of all the directors are clear and uncompromising about this. One of them said: "Everybody is special—the greater the variety, the richer a life for ourselves and the kids. School has to be all inclusive. It has to be a place where all are safe and respected— adults, parents, everyone."

PROVIDING FOR THE NEEDS OF THE "WHOLE CHILD"

Another shared principle of the CCE schools is their respect for the needs of the "whole child"—emotional, physical, artistic, and academic. Children's needs are placed before bureaucratic considerations and guide educational practice as well as policy. This is manifested in the quality of the routines that comprise the daily life of the children in these schools. The tone of voice and the gestures used by adults as they speak to children, the manner in which such daily routines as lining up for buses are conducted, the atmosphere at breakfast/lunch/ recess, the way security guards and custodians interact with students, as well as how children who are sick or lonely are treated, all demonstrate the dignity and respect that is regularly accorded to children.

Care and concern are also exhibited for other aspects of children's lives traditionally considered outside the realm of the school's responsibilities. Physical health, mental health, and extracurricular needs are considered important and addressed by the schools in a variety of ways: some offer after-school programs and make arrangements for children to attend summer camps; some refer families to service providers for health-related issues; some provide child care at evening meetings.

The Descriptive Review,[10] used by virtually all of the CCE schools, is a process in which school personnel collaboratively discuss issues, problems, or concerns of a particular child in a full and holistic way. The process, usually undertaken after school hours, begins with a description of a child developed from documented observations over time that have been collected by the child's classroom teacher. This description is followed by comments from those participating in the review process. They offer suggestions for ways the teacher and school can best support the growth of the child.

The perspectives through which the child is described are multiple, to insure a balanced portrayal of the person that neither overemphasizes some current "problem" nor minimizes an ongoing difficulty. The description of the child addresses the following facets of the person as these characteristics are expressed within the classroom setting at the present time: the child's physical presence and gesture; the child's disposition; the child's relationships with other children and adults; the child's activities and interests; the child's approach to formal learning; the child's strengths and vulnerabilities.[11]

The kind of observation and discussion that takes place during the Descriptive Review offers understandings which set the tone for a learning environment that provides for the needs of the "whole child" and makes each child visible to the school community. This is especially powerful in schools that serve diverse communities and are struggling to include all children in the ranks of successful learners. A director explains: "The value of an education will never be missed by visible and included children. They will be too excited by their own wonderful ideas to give up on learning."

ASSESSMENTS IN SUPPORT OF MEANINGFUL TEACHING AND LEARNING

CCE schools hold yet another practice in common: assessments of student work are intricately connected to and supportive of meaningful teaching and learning. One of the original directors describes how this aspect of all the schools has been woven into their structure from their inception:

From the beginning, we realized we couldn't assess in this kind of setting in any traditional way. We had to have different assessment tools which could be used to report to teachers, families, and posterity. We had to develop ways to see the work and to watch kids grow over time.

Many kinds of assessments have thus been developed to provide information to teachers, families, and communities about the progress of students and the schools as a whole. Some schools keep track of student growth through documented teacher observations collected over time. Some keep samples of student work in portfolios. Some have students demonstrate what they can do in research projects, scientific experiments, performances, exhibitions, or in interdisciplinary tasks that resemble the problems of real-life situations. Many have students engage in self-assessments. All schools report their learnings about students in detailed narrative progress reports that are sent home to families on a regular basis, followed by lengthy home/school conferences in which student work is discussed and reviewed.

At present these practices, which focus on direct evidence of students' work gathered by teachers and interwoven into the teaching/learning process, are undertaken as an addition to the indirect evidence collected by external agencies through the norm-referenced standardized tests currently mandated in New York City and New York State. Involvement in both internal as well as external assessment systems creates great tensions and problems for the schools. Not only is there not enough time for teachers to fulfill the requirements of these two very different systems, but there are significant differences in what the systems assess and in how they go about assessing it. All the directors of the CCE schools, however, expressed their optimism about the current flurry of reform in assessment practices taking place at all levels of the educational system. They see this interest in reform as public validation of the learning-centered assessment which has long been in use in their schools.

EVERYONE IS VIEWED AS A LEARNER

All the members of the Center for Collaborative Education school communities—students, staff, and families alike—are viewed as learners and are provided with continual growth opportunities. Students are encouraged to exchange ideas among themselves and with their teachers through small-group discussions, classroom meetings, and meetings of the whole school community. These model the process of "learning how to learn" and create an atmosphere that encourages inquiry and problem solving.

Teachers and other school support staff are also provided with various opportunities for ongoing learning. Staff meet together in formal as well as informal meetings, including semiannual all-school retreats, where ideas and resources are exchanged to deepen understandings of children, of teaching, and of their own personal/professional growth.

In addition, the family members of students are included in the learning environment of these schools. Two-way learning is at the heart of this relationship—teachers learning from families about their children as well as families learning from schools about education. This is accomplished by a variety of communication forms: teacher curriculum letters and homework notes, director newsletters, phone calls to family members, narrative progress reports, and school/home conferences.

These ways in which members of the school community can connect and reconnect to being a learner are facilitated by the work of the school directors. One of them explains: "Someone has to pull in the world so that teachers [and others] don't get ingrown. Someone needs to create opportunities to talk about why we do what we do, to rethink, to validate, to deal with ideas."

As directors do this, an atmosphere is created in their schools that is respectful, trusting, and facilitating for the learning of both the children and the adults involved. The comments of one of the school directors reveals more about the how and why:

We have based our theories about school on what we think to be true about human learning. Certain kinds of school environments speak to what's true about human learning and help it emerge so that in the process of teaching children, and talking about teaching children, and thinking about themselves as learners, teachers reconnect to who they are as learners.

A DEMOCRATIC LEARNING COMMUNITY

Operationalizing the principles discussed above results in a school culture and organization that promotes democratic values and that makes room for everyone to have a voice. The conviction is strong in the CCE community that schools should be organized in ways that allow students and adults to live their beliefs, not just to talk about them. This conviction is expressed by the words of the directors:

[We want] to help children learn how to cooperate and how to respect the differences among them.

We share a common belief in teaching about nonviolence, sexism, and racism. These aspects of a living democracy have always been stressed in these schools.

These beliefs are put into practice in the schools' organizational structures as well as in the development of their curricula. Culturally sensitive curricula are consciously developed which include study of people and places from nondominant cultures and which utilize the experiences and resources of the schools' diverse communities. Students engage in neighborhood studies, in community service projects, and in work that connects their daily lives to the issues and problems of the world at large. In addition, conflict resolution programs help them to develop problem-solving strategies. Student newsletters and surveys provide access to the views and concerns of their peers. (In one of the upper-grade classes in the schools a survey was developed to elicit the views held by students and parents about homework, so that assignments could be developed by the teacher to most effectively address the families' needs.)

School structures also speak to aspects of democratic living. These provide opportunities for families and teachers to participate in shaping the vision and work of the school. Many have already been mentioned here: Descriptive Reviews, faculty meetings, all-school retreats, parent meetings, conferences, progress reports, newsletters, and curriculum letters. One of the directors, who helped develop her school from its inception, explains how the vision of a democratic community, in which all participants have a say in decisions affecting their lives, has been a driving force of her school: "From the beginning, there was always the sense that these intelligent people should have a say in how the school worked."

How Leaders Lead in Learner-Centered Schools: Balancing the Challenges and Commitments

Fashioning the role of teacher-director has particular meaning in CCE schools. The directors are required to balance a variety of skills and abilities. They need both administrative skills (overseeing paperwork, buses, schedules) and political skills (educating and negotiating with stakeholders in the educational enterprise both inside and outside their schools). They also need pedagogical understandings (providing ongoing professional development and support to teachers), and a vision for the future (anticipating and preparing for new developments). This combination of attributes is difficult to find in any one individual and the directors readily acknowledge their limitations in this regard. But recognizing one's strengths and building on the particulars of personal and professional challenges seems part of the norms of these school communities. Comments like "I model decency," "I know what I can't do," "I never wanted to be a principal; I thought I would always be struggling and compromising" suggest the candor and integrity of the struggle to be "leaders *of* the community and representatives *from* the community." The strong value placed in the assumption that "everybody, absolutely everybody, is capable of having ideas, and making sense of the world and needs to be taken seriously" seems to be as much a credo for the directors as it is for other members of their communities.

The challenge of constructing a learner-centered community is made greater in the case of these particular schools by the fact that the directors and schools are trying to do this within the context of a routinized and standardized big city school system. Directors are thus required to simultaneously develop a set of skills and responsibilities that can keep their organizations healthy and growing while also developing another set of skills that can effectively maneuver the tensions and challenges posed by membership in the ranks of the public school bureaucracy.

INTERNAL CHALLENGES AND DEMANDS

In the course of their daily lives in schools, teacher-directors experience many situations that challenge their values, question their commitments, and test their educational understandings. The role of director calls upon a host of leadership attributes and dispositions. It requires school leaders to simultaneously be educators, problem solvers, crisis managers, change agents, enablers, consensus builders and networkers, as well as limit setters and authority figures. Enacting these sometimes contradictory roles and achieving a balanced performance tests even those with the strongest mettle: when to assert and when to hold back; when to intervene and how to do it right; when to deliberately lead and take a position and when to facilitate group struggle; how to handle conflict and how to make it productive; how to be accepting and respectful of differences while seeking to achieve overall agreements; how to be patient and supportive of strengths, even in the face of difficult problems; how to advocate for teachers, children, and their families while simultaneously maintaining a smoothly running school.

Supporting the growth of teachers. Directors facilitate and support teacher growth in much the same way that teachers are expected to do with children. As one director explains:

What we model for kids, I try to model for adults. Good kindergarten practice is also good leadership practice. It's about acknowledging that each has different gifts, strengths, and concerns and then finding a way to utilize them. It's about giving teachers a sense of understanding, empathy, partnership, belonging. My personal understanding of learner-centered teaching has become my model of leadership.

Expanding on this idea, another director adds:

I try to get to know each person by him/herself, as an individual. Then I find something I can relate to and support. I struggle against making judgments (the skill of observing and describing children helps a lot here). I can't let judgment get in the way of the forward movement of the teacher. It's important to always leave the teacher with respect.

Similar to the way learner-centered teaching takes place, the director functions as an observer, supporter, and reflector of individual and institutional memory for others ("Remember when you did that?"), and as a keeper of teachers' questions and comments. The director often reflects these questions and answers back to the teachers, picking up pieces of the myriad experiences taking place in and out of the classroom, and using them as a reminder and a connection to larger ideas in the outside world. One teacher explains how this has helped her growth:

The sharing that goes on in the classroom between myself and the kids is the same process that goes on between the director and the teachers. She often reflects back to us what has happened in our classrooms, helping us to see the positive things that have happened during the day rather than just the last crazy five minutes we are able to remember.

Building on strengths (a norm for students) is also the way directors support the learning and growth of adults. But there are delicate balances to maintain: how to nurture while also pushing forward by asking hard questions, raising new issues, and maintaining a standard of excellence for teaching; how to find a way to facilitate rather than dictate; how to assert leadership and assume responsibility while also building on the initiatives of others. These concerns are among the problems faced by all the directors:

I have had many conflicts about the appropriate way to enact my role. I struggle with knowing when to exert authority and when to support the initiatives of others; how to be respectful of the views and feelings of others without losing the strength and integrity of a vision which supports student learning; how to balance differences in cultures and values and to incorporate aspects of these into the community to continually build common ground.

Perhaps most important is that directors find ways to support teachers so that they can be supportive of the learning process and thereby support students and their families. Directors do this by taking care of paper work, supervising buses, breakfast, lunch, and recess times, settling disputes among students, and attending to district demands. The assumption of these responsibilities (frequently considered to be unimportant and mundane) ultimately frees teachers to concentrate on teaching and students. This dignifies the hard and intense work of teaching.

Providing staff with continual learning opportunities. Directors of these learner-centered schools have a deep conviction that growth and learning are never-ending. "Learning about learning is never finished. There is no end to the need to continue to deepen understanding."

They continually search for ways to deepen and sustain the culture of learner-centered education. They encourage teachers to try out new ideas, teach a different grade level, invest in new equipment, attend classes or conferences, or teach with other colleagues. Staying fresh in teaching is a major problem. Directors also struggle to bring new teachers into the fold, to orient them to learner-centered thinking, and to help them develop effective teaching strategies. One director deliberately places new and old teachers alongside each other in the classroom corridors so that they can learn from exposure to one another.

All of the directors have created structures to address the fact that "teachers, like students, need many different kinds of learning experiences." Directors provide opportunities for teachers to work with and support each other in a variety of ways: opportunities to visit each other's classrooms, to take trips together to other schools, to be involved in child study teams and Descriptive Reviews, to discuss professional books and articles, to meet on issues of common concern whether curriculum, world events, or special happenings in the community. These activities create an atmosphere that is described by one director as a "culture of extreme support" for individual as well as for collective learning. One director explains:

Our school is literally an institution of higher education. There are lots of opportunities for dialogue and conversation, both formal and informal. We have formal meetings—weekly grade meetings, monthly staff meetings. But the informal meetings every day after school are the best.

Teachers and staff in these learner-centered schools are thus continually engaged in talk about work, values, processes, ideas, and concerns. These conversations, facilitated by the directors, are the cornerstone of professional development through which staff members develop a powerful sense of collegiality, collaboration, and community.

Upholding the vision and values of the school. As the years have gone by and the schools have evolved, a major challenge for teacher-directors has been the preservation of the values and assumptions that form the core of learner-centered principles and practices. Directors have struggled to find ways to maintain the original school communities' intimacy and zeal as they have grown in size and brought in new people. This has entailed developing ways to avoid insularity, self-satisfaction, and nonproductive conflict as well as creating mechanisms to connect to the outside world of ideas and people.

As schools have become more established the cohesiveness of the original communities has often become diluted. Several directors are currently experiencing this phenomenon in their schools. They report that as their schools have become increasingly successful, there has been a concomitant decrease in the uniformity of their parent bodies. Only some of the families have joined their schools out of a desire for a learner-centered educational philosophy. Others have come in search of a school that is safe, well equipped, with a caring staff or a "good" reputation.

Such a diversity of reasons for attending the schools brings diverse views about future directions and priorities. Sometimes teachers or families find that they have conflicts with the fundamental values of the schools. This presents an important challenge to school leadership—a challenge to educate and build a base of support for learner-centered practices while being respectful of input and participation. Directors address this challenge by listening, evaluating, and responding to concerns in a way that incorporates professional knowledge about teaching and change. One director described a situation which highlights the need for these important skills and understandings:

A parent objected to heterogeneous grouping out of a belief that it didn't best serve her child. She wanted the school to reconsider this practice for the community as a whole. I had to find a way to help her understand that some values are inviolable and form the basis of our school.

Realizing the vision through empowerment of others. Underlying this seemingly endless array of ways that directors lead subtly or frontally is a vision that is educational, social, and fundamentally political in nature. Keeping this vision comprehensive is difficult to do. Directors must be aware that, although they have the power to push things through, it is not worth it. Instead, connecting to what people understand, want, believe, and are ready to do is the great challenge. As one director put it: "It's not enough to have good ideas. Helping others to realize their good ideas and come together to create a common vision and then to jointly make that vision a reality is the real leadership challenge."

How to be a hub and be central to all aspects of the school while not being in the center, how to be the spokesperson for all the constituencies without demanding compliance to a singular view, how to turn problems into possibilities—these are aspects of leadership style that become embodied in community belief and action: "I try to empower people, have a calming effect, model decency, and help people listen to one another. I want to help people find solutions to problems, to see that problems are solvable."

Creating these conditions calls upon directors to handle dualities, to be closely connected to people, events, and the dailiness of school, but also to have some distance: "I feel passionately for others but I also have common sense. I am a stabilizing factor in my school." To keep a school community constantly open to struggle with and develop its ideals means that directors also need to be open to change: "I value each person but also want to challenge each person. I want us to be open to change—to expose ourselves and our classrooms to that. I want people to speak up, raise issues."

All these examples give a sense of how, in attempting to put these ideas into practice, directors provide teachers with supports that are similar to those that teachers provide to their students. "I needed to let them do what they needed to do. And I needed to figure out what they needed. But I found that the more respect and trust I gave to the staff, the more they gave the same to the kids."

When teachers and students feel efficacious in their work, this becomes the real meaning of "empowerment." Rather than a slogan, it is the subtle means by which directors create the conditions for continuous growth for adults and students alike. When this happens, the momentum of change cannot be contained. It makes one director feel like shouting, "Hey, wait for me, *I'm* your leader!"[12]

EXTERNAL CHALLENGES

At the same time that the internal growth of a school community presents challenges that pull directors in different directions, problems of the outside world also present particular challenges. Even though the reform community is articulate about the need for change (and these schools are indeed a testimony to the potential for change) the contexts in which these schools are embedded require of their leaders special skills and abilities—political, practical, and pedagogical—even as these leaders are guided by their strong commitments and shared purposes.[13]

Working within contexts of contradictory values. These directors are charting the course of their schools in the context of district and system policies and politics that are often in conflict with what they value. This creates great frustration for the directors, most particularly in the areas of curriculum and assessment. Curriculum mandates and standardized testing clash directly with the developmental and holistic practices that are fundamental to learner-centered schools. While teaching and assessment in learner-centered schools are geared to the differing strengths and needs of students, the success of the schools and their practices are nevertheless measured through the use of standardized tests, well known to do a notoriously poor job of reflecting students' strengths and differences.[14] This phenomenon places directors and their staff in an inextricable bind. They must fulfill the requirements necessary for survival in the established system, while they struggle to develop and maintain an "alternate" community in which decisions are made, risks taken, and practices established that question categorization of students, fragmentation of the school program, and a standardized conception of knowledge and learning.

Working with limited resources and supports. Schools are not currently given the resources to provide enough time for teachers to engage in the kind of observing, recording, reflecting, and reporting that is required for learner-centered teaching. They also do not receive the resources needed to provide teachers with adequate opportunities for professional growth. While directors are frustrated by these limitations, they have found a number of ways to compensate for them: seeking financial supports from outside the school system, learning how to use networks external to the school, and depending on a high level of commitment from their staffs.

Network Support for Leading and Learning

The learner-centered schools described in this chapter are embedded in a network—The Center for Collaborative Education—that supports and gives meaning to their daily work. What happens in each individual school takes on a greater significance since it is part of a larger whole.

Although there has been very little empirical study of educational networks and their effects on members, Granovetter suggested in 1973 that there is a cohesive power in networks which represent "the strength of weak ties."[15] Instead of only relying on people who are friends (strong ties), networks provide a power and influence over people in organizations by connecting them to norms, values, and influences which occur indirectly (weak ties). Two examples here may help.

One director spoke of how her attendance at a network meeting encouraged her to initiate implementation of authentic assessment in her school. Through the network's discussion of the various possibilities for how the work of students could be assessed, she was able to see how these possibilities connected to all the other things that her school was doing. She left the meeting inspired to find a way to raise these issues at her school.

Still another director attending an annual network meeting participated in a discussion about the importance of standard setting for the network elementary schools. This discussion, although very contentious, made her realize that the staff of her school could indeed benefit by looking more carefully at its practices and relating them to standards held by the school but not yet formally articulated.

These examples help us to understand the critical role that networks can play in supporting both personal and professional growth. The Center for Collaborative Education network gives support to directors in articulating and practicing educational principles of learner-centeredness. This support includes developing social values that suggest what democratic schools should be. This helps them make sense of the daily struggles against bureaucratic routine and the human crises that occur so frequently, giving energy and commitment to their work. Seeking help is not seen as a weakness, but rather a part of the personal and organizational expectations of the entire community.

Networking to build knowledge and support is thus a norm of learner-centered communities, one that nurtures and encourages collective discussion and problem solving around tough issues of diversity and curriculum, as well as differing cultural and pedagogical practices.[16] Commitment to the hard work of changing schools comes from a will that cannot be imposed by policies from above; it stems from a shared belief in ideals that provide meaning and direction in the face of seemingly intractable problems.[17]

Reframing Leadership

In some ways these schools seem like many others trying to deal with changing student and parent populations and with the integration of new knowledge and approaches to learning and assessment. What makes these schools different, however, are the ideals they share that find expression in the dailiness of their work and in the way that their leaders lead: providing perspective in the midst of confusion, solving problems and setting problem-solving norms, setting priorities among competing agendas, making conflict productive, gauging the temperature of the community and acting on its needs, being respectful of each other when placing blame is easier, taking care of things backstage while the teachers and students are on stage. Teacher-directors, although their styles and strengths differ, tend to be both passionate in their beliefs and optimistic about what these beliefs will enable them to accomplish. They measure their success by the extent to which they support the collective conscience of their own school communities, as well as by the extent to which their ideas and practices influence and support the work and ideas of others.

In the traditional school, the principal is assumed to be the fount of pedagogical knowledge as well as the repository of power and control over all resources, both human and material. The principal holds power by virtue of the position. Meetings are most often for the principal to present his or her agenda. In fact, the traditional definition of a good school has often been that it is "orderly" and technically well run. While no one would dispute the need for an "orderly" and well-run school, in the Center for Collaborative Education schools order is important if it is perceived as enabling for teachers and students. Since members of the school community are part of the decision-making process, the directors organize the schools so that all members have input into decisions critical to their lives and their work.

This change redefines the role of leadership, and it is perhaps our most significant learning. In learner-centered schools the leaders are not only chosen *by* the community and are themselves members *of* the community, but are also held directly accountable *to* the community. Leadership is legitimated by following practices consistent with ideals embraced by the community, recognizing that it is an unfinished work, a culture continually in the making.

We gratefully acknowledge the contribution of our colleagues whose ideas and words are featured in this article: Mary Ellen Bosch, Director, Brooklyn New School; Sharon Fiden, Director, The New Program, P. S. 261; Blossom Gelernter, former Director/Principal, P. S. 234; Kyle Haver, Director, Central Park East II Elementary School; Sid Massey, Director, River East Elementary School; Lucy Matos, Director, Central Park East I Elementary School; Deborah Meier, former Director, Central Park East I Elementary School and current Co-director, Central Park East Secondary School; Esther Rosenfeld, former Director, Central Park East II Elementary School; Paul Schwarz, former Director, Brooklyn New School and current Co-director Central Park East Secondary School; Anna Switzer, principal, P. S. 234; Lillian Weber, Director Emeritus, Workshop Center for Open Education, School of Education, City College of New York.

NOTES

1. Roland Barth, *Improving Schools from Within* (San Francisco: Jossey-Bass, 1990); Michael Fullan and Andrew Hargreaves, *What's Worth Fighting For: Working Together for Your School* (Toronto: Ontario Public School Teachers' Federation, 1991); Jerry L. Patterson, *Leadership for Tomorrow's Schools* (Alexandria, VA: Association for Supervision and Curriculum Development, 1993); Mary S. Poplin, "The Leader's New Role: Looking to the Growth of Teachers," *Educational Leadership* 49, no. 5 (1992): 10-11; Thomas J. Sergiovanni, *Moral Leadership: Getting to the Heart of School Improvement* (San Francisco: Jossey-Bass, 1992).

2. P. S. 234 is an exception here. It began as a small school but has grown over the years into a "regular" school with its own building and its own principal.

3. The original leaders of these schools, as well as their successors, are represented in this study. The original leaders, however, all continue to engage in other leadership work. In two schools, retired directors are now involved in leadership roles in a preparatory program for urban school principals; two others are leaders in secondary schools; and one school has developed a form of shared leadership due to the particularities of the context.

4. Frederich Froebel, *Education of Man* (New York: Appleton, 1887; Englewood Cliffs, NJ: Appleton-Century-Crofts, 1974); John Dewey, *Democracy and Education* (New York: Macmillan, 1916); idem, *Experience and Education* (New York: Macmillan, 1938); idem, *The Child and the Curriculum* (Chicago: University of Chicago Press, 1956).

5. Caroline Pratt, *I Learn from Children* (New York: Simon and Schuster, 1948); Jean Piaget and Barbel Inhelder, *The Psychology of the Child* (New York: Basic Books, 1969); Jerome Bruner, *The Process of Education* (Cambridge, MA: Harvard University Press, 1966); Patricia Carini, *Observation and Description: An Alternative Methodology for the Investigation of Human Phenomena* (Grand Forks: North Dakota Study Group on Evaluation, 1975); idem, *The Art of Seeing and the Visibility of the Person* (Grand Forks: North Dakota Study Group on Evaluation, 1979); Maxine Greene, *Landscapes of Learning* (New York: Teachers College Press, 1978); idem, "How Do We Think about Our Craft?" *Teachers College Record* 86, no. 1 (1984): 55-67; Lev S. Vygotsky, *Mind in Society* (Cambridge, MA: Harvard University Press, 1978); Eleanor Duckworth, *"The Having of Wonderful Ideas" and Other Essays* (New York: Teachers College Press, 1987); Sue Bredekamp, *Developmentally Appropriate Practice* (Washington, DC: National Association for the Education of Young Children, 1987).

6. Larry Cuban, *How Teachers Taught: Constancy and Change in American Classrooms* (New York: Longman, 1984).

7. Linda Darling-Hammond, "Reframing the School Reform Agenda: Developing Capacity for School Transformation," *Phi Delta Kappan* 74, no. 10 (1993): 753-761;

Jeannie Oakes, *Keeping Track: How Schools Structure Inequality* (New Haven: Yale University Press, 1985); Lauren B. Resnick, *Education and Learning to Think* (Washington, DC: National Academy Press, 1987).

8. It is important to note that Weber's idea of a teacher advisory, as well as the values that are inherent in it, were critical to Central Park East's and later the Center for Collaborative Education's notion of a teacher-director. The efforts of this school and this organization to establish a learning community in which both students and teachers are jointly involved in inquiring how to support student and teacher learning all developed from Open Corridor practices.

9. Oakes, *Keeping Track*.

10. Prospect Archive and Center for Education and Research, *The Prospect Center Documentary Processes: In Progress* (North Bennington, VT: Prospect Archive and Center for Education and Research, 1986).

11. Ibid., pp. 26-27.

12. Barth, *Improving Schools from Within*, p. 170.

13. Darling-Hammond, "Reframing the School Reform Agenda"; Milbrey W. McLaughlin and Joan E. Talbert, *Contexts That Matter for Teaching and Learning: Strategic Opportunities for Meeting the Nation's Educational Goals* (Stanford, CA: Center for Research on the Context of Secondary School Teaching, Stanford University, March, 1993.

14. Linda Darling-Hammond, "The Implications of Testing Policy for Educational Quality and Equality," *Phi Delta Kappan* 73, no. 3 (1991): 220-225.

15. M. S. Granovetter, "The Strength of Weak Ties," *American Journal of Sociology* 78, no. 6 (1973): 1360-1380.

16. Ann Lieberman and Milbrey W. McLaughlin, "Networks for Educational Change: Powerful and Problematic," *Phi Delta Kappan* 73, no. 9 (1992): 673-677.

17. Milbrey W. McLaughlin, "Learning from Experience: Lessons from Policy Implementation," *Educational Evaluation and Policy Analysis* 9, no. 2 (1987): 171-178.

CHAPTER VIII

Thomas Edison Accelerated
Elementary School

GENE CHASIN AND HENRY M. LEVIN

A major challenge of our time is to meet the educational needs of
the large numbers of children in at-risk situations. School practices
are not neutral about who succeeds. Children from families with both
parents present, substantial parental education and income, and a middle-class version of the culture of the United States and of the English
language tend to have school experiences which value and build on
their backgrounds. In contrast, students from immigrant, minority,
and poor families often face a serious discontinuity between their out-
of-school experiences and what schools require for success. Schools
rarely find constructive ways to embrace the experiences of such children, relegating many of them to failure. Nationally, students in at-
risk situations have increased rapidly, accounting for up to 40 percent
of elementary and secondary enrollments.[1] In California, the numbers
have risen even more quickly with a majority of students perceived to
be in at-risk situations.

In this respect, Thomas Edison Elementary School in Sacramento
is a prototype of the California challenge. Edison is one of fifty-one
elementary schools among the eighty-nine schools in the San Juan
Unified School District. Over the past five years Edison and four
other elementary schools within the district have started facing
"urban" challenges. In the fall of 1989, Edison had a total of 360 students of whom 36 percent were receiving public assistance under Aid
for Dependent Children (AFDC) and Free or Reduced Cost Lunch.
The mobility rate was approximately 30 percent, and only English was
spoken. Behavior was a problem that year with a total of 103 days of

Gene Chasin is the Principal of the Thomas Edison Accelerated Elementary School
in Sacramento, California. Henry M. Levin is David Jacks Professor of Higher Education and Economics and Director of the National Center for the Accelerated Schools
Project at Stanford University.

suspension, primarily for fighting. There were seven robberies in which audio-visual equipment was stolen.

Just three years later, in 1992-93, the school's enrollment had grown by one third to 494 students of whom 80 percent were on AFDC and Free or Reduced Cost lunch. Thirteen different languages were spoken. But contrary to what might have been expected from changes in the student clientele, the mobility rate had *dropped* to 23 percent, student behavior had *improved* with only thirty-four total days of suspension, and there were *no* break-ins for the school year. And test scores of the sixth graders on the Comprehensive Test of Basic Skills (CTBS) had risen in all three areas tested.

Edison's early success in meeting its challenges are due to a major transformation of the school that has been undertaken by Edison staff, students, and parents. Edison is one of the growing number of schools that are following the Accelerated Schools process to bring all students into the academic mainstream by the end of their elementary schooling and to give them further support at the middle and secondary levels. Before describing how that process was implemented at Edison, it is important to provide background on the Accelerated Schools Project.

The Accelerated Schools Project

The Accelerated Schools Project was initiated in the summer of 1986 as a thirty-year project designed to respond to the needs of at-risk students. Although a design for Accelerated Schools had been developed by the early spring of 1986,[2] it was not until the 1986-87 school year that the ideas could be tested. In that year the project was started in two pilot schools, and by 1993-94 it had grown to include over 500 elementary and middle schools in thirty-three states. In addition to the National Center for the Accelerated Schools Project located at Stanford University, there are ten regional centers.

Four years of previous research on at-risk students and their schools had come to rather stark conclusions.[3] Such students started school without many of the skills that schools valued and they got farther behind the educational mainstream the longer they were in school. Over half of the at-risk population did not graduate from high school. The research found that the inability of existing schools to advance the education of at-risk students is hardly an accident. Most schools that enroll such children embrace organizational, curricular, and instructional strategies for remediation that lead to reduced expectations for, and stigmatizing of, at-risk students, uninspiring school experiences, and a devaluation of the rich talents of students, teachers, and parents. In the absence of change, students are subjected systematically to experiences that will assure high failure rates.

In contrast, rather than slowing the learning rate of students, the Accelerated Schools are designed to advance it by transforming the remedial emphasis in instruction to an emphasis on students' strengths. Educators usually reserve acceleration programs for students who are top performers, while remedial instruction accommodates students' weaknesses by reducing the pace and quality of learning. The consequence is that schools systematically track students to produce (perhaps inadvertently) a self-fulfilling prophecy in which those with the most educational advantages are propelled forward at faster rates than those from at-risk populations.[4]

Yet, research has found that acceleration and enrichment work for all students.[5] Recent work on the identification and nurturing of talent argues for the efficacy of enriched instructional practices and curriculum for all students.[6] Indeed, Accelerated Schools have shown substantial gains in student achievement, attendance, full inclusion of special needs children in the mainstream, parental participation, and the numbers of students meeting traditional gifted and talented criteria.[7] They have also reduced the number of students repeating grades. Their students have produced substantial numbers of research projects and have demonstrated significant accomplishments in writing.

A STRATEGY FOR CHANGE

Although the basic ideas for Accelerated Schools can be found even in our early writing,[8] application of these ideas was challenging and has required continuous refinement as experience has provided new insights. A strategy for creating accelerated institutions required three major changes in schools in the United States, changes that were in deep conflict with current practices.[9]

Unity of purpose. Most schools that educate at-risk students seem to lack a central purpose. They are comprised of a composite of programs that are largely disparate and piecemeal with no central vision. Teachers tend to see their responsibilities extending no farther than good practices in self-contained classrooms, while remedial specialists work in isolation from each other and the regular school program.

Acceleration requires the pursuit of a common purpose that serves as a focal point for the efforts of parents, teachers, staff, and students.

Unity of purpose focuses on bringing all children into the mainstream, where they can benefit more fully from stimulating school experiences. Unity of purpose, which must extend to actions, beliefs, practices, and commitments that transform school practice, demands more than just a statement posted on the wall. The development of this unity requires the combined efforts and commitment of all students, parents, and staff.

School-site empowerment. Existing schools for at-risk students are largely dominated by decisions made in agencies far removed from the school site and classroom. Federal and state governments and central offices of school districts have established a compendium of rules, regulations, directives, policies, laws, guidelines, reporting requirements, and "approved" instructional materials that serve to stifle educational decisions and initiative at local school sites. Instructional packages developed by distant publishers are often more potent determinants of the details of daily life in each classroom than the professional judgments of teachers. It is little wonder that administrators, teachers, parents, and students tend to blame factors "beyond their control" for the poor educational outcomes achieved by at-risk students.

An Accelerated School requires that school staff, parents, and teachers take responsibility for the major decisions that will determine educational outcomes. If the school is to achieve its dream of educational success, administrators, teachers, other staff, parents, and students must participate in making informed decisions regarding school activities. Important areas of school-site decisions include some or all of the following: curriculum, instructional strategies, instructional materials, personnel, and allocation of resources inside the school. Responsibility for decisions also requires responsibility for the consequences of those decisions, a system of informed decision making and accountability. Such decision making requires active support from the district's central office.

Building on strengths. In schools with large numbers of at-risk students the staff is likely to point to the inadequacies of their students, the lack of funding and of administrative support, and so on as explanations for poor performance. Heavy emphasis is placed on what is wrong with at-risk students and their parents. Preoccupation with weaknesses and deficiencies leads to low expectations and wholesale remediation. In contrast, good pedagogy begins with the strengths and experiences of participants and builds on those strengths to overcome areas of weakness.

Accelerated Schools seek out the strengths of their students and other participants and use those strengths in building school practices. In this respect, students are treated as gifted and talented students, where strengths are identified that are then used as a basis for providing enrichment and acceleration. The strengths of at-risk students are often overlooked. These include not only the various areas of intelligence identified by Gardner and his associates,[10] but also areas of interest, curiosity, motivation, and knowledge that grow out of the culture, experiences, and personalities of all children.

The process of building on strengths is not just limited to students. Accelerated Schools also build on the strengths of parents and of the entire school staff. Parents can be powerful allies if they are placed in productive roles and are provided with the skills to work with their children. Teachers bring gifts of insight, intuition, and organizational acumen to the instructional process, gifts which are often untapped by the mechanical curricula that are so typical of remedial programs.

COMBINING THE PRINCIPLES

An Accelerated School is not just a conventional school with new principles or special programs grafted onto it. It is a dynamic environment in which the entire school and its operations are transformed. The emphasis is on the school as a whole, rather than on a particular grade, curriculum, staff development approach, or other limited strategies. The goal is high academic achievement and healthy human development for *all* students.

The three principles of unity of purpose, site-based empowerment, and building on strengths are woven together in virtually all of the activities of the Accelerated School. The school is governed by its staff, students, and parents, and priorities are pursued by task groups that follow a systematic inquiry process for problem solving, implementation, and evaluation.

Accelerated Schools use a "powerful learning" approach that reflects high expectations for student success and a close link to student culture, experience, and interest. Active learning experiences are provided through independent projects, problem solving, and applying learning to concrete situations. By applying academic concepts and skills to real-life problems and events, students see the usefulness of what they are learning. The creative arts are viewed as vehicles which build on and enhance students' strengths.

The organization of Accelerated Schools allows for a broad range of participants and a collaborative approach in which students' families play a central role. Indeed, success depends on parents working with staff and students, helping to make school decisions by participating in the decision-making bodies of the school.

DECISION MAKING IN ACCELERATED SCHOOLS

At the heart of the Accelerated School is the emphasis on site responsibility for the educational process and outcomes.[11] To make this a reality, there must be an appropriate decision structure built around the school's unity of purpose and an effective process for decision making. We have found that three levels of participation are necessary to encompass the range of issues that must be addressed in a democratic and productive way: the School as a Whole, the Steering Committee, and Cadres.

The School as a Whole (SAW) refers to the principal, teachers, teachers' aides, other instructional and noninstructional staff, and parent representatives as well as student representatives. The SAW is required to approve all major decisions on curriculum, instruction, and resource allocation that have implications for the entire school.

At the opposite extreme in terms of group size are the Cadres. These represent small groups organized around particular areas of concern for the school. Where the concern is a continuing one, such as curriculum or parent participation, a Cadre is formed. In the case where the concern is episodic, such as the planning of new facilities, an ad hoc committee is formed for the duration of the task. The major guideline for forming Cadres or committees is to create as few as possible, always looking for ways to combine related responsibilities and to dissolve entities that are no longer needed so as to avoid an overburden on staff.

The Cadres are the groups that do most of the analytic and preparatory work such as defining specific problems that the school faces and searching for and implementing solutions. Before implementation begins, the recommendations of task and policy committees must be approved by the Steering Committee and in some cases the School as a Whole. The Cadres build on the camaraderie, ease of communication, and motivations associated with small teams working together on a regular basis and building expertise through sustained exploration and investigation.

The Steering Committee consists of the principal and representative teachers, aides, other school staff, and parents. The purpose of the

Steering Committee is to monitor the progress of Cadres and ad hoc committees, and to develop a set of recommendations for consideration by the SAW. Steering Committee members include representatives of each of the Cadres in order to assure that the work of the Cadres is coordinated at the level of the school. Cadres are expected to meet on a weekly basis, the Steering Committee on a bi-weekly basis, and the School as a Whole on a quarterly basis or as needed.

The principal is responsible for coordinating and facilitating the activities of decision-making bodies as well as for obtaining the logistical support that is necessary in such areas as information, staff development, assessment, implementation, and instructional resources. A good principal in an Accelerated School is an active listener and participant who can identify and cultivate talents among staff, keep the school focused on its mission, and work effectively with parents and community. This principal is also dedicated to the students and their success, can motivate the various actors, can marshal the necessary resources, and is "the keeper of the dream."

Accelerated Schools require that school districts play a greater service role for individual schools than they normally do.[12] Instead of serving as regulators to ensure compliance of school activities with some centralized plan, the school district must provide support services to assist Cadres and the Steering Committee in identifying challenges and obtaining information on alternatives, implementation, staff development, and evaluation.

While schools for at-risk students need considerable additional resources,[13] transformation to an Accelerated School is a qualitative change that can be made largely within existing resources. The major need is adequate staff time for meetings, staff development, discussion, reflection, planning, and exploration of alternatives. In addition, a coach is needed to assist in building the school's capacity to accelerate the education of its students. The Accelerated Schools Project has a training program for such coaches, and it mentors their progress at the school site.

BUILDING SCHOOL CAPACITY

Accelerated School philosophy, values, and practices are largely alien to the culture of existing schools. Much of the transformation process in an Accelerated School results directly from exposure to a new set of values and practices followed by daily reinforcement through learning by doing. As school staff and community work at it, they become experts at the process. The goal is nothing less than the "internal transformation of school culture."[14]

The entire school (all staff, representatives of parents, and of students) participates in all training. Between training sessions the school undertakes tasks that develop its capacity to grow and practices a set of empowering skills in making decisions in areas of concern. The overall training approach is based upon a constructivist model which assumes that human beings learn most effectively when they actively construct their own understanding of phenomena rather than passively receiving someone else's understanding.[15] The training is built around a range of interactive endeavors in which groups reflect on a range of issues and respond by creating activities in which they must introduce the various dimensions of the Accelerated School process to students or to parents. Coaches guide the participants through constructivist activities and help them use questioning approaches rather than criticisms or directives.

Inherent in all the training and school activities are the three principles to which we have already referred (unity of purpose, school-site improvement, building on strengths). Specific values such as risk taking, community participation, experimentation, equity, and the school as center of expertise are embedded in the training. The school is also devoted to the continuous development of powerful learning strategies, in which educational content, instructional strategies, and context (school climate and organization) are integrated to maximize learning by building on the strengths and experiences of children. These powerful strategies are heavily constructivist in nature and often constitute many domains which are usually viewed independently in traditional schools.[16] Since much of the work at school sites is done in groups, it is necessary to provide considerable training in group process and decision making in a team context.

Applying the Model at Edison School

Staff development for an Accelerated School is initiated in phases. In the awareness and buying-in phase, the entire school becomes informed about the Accelerated Schools model by discussing the ideas contained in a video tape and in reading materials provided by the National Center for the Accelerated Schools Project or one of the regional centers. This is followed by visits to Accelerated Schools and extended discourse on what is learned and observed there. At some point 90 percent of the entire school staff and student and parent representatives must support the commitment to move forward (an accomplishment that is met eventually by over 90 percent of schools that explore the model).

AWARENESS AND BUYING-IN

In the fall of 1990, a "futuring" group of parents, students, and staff was formed to chart a course for Edison School. This group spent its first meeting developing a comprehensive parent survey which was administered at the school's back-to-school night. This survey helped identify the challenges and goals the school faced. Key concerns identified were:

- dissatisfaction with the lack of continuity across the grades for curriculum and behavior management and with the way the imposed curriculum failed to meet the diverse needs and abilities of the school community with its increased numbers of limited-English-speaking students and at-risk students.
- declining test scores despite the liberal use of time and materials for remediation;
- a school climate which was not fostering students' decision making; and
- limited community involvement and ownership of the school.

In response the group developed the following goals:

- find an "umbrella" for all the programs at the school that would also enable the school community to help make decisions about which programs to implement;
- "dream" about the ideal school for the students, especially in light of the rapidly changing school population and the need for students to be empowered as decision makers;
- involve parents and students in meaningful ways in order that they begin to take ownership of their school.

After four months of meetings and research on major restructuring efforts nationwide, the Futuring Committee decided to view firsthand the Accelerated Schools model by sending three teams of parents, school staff, and district administration on visits to two Accelerated Schools. After several more site visits the Futuring Committee decided that the Accelerated Schools model fit the goals of the school community, and they spent six months building consensus among the staff. The entire staff finally agreed to implement the Accelerated Schools model in the late autumn of 1991.

The principal, Gene Chasin, had been in contact with the National Center at Stanford and now requested a coach. Normally the National Center would arrange with the school district for nominations, interviews, and selection of a local coach who would be trained using constructivist methods and would commit to weekly coaching visits to the school as well as to formal staff development days. However, Chasin persuaded the Assistant Director for Training at the Center, Pilar Soler, to serve as a coach to the school until the school could build its own capacity.

INITIATING THE PROCESS AND TAKING STOCK

Training of the Edison Community began in January of 1992. All of the staff development and activities incorporated both the full staff and parent representatives in a set of constructivist activities in which were embedded the Accelerated Schools' principles, values, and the focus on children. These first days of training provided the school with its first opportunity to engage in serious and widespread discussion about school philosophy and focus instead of just applying band-aids to solve problems. These two days culminated with an introduction to "Taking Stock."

Taking Stock requires staff, parents, and students to work together in establishing baseline information about the school through group research that takes two months or more.[17] Edison formed teams to explore each dimension of the school, establish research questions in each area, and identify and implement methods for answering the questions with the guidance of the coach. Using available documents and direct observations as well as tailored surveys and interviews of staff, parents, students, and community members, the teams worked together to compile a Taking Stock report.

The purpose of this activity is to begin the Accelerated School process through a self-examination and the preparation of a written record of the school's status at the start to be used later to assess progress. The process of collecting, reporting, and discussing the baseline information contributes to a unity of purpose, empowers the school community to work together, and identifies strengths as well as challenges. The process also builds collegial cooperation and the capacity of the school staff to do research.

Nine weeks were spent conducting surveys and collecting data. Many of the staff found the process frustrating initially because they wanted to start immediately to change the school without the time-consuming burden of taking stock. However, over time the staff recognized this step to be vital in providing baseline data and in creating a meaningful training ground for working together. This process also gave the school staff, particularly its teachers, an overview of the entire school and of what was happening in all classrooms. The walls started to come down. The majority of the staff were excited and challenged because they found the process running contrary to traditional school governance.

DEVELOPING A LIVING VISION

While Edison was gathering data to respond to its taking stock questions, it began to project a new vision of the school.[18] In a series of meetings of both the School as a Whole and smaller components of staff, parents, and students, the participants focused on designing a dream school that would work for all members of the school community. Since the Accelerated School transitional process is expected to take about six years, the participants projected a new vision of their school as they would like it to be after six years. This phase required considerable reflection, discussion, and decision making. It also drew heavily upon the dreams of individual staff members, students, and parents and their abilities to work together.

The fact that the development of this vision was part of an ongoing process that included parents, students, and staff meant that, unlike past mission statements, this one was a living document rather than just a collection of words. The vision statement has evolved over time as the school has achieved its earlier goals and established more ambitious ones. It took participants a great deal of time and some emotion-charged discussion to understand this difference and to agree on a statement. The school's first statement of the vision was:

The vision of Thomas Edison Accelerated School is to achieve:
- High academic standards for all
- A nurturing, safe environment
- Active community involvement
- Respect for individual differences
- Students educated to become confident productive citizens

Although these words may not differ much from past statements or those of other schools, the concrete understanding and commitment behind the words have made it an active vision for Edison.

This meaning was very evident as Edison celebrated its "Vision Day," when the vision was unveiled to the community and student body. The staff and students presented a performance called "Working Together" which explained the school vision. The day was an emotional one in which all students and staff and many parent and community representatives became personally involved in the Edison dream. All of the classes of the schools performed their own versions of the dream as interpreted through songs, raps, readings, art, dance, and discussions about the future for Edison Accelerated School.

CHOOSING PRIORITIES AND GOVERNANCE

Having finished its taking stock and its vision statement, Edison began the process of identifying its top priorities and establishing its system of governance.[19] With the assistance of its coach, a staff development day was devoted to comparing the details of the vision (not just the abbreviated vision statement) with the details of the Taking Stock report. It was obvious that there was a large gap between the vision and the existing situation. School staff were asked to work on setting out everything that would have to be done in order to move from the present situation to the future vision.

The whole school met to consider the list of what needed to be accomplished. No organization can work effectively on more than three or four priorities at a time. Through discourse and discussion, the staff identified the following areas of priority: self-esteem, curriculum and instruction, budget and public relations, and community involvement. This agreement on priorities was followed by the establishment of the first Cadres, one for each priority area and the assignment of staff to each group, usually through self-selection. The Steering Committee was established with participants from each Cadre as well as the principal, parents, and at-large representatives of teachers and support staff.

At this point in the training it became clear that several of the teachers were becoming uncomfortable with their understanding of the type of instruction desired for all of the school's children. Four teachers opted to leave during the first year—two transferred to other schools and two retired. New teachers were hired who believed in and were committed to the philosophy and process.

STAFF DEVELOPMENT AND PRACTICE

By this time almost five months had elapsed from the beginning of the process, and four full staff development days had been used as well as weekly meetings and a few early release days. The school was now ready to adopt the full decision process. This process must be gradually embraced by school staff, students, and parents and practices in an exemplary way by the principal, Cadres, the Steering Committee, and school district liaison personnel. It requires training and regular practice in working together to address challenges through a process of systematic inquiry that defines clearly the issues and specific hypotheses on why the problem exists. Data are collected to see which hypotheses hold water. Once the Cadre narrows the problem to a specific cause or causes, it needs to seek out alternatives for addressing it. Finally, it chooses a solution or strategy, which if ratified by the Steering Committee and the School as a Whole is implemented and evaluated for results.

The Edison staff was trained in both the inquiry process and group dynamics to launch the work of the Cadres and Steering Committee.[20] Such capacity building is an ongoing activity, particularly over the first year where formal training is followed by daily practice and assessment. The staff also received continuing training in constructing "powerful learning situations"—situations in which an integrated approach to curriculum, instructional strategies, and school climate and organization build on strengths and accelerate learning.[21]

The Edison staff's familiarity with the governance model of Accelerated Schools proved critical to its early success in following the process. Through active involvement on Cadres, representation on the Steering Committee, and periodic meetings of the School as a Whole, all of the stakeholders perceived their roles as influential. Having all stakeholders actively involved was also critical to the incredible energy and momentum that was generated. The inquiry process has proved very appealing to site administrators and district office staff because it ensures that all decisions are made only after thoroughly researching the situation and are based on what is best for the students. The school community found that practice was needed to firmly imbed the process since the school had been habituated to quick decisions and short-term solutions.

Initially, many participants did not see the need for school research until they experienced success with the process. After more than a year it is now second nature. Early struggles with this problem-solving process included distrust of peers and concern about the amount of time required to carry out inquiry. Only after repeated experience with the process did these concerns diminish.

Throughout the 1992-93 school year the Cadres met regularly to work through the inquiry process in their areas. During the problem phase of inquiry they did considerable research using the library, consulting experts, and surveying students, parents, and staff. Above all they focused on how to bring "powerful learning" into the school through identifying strengths of students, staff, and parents and building on those strengths by transforming the overall dimensions of the school: organization and climate, curriculum, and instructional strategies.[22] Powerful learning represents an important overall focus of the Accelerated School and permeates the activities of every Edison classroom and Cadre, the Steering Committee, and the School as a Whole.

The Cadre on family and community involvement focused on ways to improve home-school communication. In the problem phase of inquiry they found that staff and parents felt that the system for communicating pupil progress was inadequate. Specifically, concern was raised about the effectiveness of the mid-quarter deficiency notice issued to all students receiving unsatisfactory grades. The Cadre explored potential solutions that would encourage a dialogue between the parents, student, and staff and provide information which ultimately would empower the child. These solutions were put into an action plan that was approved by the Steering Committee and the School as a Whole for pilot testing and evaluation. After the pilot period the plan was further revised to address needs identified by the pilot evaluation. This revised plan was returned to the Steering Committee and School as a Whole for final approval.

During 1992-93 many changes took place that derived from the early work of the Cadres and the overall philosophy and practices from the Accelerated Schools training. For example, the move to active learning was pronounced as was a far more supportive emotional climate for students and staff. Parent participation expanded along with schoolwide multicultural events and the introduction of multicultural awareness across the curriculum. Cadres were exploring establishment of a very active learning approach to science and a new reinforcement system for good attendance and behavior.

EARLY RESULTS

At the time that this chapter was prepared, Edison had been in the Accelerated Schools process for only eighteen months. This is a short period compared to the five to six years that the National Center believes are required for complete transformation of a school. To get an idea of the rapidity of change at Edison the reader should have a glimpse of what the school was like immediately prior to the introduction of the Accelerated Schools process. Perhaps the most important adjective to describe the school would be "traditional." For example, as recently as 1991-92 the school had sponsored pull-out services for Chapter 1 programs and specialist programs. By the end of 1992-93 these services were offered in classrooms, resulting in a smaller effective class size. A schoolwide writing program as well as an integrated and thematic curriculum became common.

In 1991-92 Edison operated under a traditional style of management. Many decisions were being made at the state and district levels with the school responsible only for implementation. The principal and school staff did not have a method for addressing specific school needs and concerns. The school community felt little ownership of the school. Parent participation was minimal despite newsletters and family events. By the end of 1992-93, decisions had moved to the Cadres, Steering Committee, and the School as a Whole. With regular meetings and the use of an inquiry process, these groups were taking responsibility for both decisions and their consequences.

Prior to the launching of the Accelerated Schools process, traditional teaching methods were used in self-contained classrooms with a heavy reliance on textbooks and curriculum. Active student involvement and input were minimal. Teachers were working in isolation within their classrooms with little knowledge of what was being taught in the room next door. By the end of the 1992-93 school year, teachers were working together to develop new approaches around the powerful learning concepts that had been introduced. Teachers and students reported in a survey that classes were more exciting, stimulating, and challenging.

In the Accelerated School Project it is not expected that the mere launching of an Accelerated School will create an immediate payoff in terms of systemic change. Implementing the Accelerated Schools process and transforming decisions into school change take time as does the move from a traditional to an accelerated culture.[23] However, Edison had an especially high level of readiness because of the wide dissemination of information and excitement generated at the time of its "buy-in" to Accelerated Schools. In addition, it had the benefit of strong leadership, a principal and staff who had mastered the concepts of Accelerated Schools so fully that they have participated recently in the training of new coaches for Accelerated Schools. These two factors have resulted in strong early results. For example:

• Enrollment grew from 371 in 1990-91 to 489 in the fall of 1993-94. The additional enrollment was due mostly to parents from other attendance areas who decided to enroll their children at Edison under the district's open enrollment plan.

• Student suspensions declined from 103 in 1991-92 to only 34 in 1992-93.

• Uncleared absences declined from 866 in 1991-92 to 59 in 1992-93, and tardy or truancy referrals fell from 47 to 34 over the same period.

• Despite rising numbers of at-risk students, test scores rose. Scores for reading on the Comprehensive Test of Basic Skill for grade 6 rose from the 44th percentile on national norms in the spring of 1991 to the 55th percentile in the spring of 1993. During the same period, language scores rose from the 42nd to the 46th percentile, and mathematics from the 38th to 47th percentile.

As impressive as these changes are, it should be noted that Edison was a relatively new Accelerated School at the time that this chapter was written. The transformation process is a continuous one in which the School's understanding of its needs, its proficiency at using the inquiry process, its ability to apply powerful learning, and its embrace of the philosophy and values deepen considerably over time. The sense of excitement, inspiration, and dedication has been translated into the belief that Edison's dream for all of its children is also its destiny.

NOTES

1. Gary Natriello, Edward L. McDill, and Aaron Pallas, *Schooling the Disadvantaged* (New York: Teachers College Press, 1990); Henry M. Levin, *Educational Reform for Disadvantaged Students: An Emerging Crisis* (West Haven, CT: NEA Professional Library, 1986).

2. Henry M. Levin, "Accelerated Schools for Disadvantaged Students," *Educational Leadership* 44, no. 6 (1987): 19-21.

3. Levin, *Educational Reform for Disadvantaged Students.*

4. Jeannie Oakes, *Keeping Track: How Schools Structure Inequality* (New Haven, CT: Yale University Press, 1985).

5. John M. Peterson, "Remediation Is No Remedy," *Educational Leadership* 45, no. 6 (March 1989): 24-25; Michael S. Knapp, Patrick Shields, and Brenda J. Turnbull, *Academic Challenge for the Children of Poverty*, 2 vols. (Washington, DC: Office of Policy and Planning, U.S. Department of Education, 1992).

6. John Feldhusen, *Talent Identification and Development in Education (TIDE)* (Sarasota, FL: Center for Creative Learning, 1992).

7. Richard A. English, *Accelerated Schools Report* (Columbia, MO: Department of Educational and Counseling Psychology, University of Missouri, 1992); Jane McCarthy and Suzanne Still, "Hollibrook Accelerated Elementary School," in *Restructuring Schools*, edited by Joseph Murphy and Philip Hallinger (Monterey Park, CA: Corwin Press), pp. 63-83.

8. Henry M. Levin, "New Schools for the Disadvantaged," *Teacher Education Quarterly* 14, no. 4 (1987): 60-83; idem, *Towards Accelerated Schools* (New Brunswick, NJ: Center for Policy Research in Education, Rutgers University, 1988); idem, "Accelerated Schools for Disadvantaged Students."

9. Wendy Hopfenberg, Henry M. Levin, and Associates, *The Accelerated Schools Resource Guide* (San Francisco: Jossey-Bass, 1993), pp. 20-30.

10. Howard Gardner, *Frames of Mind: The Theory of Multiple Intelligences* (New York: Basic Books, 1983).

11. John I. Goodlad, *A Place Called School* (New York: McGraw-Hill, 1984); Philip Schlechty, *Schools for the Twenty-first Century* (San Francisco: Jossey-Bass, 1990).

12. Hopfenberg, Levin, and Associates, *The Accelerated Schools Resource Guide*, pp. 271-276.

13. Henry M. Levin, "Financing the Education of At-Risk Students," *Educational Evaluation and Policy Analysis* 11, no. 1 (1989): 47-60.

14. Christine Finnan, *Becoming an Accelerated Middle School: Initiating School Culture Change* (Stanford, CA: National Center for the Accelerated Schools Project, Stanford University, 1992).

15. Jacqueline G. Brooks and Martin G. Brooks, *The Case for Constructivist Classrooms* (Alexandria, VA: Association for Supervision and Curriculum Development, 1993).

16. See Hopfenberg, Levin, and Associates, *The Accelerated Schools Resource Guide*, chaps. 6-9.

17. Ibid., pp. 60-73.

18. Ibid., pp. 74-81.

19. Ibid., pp. 82-84.

20. Ibid., chap. 2.

21. Ibid., chaps. 6-9.

22. Ibid.

23. Finnan, *Becoming an Accelerated Middle School*.

CHAPTER IX

CityWorks: Redefining Vocational Education

ADRIA STEINBERG AND LARRY ROSENSTOCK

Some people seem to have a problem with the Rindge School of Technical Arts. They are always putting RSTA down and stereotyping us. . . . the students in RSTA are dumb; they will not go to college; they are going to drop out. Well, I will not take this any more. . . . Being a freshman in RSTA, I am positive that I will go to college, and a lot of my confidence has come from my teachers. RSTA students have worked hard, demonstrated enthusiasm and displayed some great exhibits. We are smart, not only in mind, but also with our hands. We have, or will have shortly, an advanced technological mind as well as an academic mind. . . . We give respect, so we expect respect. Success demands it!

In March, 1993, Paulina Mauras published this statement in the newspaper of the Cambridge Rindge and Latin High School. Her anger is not surprising. Why would anyone want to be labeled "non-college-bound"—especially in Cambridge, Massachusetts, the premier college town in the United States? As a ninth grader in the Rindge School of Technical Arts, the vocational wing of Cambridge's comprehensive high school, Paulina suffers from the low status accorded to vocational education and all who enter it.

What is worth noting is that this fourteen-year-old is ready to do something about it. She knows she is smart; she feels ready to tackle anything or anybody at the high school; and she believes that she has the right to voice her thoughts and feelings in a public forum. Perhaps most striking, Paulina has become an articulate spokesperson for a new definition of vocational education—one that is not based on a prediction about a child's future (for example, non-college-bound) but rather on challenging the conventional conceptions of ability.

The authors of this chapter are associated with the Rindge School of Technical Arts in Cambridge, Massachusetts, where Adria Steinberg is the Academic Coordinator and Larry Rosenstock is the Executive Director.

Not surprisingly, this reconceptualization is difficult to achieve in daily practice. Paulina puts particular blame on the "put downs" of those outside her school program. Certainly she is right that old stereotypes must be attacked. But in this chapter we focus on another more subtle and difficult challenge: how to help a veteran vocational faculty to move outside the century-old paradigm of training workers for industrialization and to embrace new curricular priorities and instructional policies and practices.

Like Paulina, the authors of this chapter are writing "from the inside." In 1990, Larry Rosenstock became the executive director of the Rindge School of Technical Arts (RSTA), where he had previously worked for eight years as a carpentry teacher. He entered this new role with the explicit goal of tearing down the walls between academic and vocational education—a goal he had just spent two years helping to embed in federal law as a staff attorney for the Center for Law and Education. Adria Steinberg, then editor of the *Harvard Education Letter*, entered first as a consultant to the process and then stayed on as the full-time academic coordinator. Combining an intimate knowledge of "business as usual" with a strong vision of a very different kind of vocational education, the authors have worked with a veteran faculty to put the rhetoric of academic and vocational integration into daily practice.

We decided to begin with the ninth grade program, the entry point for students into our vocational school. In the spring of 1991, a small design team of faculty created the framework for a new program called "CityWorks." The idea was to replace the traditional ninth grade exploration of different shops and trades offered at the school with an exploration of local community needs and resources. Although we began without a blueprint of what we hoped to accomplish, we were guided by a key assumption about school change: if we wanted a school where all students could be smart, we would have to restructure it in ways that would call upon all teachers to be smart. While this statement seems almost a truism, teachers have a very hard time believing that anyone really wants them to think or will listen to their ideas.

Acutely aware of their low status within the comprehensive high school, Rindge teachers were especially cynical. They had seen reforms and reformers come and go. What they had never experienced was a change effort in which they would be encouraged to use everything they knew and understood, not just about students, learning, and schools, but about the world outside of school, where they had developed considerable expertise as parents, community members, and, in many cases, as entrepreneurs and independent contractors.

The pages that follow provide an account of what happened when teachers at Rindge became engaged in redesigning the ninth grade program. In the first section we focus on the technical aspects of this innovation, the curricular projects, activities, and content that give CityWorks its definition and that differentiate it from the model of vocational training it replaced. The second section provides a sketch of how political and economic events have shaped vocational education, and how recent changes at the federal level are helping to create fertile ground for "growing" this local innovation. In the remainder of the chapter we focus on the process of change, outlining both the strategies we used to try to create a professional culture within a vocational school and the lessons we learned about the dynamics of political and normative change.

Beyond Shop Class: Reinventing Curriculum

THE CITY IS THE TEXT

Paulina's notion of combining hands and minds comes directly from her experiences in CityWorks, the centerpiece of the ninth grade program at the Rindge School of Technical Arts (Rindge). Cambridge is the "text" as students investigate the neighborhoods, the systems, the people, and the needs that comprise an urban community. Students work on individual and group projects, bringing aspects of their community into the classroom by creating numerous "artifacts" of Cambridge—maps, photographs, tapes, oral histories, and three-dimensional models.

Several features make this program unusual. First, CityWorks combines key characteristics of vocational programs—a project approach, apprentice-master relationships, and real clients—with the broader content and essential skills of academic education. Projects involve "hands on" work, like making a wall-sized map of the city and wiring it to light up selected landmarks. At the same time, students engage in problem solving, like deciding where on the map to locate a new teen center that would attract youth from all ethnic and racial communities of the city.

Second, CityWorks is taught in a space designed for collaborative learning projects. Looking for an alternative to both shops and classrooms, we borrowed the notion of "studios" from design schools. An open area at one end of the room is used for large-group activities such as demonstrations and exhibitions, but most of the room is subdivided into studios where teachers work on projects with small groups of students. This arrangement gives participants the flexibility to regroup, team up, or borrow tools and materials as the project necessitates.

Third, community representatives are invited to help create a context for students' efforts. Staff members from city agencies and programs identify unmet community needs that students could address and also serve as an authentic audience for students' finished products and presentations. For example, at a recent exhibition of students' work, several teams of students displayed drawings and scale models of a heritage museum they had designed for Cambridge. Each group had a different conception of where the museum might be located and how it should be designed. The museum builders sat with their models to explain their ideas as audiences of parents, city officials, and local businesspeople wandered through the exhibit.

In making the models, the museum builders were responding to a request from the city's tourist agency that is actually in the process of raising funds for a museum. Six weeks before the exhibit, the agency director had come to speak to CityWorks students and ask for their help in this effort. With thousands of people visiting the city each year, it was important for students to understand the tourism industry and to help plan its development in a way that would take the needs of residents into account.

In addition to the museum builders, several other groups of students involved themselves in the question of what visitors to the city should see and do. Rejecting existing brochures featuring "Old Cambridge" and Harvard University, one group designed a tour featuring places of interest to visiting teens, while another created a "Sweet Tour" for visitors seeking the best desserts in town.

A third group of students liked the idea of highlighting the efforts of a "local hero." They videotaped an interview with John E. Gittens, a founder of the Cambridge National Association for the Advancement of Colored People, and learned that he had led a neighborhood organizing effort to get the city to open a new playground named after a child who was struck by a car because he was playing in the street. Their brochure featured a map locating the playground as well as the story of its creation. All three brochures, along with a T-shirt that another group of CityWorks students designed, have since been adopted by the board of the tourist agency as products they will distribute and market.

The goal of CityWorks projects is to help students understand their community and its needs, and ultimately to see themselves as people who can affect that community and create new opportunities for themselves and others who live or work there. Through the lens of community development, students arrive at a very different and more positive vision of what it means to be a vocational student. The point is not just to make things, learn some skills and get a job, but rather to become thinkers and solvers of problems, who work well together in teams and communicate well with various audiences.

WRITE IT DOWN; WRITE IT UP

The work that Paulina and her classmates do in CityWorks is complemented and reinforced by two other multidisciplinary courses: CityLife (humanities) and CitySystems (integrated mathematics and science). This means that freshmen at RSTA spend five of their seven periods each day in integrated study.

In CityWorks, students explore the dynamics that affect them and their community. In CityLife, a double-period humanities course, they read texts describing how young people in other times and places have thought about and fashioned their lives and futures—from Benjamin Franklin's "Advice to a Young Tradesman" to Jay MacLeod's ethnographic portrayal of the "Hallway Hangers" in a housing project in Cambridge.[1] The model building and other hands-on skills emphasized in CityWorks are reinforced in CityLife through group projects in which students are required to combine library research, construction, and public presentation. For example, in one project students investigate cities in other countries and time periods, building models to illustrate what they have learned. These, too, become part of the CityWorks exhibitions.

Because many students entering Rindge are reluctant writers, emphasis is also placed on giving them a new way to think about what is involved in putting pencil to paper. The approach is two-pronged: "Write it down" and "Write it up."[2] Students learn the habit and value of reflection and thinking on paper through keeping journals and work logs (write it down) and they also learn what is involved in preparing their writings for public presentation (write it up). The work logs students keep in CityWorks can also be brought to the humanities class if they want to "write up" any of the entries in more finished form for either an exhibition or inclusion in a final portfolio.

CitySystems is ambitious not only in its integration of academic with vocational education, but also as the only course in the high school to attempt a full integration of mathematics and science. Studying many of the same concepts covered in the schoolwide freshman course, Scientific Principles, students learn to use mathematical reasoning, patterns, and equations as a quantitatively accurate "language" for describing these principles. Whenever possible, the vocational shops are used as the laboratories for this learning.

For example, the voltage meter in the electrical shop becomes a tool for teaching positive and negative numbers. Visits to this shop also feed into a study of mechanics: students build small electric motors, using only wire, batteries, cups, rubber bands, and copper wire. The autobody shop is a place to begin the study of the principles of force. Students puzzle over why it is easier to break the window of a car than the fender. ("We took a beat-up car and started hitting it with a sledge hammer to see how force works," explains one delighted student in his photo essay of this trip). Visits to the autobody shop also afford an opportunity to compare the structure (skeleton) and organic systems of a human body to the frame and systems of a car.

Such visits are intended to serve a dual purpose. By exposing students to "real world" applications, lessons taught in the shops help them to understand scientific theories and concepts as well as the importance of quantitative accuracy. At the same time, investigations in the shops help students to see the high level of academic skills required in technical work.

The Dual System: Changing the Rules

THE OLD RINDGE

If Paulina had entered Rindge several years ago, her experience would have been almost totally different. She and her classmates would have been placed in an "exploratory," spending two periods per day, for two to three weeks at a time, rotating through each of the shops offered in the school. The rest of the day would have been spent in the typical fragmented, academic schedule of a high school freshman. At the end of the year Paulina would have chosen a "major"— the shop in which she would spend half of her school time for the next three years in narrow skill training for a specific occupation.

There was virtually no integration of the exploratory with academic subjects. In fact, Rindge students "went out" to the other parts of the high school for academics. Although this was supposed to eliminate social isolation and bring vocational students into contact with a wide range of peers, the reality was that they were mixed primarily with other low-income students in low-level academic classes. Rindge students faced all the problems associated with the bottom track in high school: watered down curriculum with minimal academic content, teachers who would rather be working with a more motivated set of students, and negative labeling (such as Paulina describes) by other students and teachers.

The traditional Rindge program was justified in terms of appropriateness for its clientele. Since they were considered non-college-bound, Rindge students had to choose—at age fifteen—what they were "going to be" for the rest of their lives so that they could work on the skills necessary to their chosen occupation. The justification harked back to 1888 when Frederick Rindge bequeathed money and land to the city with the stipulation that it be used for a manual training school for boys. The sons of the city's merchants, businessmen, and professors already had their school (Cambridge High and Latin). The philanthropist Rindge wanted to ensure that a broader base of young men would be prepared to work in the rapidly growing manufacturing industries of New England. The now merged comprehensive high school (Cambridge Rindge and Latin) still displays his sentiments, carved in granite over the front door: "Work is one of our greatest blessings. Everyone should have an honest occupation."

ORIGINS OF THE DUAL SYSTEM

Massachusetts was one of the first states to institutionalize two separate curricula: one to educate middle and upper level managers for the new industrial firms, the other to train laborers and clerical workers. But the early history of vocational education also contained a more democratic impulse. Seeking to realize Horace Mann's vision of a common school system that included children from all backgrounds, local school boards found that they could attract Irish immigrant and rural families by introducing vocational programs focusing on agriculture and mechanical trades.

By the late nineteenth century the fundamental contradiction of vocational education was evident. On the one hand, it was and remains a means of providing an education to students who would not otherwise attend school. The Massachusetts Commission on Industrial and Technical Education reported that high school enrollment in Massachusetts rose from 6.7 percent of those fourteen to seventeen years old in 1888 to 32.3 percent of that population by 1906.³ On the other hand, it created a dual system in which lower-income students were tracked into vocational classes and away from the academic courses which prepared others for future education and higher income, white-collar jobs.

A 1906 report by the Massachusetts Commission on Industrial and Technical Education triggered a debate between John Dewey and David Snedden, the Commissioner of Education in Massachusetts. Believing that vocational education could "do more to make public education truly democratic than any other agency now under consideration," Dewey argued vehemently against Snedden's defense of the efficiency of a dual system.⁴ As Dewey noted: "Nothing in the history of education is more touching than to hear some successful leaders denounce as undemocratic the attempt to give all the children at public expense the fuller education which their own children enjoy as a matter of course."⁵

Despite such deep disagreement about the direction of vocational education, it garnered wide support. A powerful lobbying organization, the National Society for the Promotion of Industrial Education, was supported by a broad range of groups, including educators, the Chamber of Commerce, the National Association of Manufacturers, major farm organizations, and settlement workers. After initial suspicions about vocational education, even organized labor jumped on the bandwagon. Sensing the inevitability of vocational education, the American Federation of Labor wanted a voice in redirecting its antiunion bias.

The campaign culminated in the passage of the Smith-Hughes Act in 1917. For the first time, federal money was available for high schools to use in preparing students for employment in the major occupations of an emerging industrial society. In addition to the availability of federal money, two other factors assured the growth of vocational education. First, the compulsory education laws of 1923 captured into vocational programs many students who were now required to go to school. Second, intelligence tests such as the Stanford-Binet were developed and used to justify relegating some students to "work with their hands," separated from those who would presumably benefit from academic pursuits.

THE PERKINS ACT OF 1990

The Carl D. Perkins Vocational and Applied Technology Education Act of 1990 created a federal legislative mandate to reopen the conversation about the purposes and content of vocational education.

As recently as the previous reauthorization hearings in 1984, it was practically blasphemous to suggest that schools integrate vocational and academic education. But by 1990 some disturbing facts had begun to emerge. The job entrance rates and wage rates of vocational school graduates were only marginally better than those of students graduating from the high school's general track; only 27 percent of all secondary students in the United States who were majoring in a technical area ever worked in a related field. Widespread dissatisfaction with the outcomes of vocational education, combined with strong pressure from a coalition of national advocacy groups led by the Center for Law and Education, galvanized support for change.[6]

In its final form the Perkins Act requires that vocational and academic education be broadly integrated and that vocational programs move from occupationally specific, narrow, skill-based training to offer instruction in "all aspects of an industry." Through its participatory planning mechanisms the Act also increases the opportunity for vocational education to forge links with community economic development efforts.

In theory, the Perkins Act makes available federal money that could potentially affect the direction of schooling for 4.3 million vocational students. CityWorks is one of the first efforts to work out the ideas embodied in the Perkins Act in a real school setting. As the mandates of the Perkins Act trickle down to the local level, educators call and write, asking us to please "send CityWorks." Although we oblige such requests by mailing out curriculum packets, we suspect that these materials by themselves will do little to help our colleagues.

What is important about CityWorks is not the lesson plans or the specific projects that each group of teachers and students does. At best, these represent a way to bring technical improvements to a school. The process of detracking, staff development, and restructuring that CityWorks exemplifies and necessitates is much more at the heart of what it means to put the Perkins Act into practice. Vocational programs supposedly exist for the benefit of those who wish to enter the skilled labor market. But in too many cases, such programs have become dumping grounds, barely distinguishable from the "general track." The Perkins Act could be a powerful tool, not just for improving vocational education, but for challenging the social class biases and assumptions about intelligence that lie behind the sorting itself.

Changing the Norms

VOCATIONAL EDUCATION FOR EVERYONE

In Cambridge Rindge and Latin High School, as in most urban comprehensive high schools, the measure of quality is in the percentage of students going on to higher education. The Cambridge Public Schools pride themselves on having eliminated the general track and having achieved a 75 to 80 percent college-going rate. Basically, it is assumed that the non-college-bound go into the vocational track, and everyone else is preparing for college.

But these statistics are deceiving. What happens to the students who are supposedly college bound? How many leave high school really prepared to succeed in college and how many ever attain a degree? Although not collected on a local level, the national data tell a depressing story. Of those entering two-year colleges, the majority leave within the first six months. Only about half of those entering a four-year college or university graduate within a six-year period.

As we thought about who would benefit from a redefinition of vocational education, we looked not just at the students coming into our program but at the much larger group of young people who could benefit from broadly integrated academic and vocational education, from the creation of new career pathways and apprenticeships, from opportunities to contribute to the revitalization of their own depressed communities. In a very real sense, we saw our potential clientele as encompassing the whole student body, rather than the 15 to 20 percent willing to identify themselves with a program for the "non-college-bound."

We began with the ninth grade, not simply because it is the entry point for students into the social sorting mechanism of the high school, but also because changes in the ninth grade program would, of necessity, involve most of the vocational teachers. Although they taught the "exploratory" course in the autonomous isolation of their own shops, these teachers each had a strong interest in getting to know all of the freshmen. The exploratory course had long been the recruiting ground for future shop "majors."

The system functioned rather like a series of blind dates: students went from shop to shop trying to decide with which teacher (and technical area) they would enter into a relationship. Not surprisingly, this bred competition among the areas. Teachers in each area suspected the other areas of "courting" students too vigorously and of making unrealistic promises. Although teachers did not propose a change, there was a recognition that a competitive norm was not particularly healthy. There was also a growing feeling of futility and desperation as the total enrollment continued to drop, and students who entered seemed less and less interested in vocational pursuits.

SETTING GROUND RULES

In January, 1991, we took our first step: informing the staff about key provisions of the Perkins Act and explaining a proposed strategy for addressing these at Rindge. We would begin by undertaking a complete overhaul of the ninth grade program, and then, as the first group of freshmen proceeded through the school, revamp the program offerings in each successive grade level. It was, we hoped, a suitably ambitious, but not totally overwhelming way to proceed. The superintendent supported us by publicly declaring her desire for Rindge to be "turned on its head."

According to our timetable, the staff had the spring and summer of 1991 to design a new ninth grade program for the fall of 1991. For the plan to succeed, the new ninth grade program not only had to work for students but also had to function as effective staff development for teachers. A curriculum had to be designed that would introduce the whole staff to what we envisioned as the core idea of a revamped four-year program: academic-vocational integration within a community development framework. As soon as possible, staff needed not just to talk about but to *experience* what it was like to work together across trades and to combine methods that they used regularly in their shop with content that was less familiar.

In embarking on program redesign, we set ourselves three ground rules. The first was to keep everyone in the department informed of all that we were doing. The second was that no one would have to participate who did not want to. And the third was that those who did not want to participate would not be allowed to interfere with the efforts of those who did. When the first call went out for teachers to join a design team, six volunteered.

By the fall of 1991, the team had come up with an overall conceptual framework for CityWorks, had fiddled with the schedule to create unprecedented daily meeting time for teachers, and had begun the construction of a space that would house the new program. Although our goal had been to establish a full academic program, in the first year students continued to go to the main campus for most of their academic subjects. It took us until the fall of 1992 to find a way to fund and schedule the CityLife and CitySystems components.

In all, we began the school year in 1992 with enough classroom activities to last only about one month. The rest would have to come from the CityTeam meetings in which everyone teaching the course would participate. Although it was a bit terrifying not to have all of CityWorks plotted out, we also knew it would be a mistake to hand teachers a finished curriculum. Teachers, like students, are not empty vessels into which the current wisdom can be poured.

For years vocational teachers at Rindge had spent virtually all of their time at school teaching narrow technical skills that were occupationally specific. Most believed that this is what it meant to be a vocational teacher. State mandated curricula reinforced this notion. Vocational teachers received manuals for their shop areas listing duties and tasks that students in that area were expected to undertake. If we wanted our school to be a place where all students could be smart, we would have to structure a program where all teachers could be smart. This meant encouraging teachers to unearth the reasons behind their current practice, and to reconsider that practice in the light of changing economic and social realities. In other words, it was important to respect and make room for them as thinkers as well as doers.

We suspected that Rindge teachers were experiencing a kind of cognitive dissonance. Certainly the curriculum they were teaching at school left out much of what they knew to be important in their own work and lives outside of school. This was brought home to us early on in our reform efforts in a conversation with a teacher who had taught carpentry at Rindge for many years. Like many vocational teachers, he was an independent contractor outside of school. He explained that he would very much like to turn his business over to his sons, both of whom were skilled carpenters. The problem was that neither seemed to be good at most of the other tasks associated with running a successful contracting business, for example, making good estimates, writing contracts, dealing with clients and subcontractors, and getting variances from the local zoning board.

This teacher held within his own experiences the seeds of a new approach to practice. The challenge for us has been to create a professional culture which encourages teachers to share their experiences and reflect on their practice. Three strategies have been particularly critical to that effort. These are described below, with further discussion of the political and normative dimensions of such strategies in the sections that follow.

1. *Carving out time and space for teachers to meet.* The most basic thing that we have done is to give teachers both informal and formal opportunities to work together. Their close physical proximity in the CityWorks room opens up the possibility of joint projects. Required daily CityTeam meetings ensure that such possibilities will be discussed.

To create a meeting time in the daily schedule necessitated closing the shops for a period, not a popular move either with our own teachers or counselors who signed students up for shops as personal-interest electives. But it is critical to what we are trying to accomplish. The meetings are a time to reflect on what is happening in CityWorks, to review, revise, and propose curriculum activities, and more generally, to get to know one another and explore the possibilities for collaboration. As the facilitators of the daily meetings, the authors have played a key role in steering the meetings away from gripe sessions and a focus on logistical concerns to a broader conversation about teaching and learning.

2. *Including people from outside the department and the school.* From the beginning, the vocational teachers who staffed CityWorks have been joined by a variety of people from very different backgrounds who bring other perspectives and experiences to the task. The "others" have included several academic teachers, a loaned employee from the Polaroid Corporation, bilingual technical assistants, and, as needed, consultants to assist staff, first in their work on curriculum, later on group dynamics and issues of organizational development.

This mixture creates a forum for reexamining assumptions and for moving beyond the specific skills involved in particular trades or subjects to what it is important for all students to know and be able to do by the time they leave the program. At one critical juncture, for example, when vocational teachers were resisting collaborative projects in the name of craft specialization, the Polaroid employee talked about the multicraft perspective at his company and at other high-performance workplaces.

3. *Creating a situation of genuine interdependence.* The meetings are productive because they have to be. Everyone knows that they are about to go in and teach CityWorks the next day (or the next hour). In a very real sense, they sink or swim together. If the program works, it will eventually increase enrollments and attract a broader clientele of students. If it does not, Rindge will suffer the kinds of staff cutbacks of other vocational programs. As of this writing, the program *has*

worked. Freshman enrollments at Rindge for 1994-1995 have doubled. The competitive ethic of the old exploratory does not die easily, but it really is counterproductive in the new structure. It makes much more sense to collaborate, to nurture and support new ideas, and to look to one another for project ideas and strategies.

Learning the Politics of Change

NOT A SECRET

There is a tendency in school reform efforts to build a protective wall around what you are doing. If you do not, you might get accused by parents, or worse, by school board members of "experimenting with our children." Although it is possible to hide for a while, in the long run the only real protection is in convincing key stakeholders of the value and perhaps the inevitability of what you are doing.

CityWorks has never been a secret. Staff members and students have made presentations at parents' nights, spoken at each of the junior high schools, and hosted hundreds of people at the exhibitions of student work. The interest in CityWorks expressed by the larger community has given an added impetus to the staff both to make the new program work well and to be able to describe it well to others.

The "publicness" of what we are doing has caused political problems locally. Speaking for a small but vocal constituency of parents, one school board member accused Rindge of misdirecting working-class students by offering them liberal arts rather than the manual training that they need. One critic noted that Rindge is preparing "Renaissance people, not plumbers." There has also been an attempt to get the state to decertify our program.

Thus far, such attacks have tied up time and energy, but they have also solidified the staff, students, and parents behind the new program. Fortunately, we also receive very positive feedback about what we are doing, both from within the district and around the country. As awareness of the Perkins Act has grown, so have requests to visit our program or to send our teachers out as workshop leaders and presenters. In fact, the requests became so great that we set up our own formal mechanism for handling them: the Hands and Minds Collaborative[7]—a joint effort of Rindge and the Center for Law and Education.

YARDSTICK FOR MEASURING CHANGE

Contact with "outsiders" has brought major benefits to our staff. The attitudes, questions, and comments of teachers from other districts have become yardsticks against which Rindge teachers can measure the distance they have come. In June of 1993, a dozen Rindge teachers served as workshop leaders at a national conference cosponsored by the Center for Law and Education, the Massachusetts Institute of Technology, and the Hands and Minds Collaborative. It was the job of the workshop leaders to assist the nearly two hundred participants in developing projects that would help them implement the Perkins Act in their own schools.

At the last session, after listening to a number of teachers express concerns about the loss of time for trade-specific training, Tom Lividoti, the electrical teacher at Rindge, spoke up: "I used to sound just like that. I was the loudest one complaining about fewer hours in the electrical shop. But what we're doing now brings out creative juices I didn't know kids had; I see developments on the academic end that I never dreamed were possible. I may not be able to turn out second-year apprentice electricians, but I know we are turning out better all-round students."

Academic teachers working with the CityWorks program have also found that they have important messages to share with their colleagues. Alif Muhammad, the CitySystems teacher, convened a workshop series for Cambridge teachers called: "Put the action back into math and science." In these sessions mathematics and science teachers learned to use new tabletop physics equipment being constructed by students in the woodshop. Rob Riordan, a member of the Rindge humanities team, echoed Dewey last year when he addressed teachers and scholars at a national meeting sponsored by the American Council of Learned Societies: "I started the year thinking it was my mission to bring humanities into vocational education. Now I believe we must bring vocational methodologies into the humanities."

TOWARD INTERDEPENDENCE

During the first few months of CityWorks team meetings, teachers would almost never comment on a teaching or learning issue without prefacing it with a disclaimer: "I would never say what's right for anyone else" or "This is just the way I do things" or "I know that everyone has his or her own way of doing things and that's fine." The frequency of such statements provided clues to an underlying group norm that can best be characterized as "noninterference" (that is, I won't look too closely at what you're up to or tell you what to do; and you won't scrutinize me).[8] The conditions of teaching make teachers view their work with the sometimes fierce independence of artisans.[9] For vocational teachers, this perspective is reinforced by their highly specialized work within the school (and outside) as trade artisans.

In the past, Rindge teachers defended the separateness of their shops in terms of the differences among their trades, each with its own specific skill requirements. Shop autonomy seemed a natural and even necessary condition of vocational education. The most obvious negative side effect was the competition for students noted earlier. But perhaps an even more serious problem was that teachers had no reason to identify the broader educational needs of their students, nor any real way to address those needs. They focused on finding ways to interest students in a specific technical area, but did not feel responsible for ensuring that all students become better problem solvers or communicators, or gain a good solid basis of reading, writing, and quantitative and scientific reasoning skills.

It is impossible to pinpoint a moment when the focus changed, but after two years of team meetings a sense of broader responsibility is now evident within the group. It can be seen in an increased sharing of information and in a willingness to identify competencies that students need regardless of their schooling or career choices. Staff members are more likely to team up for multicraft projects, and, sometimes even design classroom projects that do not involve their trade specialty at all.

In early planning stages for CityWorks there was a tendency to swing from cynical skepticism ("This will never work") to unrealistic enthusiasm ("We're almost done"). Now teachers approach the task of restructuring with a kind of rolling up of the collective sleeve. There is a noticeably greater tolerance for ambiguity. People are more willing to bring issues to the team for group problem solving and have found ways to deal constructively with disagreements. Teachers are evolving a shared language for talking about how they work together and for getting through the inevitable crises. Perhaps more important, we now have a picture of what we could and should become: a high performance workplace where staff members are highly interdependent yet each is an active participant, focusing energy on the tasks at hand.

WHEN TEACHERS CARE

The amount of time devoted to meetings and the intensity of the staff work have, at times, created a worry that we might become too adult-focused. Fortunately, this is not what students seem to feel. When freshmen are asked what is most noticeable or important to them about Rindge, most students begin with the simple statement: "The teachers here really care about you."

Of course, the teachers cared about students before too, but the scope of what they care about has broadened considerably and hence is more evident to the students. In the old way of doing business, teachers had little patience with students who were not ready to make a choice about what they wanted to be and were not motivated to learn all of the skills of that particular trade. They felt their identities as skilled craftspeople slipping away, to be replaced by a much less desirable identity as "caretakers of marginal students."[10]

CityWorks gives teachers a new identity. Even if students do not express interest in particular trades, teachers no longer feel like mere caretakers. They know that they can help students develop competencies, interests, and attitudes that will serve them well in future schooling or work. This feeling of self-efficacy on the part of their teachers is evident to students. Several freshmen recently surprised a visiting reporter by telling her that what makes CityWorks teachers different is that they *like* what they are doing.

Not surprisingly, students respond by becoming more engaged with school; their "creative juices" get going and teachers see them at their best. The caring and mutual respect go beyond the classroom walls. For example, during the summer a group of students who had just completed their CityWorks year responded to the invitation from one of their teachers to come up with ways to smooth the entry of incoming freshmen. Using the acronym R.S.T.A. (the abbreviation for the Rindge School of Technical Arts), they named themselves "Responsible Students Take Action."

When Paulina and her cohort entered Rindge, they received a new student handbook, covering all of the things the older students wished someone had told them, and they found immediate support in the form of R.S.T.A. student mentors who had set up a table in the hall to help freshmen with everything from coping with sticky locks on lockers to dealing with hazing.

Impressed by such efforts, staff members have become willing to carve out even more unusual forums for student participation and input. Rindge is probably the only vocational school in the United States to have its own Innovations Board, with equal membership (and votes) of students and staff. The Board was created in late 1991, soon after CityWorks received an Innovations Award from the Ford Foundation. One of ten innovations in state and local government selected nationally from over 1,700 applicants, CityWorks was given $100,000 to "broaden and deepen" the work.

The staff agreed to set aside one third of this award to be given out over three years in small grants to other innovations in the Cambridge Schools that would further the CityWorks mission. The process would be overseen by a board with equal representation of students and staff, and several slots reserved for community representatives. At its first few meetings, the board hammered out a mission statement and a set of priorities. Student members were outspoken in these discussions, insisting, for example, that all proposals be submitted by at least one teacher and one student, and that proposals specify the ways in which students would be involved in carrying out the program.

By the spring, board members were reading and evaluating nearly two dozen proposals from all over the school district. After selecting and interviewing the finalists, the board selected nine winners, with proposals ranging from a new student-run radio program to a special summer school for bilingual students. Questioned by teachers and classmates as to why they did not use more of the money internally for Rindge projects and programs, several students spoke passionately of the need to end the isolation of the vocational program. They want the Innovations fund to encourage teachers and students throughout the school district to try new ways to join hands and minds. Their hope echoes the note sounded by Paulina at the end of her statement to the school: "We give respect, so we expect respect. Success demands it!"

NOTES

1. Jay MacLeod, *Ain't No Making It* (Boulder, Colorado: Westview Press, 1987).

2. Rob Riordan, English Department Coordinator of the Cambridge public schools, coined this phrase.

3. Edward Krug, *The Shaping of the American High School, 1880-1920* (Madison: University of Wisconsin Press, 1969), p. 220.

4. John Dewey, "Some Dangers in the Present Movement for Industrial Education," *Middle Works* 7 (1913): 99, 102.

5. Robert Westbrook, *John Dewey and American Democracy* (Ithaca: Cornell University Press, 1991), p. 178.

6. The Center for Law and Education, based in Cambridge, Massachusetts and Washington, D.C., provides support services on education issues to advocates working on behalf of low-income students and parents. Paul Weckstein of the Center played a lead role in advocating academic and vocational integration in the 1990 reauthorization of the Perkins Act.

7. The Hands and Minds Collaborative is open to educators and community partners interested in redefining vocational education. It is based at the Rindge School of Technical Arts, and is funded by the Dewitt Wallace-Readers Digest Fund and the Stewart Mott Foundation.

8. Judith Warren Little, "The Persistence of Privacy: Autonomy and Initiative in Teachers' Professional Relations," *Teachers College Record* 91, no. 4 (Summer 1990): 509-535.

9. Michael Huberman, "The Social Construct of Instruction in Schools," *Teachers College Record* 91, no. 1 (Fall 1989): 32-58.

10. Judith Warren Little, "Two Worlds: Vocational and Academic Teachers in Comprehensive High Schools," National Center for Research on Vocational Education, University of California at Berkeley, June 1992.

CHAPTER X

Complementary Energies: Implementing MI Theory from the Laboratory and from the Field

MARA KRECHEVSKY, THOMAS HOERR, AND HOWARD GARDNER

The Yin and Yang of Multiple Intelligences

When Gardner published *Frames of Mind: The Theory of Multiple Intelligences* in 1983,[1] he was unprepared for the reception that it received. A developmental psychologist and neuropsychologist by training, Gardner had expected that his book would be read primarily by psychologists, and these behavioral scientists might be expected to debate whether his definition of intelligence was appropriate and whether the proposed list of intelligences made sense. The book contained some concluding but largely speculative material on the educational implications of the theory.

While the book has received some attention and has generated some controversy within psychological circles,[2] it has been much more widely read and discussed by educators. Indeed, by the end of the first year following publication, it had become clear that the book was of considerable interest to administrators and teachers, and that it spoke to a wide range of educational audiences, including those involved in gifted education, special education, arts education, as well as to those in the mainstream of precollegiate education. The assertion that all normal human beings possess at least seven separate intellectual potentials—only two of which are normally covered by the psychological concept of *intelligence*—apparently struck a responsive chord among educators. By the same token, the vociferous attack on short-answer standardized tests and the call for the assessment of the range

Mara Krechevsky is Director of Project Spectrum at Harvard Project Zero in the Graduate School of Education, Harvard University. Thomas Hoerr is Director of the New City School in St. Louis, Missouri. Howard Gardner is Co-Director of Harvard Project Zero and Professor in the Graduate School of Education at Harvard University.

of human intelligences in an "intelligence-fair" way were messages that many American educators were ready—even eager—to hear.

Scholars in the sciences like to think that their work follows a course of its own, uninfluenced by social and cultural factors. But this view is naive. The interest of educators in multiple intelligences (hereafter, "MI") has had a profound effect on Gardner and his colleagues at their research group, Harvard Project Zero. On the one hand, it has given rise to at least a dozen separate research projects, each exploring one or another facet of the theory of multiple intelligences. We refer to this as the "laboratory" wing of MI theory. On the other hand, it has spawned considerable interest beyond the university setting. There are now dozens, possibly hundreds, of experiments underway in educational institutions all over the country. By and large these efforts have been initiated by educators who somehow learned about MI theory and thought that it might help to enhance their educational programs. As part of their own research efforts at Project Zero, Gardner and his colleagues have informally monitored the progress of these various efforts that have arisen in what we here term the "field" wing of MI theory.

Before looking in detail at developments in these two lines of work, it is important to consider the background against which MI theory was developed, the major lines of work that it suggested to educators, and the ways in which progress in these lines of implementation might be charted. Educators have always been aware that youngsters have different interests and learn in different ways. Despite this widespread awareness, however, most schools have been so set up that children are often taught the same thing in the same ways and are assessed using the same kinds of instruments. Resistance against a more personalized kind of education has stemmed in part from the apparent impracticality of crafting an education for each youngster, and in part from a curious belief that, despite differences, students are best educated if they are treated in the same, presumably "fair," way.

As a psychological theory, the MI perspective does not in itself dictate a particular way to proceed. Rather, as detailed in *Frames of Mind* and many other publications, MI theory is a claim about the evolution of the human mind/brain. Over the millenia, humans have evolved so that they are sensitive to, and can process information about, at least seven separate forms of information in the world: linguistic signals (linguistic intelligence); musical signals (musical intelligence); information about objects, numbers, and causal relations among them (logical-mathematical intelligence); information about the large-scale and more local spatial environment (spatial intelligence); data about one's body and parts of one's body (bodily-kinesthetic intelligence); sensitivity to other persons (interpersonal intelligence); and sensitivity to oneself (intrapersonal intelligence). All human beings possess all intelligences and all can enhance the ensemble of intelligences through practice; yet because of genetic and environmental factors, no two individuals exhibit exactly the same profile of intelligences.

For the purpose of scientific inquiry, it makes sense to isolate and describe each intelligence. Moreover, there are individuals who—usually as a consequence of pathology—exhibit single intelligences that have been spared or destroyed in isolation from others. Yet, for most of us working in ordinary environments, intelligences work together to accomplish tasks and goals. Intelligences do not operate and cannot be seen in isolation; rather we take cognizance of intelligences as we see individuals engaged in roles in the world in which they are solving problems or making products.

In school, linguistic and logical-mathematical intelligences are clearly at a premium. On the other hand, once one leaves school many combinations of intelligences prove to be serviceable. Moreover, even within schools individuals can, should, and do make use of a variety of intelligences. Intelligences can be used to "enter" into a subject: thus some individuals learn about history primarily through a narrative-linguistic entry point, while others approach history in a more logical or a more personal manner. Student projects can showcase a variety of intelligences and combinations of intelligences; in contrast, texts and tests highlight but a narrow band of human intellectual competencies. A variety of school subjects clearly call on a range of intelligences, with artistic subjects being different from those in the natural sciences, the social sciences, or the humanities. Finally, even the most "core" aspects of a subject—such as the theory of evolution in biology, Newton's laws in physics, or the constitutional processes in American history—can be expressed, learned, and critiqued in terms of a number of different intelligences and combinations of intelligences.

This much can be considered a relatively noncontroversial reading of the educational implications of MI theory. Yet, in many education milieus, MI theory has in part proved to be a kind of Rorschach ("inkblot") test, with some readers calling for an education that touches equally on each intelligence, while other readers infer that it is preferable to ferret out, and to teach to, particular strengths (or deficits). In general, however, MI theory has been seen as a charter for personalizing education—for making sure that each child's own strengths (and weaknesses) are taken into account in and outside of school and, correlatively, for nurturing the child's strengths as the optimal means of education.

Taken seriously, this line of thought has profound consequences for schooling. It means that one needs to know a great deal about each child; moreover, this knowledge needs to be secured in an "intelligence-fair" way (not simply through paper-and-pencil tests) and it needs to be monitored over time. For example, if we want to find out about a child's musical intelligence, we cannot simply give the child a written test asking her to define musical terms or have her answer essay questions about a musical work. Rather, we need to design and regularly administer tasks using real musical instruments or authentic problem-solving in the domain.

Building on specific knowledge of each child, educators are responsible for delivering materials that are appropriate to the child's modes of learning and for making sure that the child has the opportunity to demonstrate learning and understanding in an appropriate way. At the same time, radical shifts of emphasis cannot simply be imposed on a system that has long embraced different practices and values. In the end, for an approach like MI to last, teachers need to feel that it helps them to accomplish both their own goals and those of the wider society.

It has been quipped that an appeal of MI theory is that one can endorse it and yet continue one's current practices: lip service is readily paid to individual differences. Yet an effort to take the differences among human beings seriously will ultimately lead to a new kind of educational system. Initially, to be sure, any educational innovation is likely to be adopted in a superficial way; this is inevitable and not in itself troubling. The better test for an innovation like MI theory is the "five years later" test. When one returns to the site of the innovation after half a decade, will one find that the innovation is still being utilized in the same superficial manner; that the innovation has long since been forgotten; or that understanding of the innovation has deepened, been transformed, and has now been assimilated into the expert practice of the educator?

By the same token, and relatedly, just as one must examine the depth with which an innovation has been assimilated, so too one needs to notice the extent to which it has permeated other facets of education. In the case of MI, one wants to see attention to individual differences as part of a more pervasive systemwide approach to teaching and learning, not just the focus of a single subject, a single teacher, a single line on the report card, or a single MI activity room. And so the test of breadth needs to be applied as well.

It would take many pages to chronicle all of the "lab" and "field" efforts that have grown out of MI theory during the past decade. We have ourselves begun this task in a number of separate writings. In *Multiple Intelligences: The Theory in Practice*,[3] we summarize the results of several major lines of research that have been undertaken at Project Zero; we also provide an inventory of some of the fledgling efforts that have been undertaken by colleagues throughout the country. In a complementary set of papers, we have begun to report the major findings that have emerged as we have surveyed various applications of the theory undertaken by educators who have been kind enough to allow us to observe the fruits of their labors.[4] Finally, there have been correlative writings by the educational pioneers themselves.[5] In what follows, we look in somewhat greater depth at two prototypical efforts: Project Spectrum, Project Zero's first "lab" effort to investigate some of the implications of MI theory for the assessment of the strengths of young children; and the New City School, an ambitious "field" effort to implement MI theory throughout an urban elementary school. We conclude with an accounting of some of the lessons that we have drawn from these two strands of application, in terms of the criteria of effectiveness that we have just outlined.

Project Spectrum: The View from the Laboratory

Project Spectrum began in 1984 as an attempt to investigate whether distinctive intellectual profiles could be identified in children as young as three and four years of age. At issue was whether one could create materials that could elicit children's intellectual strengths and, if so, whether the resulting profiles provided support for the claims of MI theory. If it turns out that significant differences can be discerned at the time of the first formal schooling, educators are accordingly challenged to create approaches and milieus which are sensitive to the differences, say, between a child who exhibits a standard "scholastic" profile, and a child who is strong in musical, spatial, or personal intelligences.

MAJOR IMPLEMENTATIONS

Based on Gardner's theory and the work of psychologist David Feldman[6] on development in nonuniversal domains, the research team created a set of fifteen assessment activities in seven domains of knowledge that draw on a variety of intelligences and that are valued in our society (science, mathematics, language, music, movement, visual arts, and social understanding). (See figure 1.) During this phase of the project (1984-1988), the team worked at the Eliot-Pearson Children's School, a laboratory school connected to Tufts University.

ACTIVITIES

MOVEMENT

Creative Movement Measure:
  Biweekly Movement Curriculum

Athletics Measure:
  Obstacle Course

LANGUAGE

Invented Narrative Measure:
  Storyboard Activity

Descriptive Narrative Measure:
  Reporter Activities

MATHEMATICS

Counting/Strategy Measure:
  Dinosaur Game

Calculating/Notation Measure:
  Bus Game

SCIENCE

Naturalist Measure:
  Discovery Area

Logical Inference Measure:
  Treasure Hunt Game

Hypothesis-Testing Measure:
  Sink and Float Activity

Mechanical Measure:
  Assembly Activity

SOCIAL

Social Analysis Measure:
  Classroom Model

Social Roles Measure:
  Peer Interaction Checklist

VISUAL ARTS

Art Portfolio:
  Yearlong collection of
  children's artwork
  supplemented by structured
  activities

MUSIC

Production Measures:
  Happy Birthday
  New Songs—Up in the Air
            Animal Song

Perception Measures:
  Pitch Matching Games
  Song Recognition

WORKING STYLES

Working Style Checklist

Figure 1. Project Spectrum activities in seven domains of knowledge.
© 1986 Project Spectrum.

Characteristic features of Spectrum's approach to assessment include: emphasizing children's strengths; blurring the line between curriculum and assessment by assessing children as they play with rich materials; using "intelligence-fair" materials (for example, having children work with real mechanical objects instead of answering questions about how the objects work); embedding the assessments in meaningful, real-world activities; and attending to the stylistic dimensions of performance as well as sheer computing power.[7] Rather than generating a single number (or a set of "scale scores") that sums up a child's intellectual worth, the Spectrum assessments lead to a one- or two-page narrative profile that focuses on describing a child's strengths. Along with this profile, parents receive a Parent Activities Manual and a Community Resource List, identifying related activities and resources in each domain, for use in supplementing the child's normal educational regimen. The research results from this phase of the project suggest that the Spectrum measures did, in fact, identify a number of domain-specific strengths in preschool children.[8]

In the next phase of the project, the researchers moved from a research model to an applied design that could be used by classroom teachers. The goal of this phase was to help teachers identify strengths in children not typically addressed in school, and then bring these strengths to bear on academic areas like reading and writing. In 1991–1992, the team worked with four first grade teachers in the public school system in Somerville, Massachusetts. We maintained the assessment component from the preschool phase through identifying key abilities in eight domains and designing learning center activities to tap and nurture those abilities. The team developed small-group and whole-group activities, child- and teacher-initiated activities, and structured and free play activities (see figure 2 for a sample activity). Each learning center also had a set of corresponding take-home activities to involve parents. Children with a strength in an area served as leaders for the related learning center.

The Somerville program was implemented in four phases:

(1) exposing children to different domains through a variety of activities;

(2) identifying children's strengths (focusing on at-risk children) through observations of domain-specific key abilities;

(3) nurturing children in their areas of strength by providing activities in different domains;

(4) bridging children's strengths to areas of weakness, with a focus on at-risk children.

WORKING WITH TOOLS

Objective: Learn to use different tools

Core Components: Attention to detail
Eye-hand coordination
Visual-spatial relations

Materials:

Group One: Wire Design
4 wire cutters
Assorted wires
Contact paper

Group Two: Driving Screws
4 regular screwdrivers of different sizes
4 Phillips screwdrivers of different sizes
Assorted screws of various sizes and different heads
4 pieces of board with pre-drilled holes of different sizes

Group Three: Woodworking
4 hammers
Assorted small pieces of wood
Small nails
Wood glue

Group Four: Straightening Paper Clips
4 pliers
Paper clips of different sizes

Procedures:

1. Teacher's preparation
A. Divide the class into four groups of children.

B. Put the four groups of materials on four separate trays.

C. Remind children of the rules for using tools.

2. Whole class introduction and demonstration
A. Place four trays in front of the children and explain, "Today, our mechanical activity is called working with tools. You will be able to use four different kinds of tools: pliers, hammers, wire cutters, and screwdrivers."

B. "The first group of children will use wire cutters to cut all sorts of wires. These wires are made of different materials. They also vary in size. I will give each of you a piece of special paper called contact paper. If you put wires on the paper, they will stick to it and then you can make a wire design."

C. "The children in the second group are going to use screwdrivers to drive screws into this piece of board. Here are different-sized screws with different types of heads. You need to find the screwdriver that works best to complete the job."

D. "The third group of children will work like carpenters. The tools you will use are hammers and nails. You can make anything you like and you can also use glue to help your construction work. I can also help you write your name on a piece of wood, and then you can nail it."

E. "The fourth group will use pliers to straighten these paper clips. Then, you can take the straightened clips and twist them together or make different shapes, like a circle."

3. Small group work
A. Children should stay with their assigned activity for at least fifteen minutes. Groups may then change to another activity upon the teacher's approval.

B. Teacher rotates to supervise the four groups.

Variations:

1. Invite children to explore the mechanics of the classroom. Inspect what makes the cabinet door stay closed and how the drawers roll. Let the children try locking and unlocking the door. Investigations can also be conducted in other areas of the school, such as the playground or teacher's office.

2. Make a sample of geometric shapes from straightened paper clips. Ask children to make any geometric design except the design that the teacher demonstrated.

3. Invite some parents who work with tools to come to the classroom and demonstrate the ways they use different tools.

4. Take a field trip to a hardware store to examine uses of simple hardware, such as springs, hinges, nuts, and bolts. Have the children guess the uses of various parts of different tools.

5. Read books about tools and machines to children. Discuss tools with which they are familiar, including those you have not yet introduced.

6. Encourage children to draw their favorite tools and write about their experiences working with different tools. Ask children to create their own tool dictionary.

Figure 2. A sample activity: "Working with Tools."
© 1992 Project Spectrum

A feeling for the potential of this approach can be conveyed through the example of Jacob, an at-risk student who exhibited serious difficulties in language, but unusual strength in the mechanical area. When Jacob's teacher suggested that he create a tool dictionary, he began to make steady progress. Over time, Jacob's dictations became longer and more detailed, and his pictures more elaborate. Reviewing "his dictionary" became Jacob's first successful reading experience. It was also the first in-class exercise in which he was self-directed. Jacob's teacher further noted that he demonstrated leadership skills in the mechanical center, helping other children with the tools and materials.

This example illustrates the power of MI in at least two ways. First, the teacher came to value mechanical skill as involving cognitive problem-solving and "intelligence," just like the other more standard parts of her curriculum. She told us that now she felt as though she had something positive to say to Jacob's parents in the parent-teacher conference. Changing this teacher's belief system led to more children having the opportunity to feel successful in her classroom. Second, she used her knowledge of Jacob's strength to help him in an area essential to being effective in the world—reading and writing. To be sure, not all bridging examples can be individually fashioned. Still, an approach that builds on children's strengths offers a way to assess both the relative strengths of the student body and one's classroom curriculum in order to determine whether sufficient opportunities for nurturance or bridging exist.

One must note several obstacles to this type of approach, ranging from lack of time or support outside the context of a research project to confer with colleagues, to the daunting task of trying to create bridging experiences if one is dealing with a large number of students who could be considered "at-risk for school failure." Moreover, although results from this phase of the project suggest that working in one's area of strength was the most significant factor associated with at-risk children's improvement in self-esteem, classroom adjustment, and working style, no significant improvement occurred on standardized measures of academic achievement when compared to a control group.[9]

Spectrum has been extended in a number of ways in recent years. For example, the research team developed a classroom-based mentorship program in an inner-city school in Boston to connect Spectrum more directly to the community. The goals of the project were (a) to introduce children to alternative role models who represent different intellectual strengths and styles in their vocational and avocational roles, and (b) to help children make connections between their own personal interests and strengths and the adult roles in the community. Moreover, a number of schools and programs besides the original research sites learned about Spectrum and adapted it for their own settings. Because these schools and school districts launched their own efforts from the field, there was often a great sense of excitement, ownership, and commitment to applying, and even extending, the approach beyond the original participants and sites. In some circumstances, Project Spectrum researchers provided materials, workshops, and logistical support, thus linking the "lab" and "field" wings of MI activity.

LESSONS

Several lessons can be drawn from the application of MI/Spectrum to research and other settings. First and foremost, the Spectrum philosophy serves as a constant reminder to seek out a child's strengths.

For example, in the mentorship program, teachers and researchers agreed to spend the fall semester identifying children's strengths through classroom observations. In one of the early meetings, a first grade teacher commented that one of her students did not know the word for "leaf." When other members of the group reminded her that the focus of the observations was supposed to be on strengths, she realized with a shock how conditioned she had been to look for deficits in her students' learning.

As another example, in many of the schools that adopted the MI/Spectrum framework, the referral process for special education was altered to reflect an emphasis on strengths. In one school, teachers are now asked to describe explicitly a child's strengths in addition to identifying the reasons for referral.

Second, many teacher education programs focus on language and mathematics instruction, and do not provide much training in close observation of domain-specific skills. Spectrum provides a vehicle for observing, identifying, documenting, and classifying children's abilities and interests across a range of content areas. For example, one first grade teacher commented that, after Spectrum, instead of just saying that she liked a child's picture, or that she thought that it was good, she could now refer to the child's sense of detail, or positioning of objects on the page, or use of color.

Third, the MI/Spectrum terminology also provided a common language or vocabulary for conversations among teachers, students, parents, and administrators. A second grade teacher in one school reported that instead of referring to a child as a behavior problem ("he just won't sit still"), the staff are more likely to talk about children on a higher level ("he's a 'B-K' [bodily-kinesthetic] kid"). In designing curriculum, she said you often hear people asking, "What would be a B-K thing I could fit in here?" or, "Where is the musical piece that I could put in here?" Labeling ability in music, movement, and art an "intelligence" is an important linguistic shift, one which elevates the traditional "nonacademic" subjects to a higher status both in and outside the classroom.

Finally, the Spectrum approach can be used as a framework for assessing the classroom environment. When a teacher or school sets out to apply Spectrum, a natural first step is to assess the human and physical environments to determine which cognitive domains are already sufficiently covered in terms of experience, areas of expertise, comfort level, and materials, and which can be enhanced. This self-examination often leads to teacher collaboration, or teaming with specialists, as well as drawing upon resources in the community (bringing in artists, mathematicians, mentors, or other "domain experts" from the community). These experts are often brought in to work not just with children, but with teachers to explore and develop their own expertise in a number of areas. Many people who have been exposed to the Spectrum approach and who are familiar with Gardner's work in general describe the environment they are trying to create as resembling a children's museum or a discovery museum. Such classrooms offer a variety of stimulating hands-on materials and experiences drawn from the nonschool world that encourage children's investigation over time. Thus, the lines separating school and community are further blurred.

The New City School: The View from the Field

Once ideas have been released into the world, they often take on a dynamic of their own. While Gardner's interests were initially psychological, for the teachers at New City School MI has served as far more than a theory of intelligence; it resembles instead a philosophy about education, student learning, and the responsibilities of educators. Members of the New City staff have found that its implementation of MI has provided many benefits to students and faculty.

To understand any particular implementation of MI it is important to understand the school setting. New City School, located in St. Louis, is an independent school of 355 pupils, beginning with students who are three years old and ending with sixth graders. New City features experiential learning, a developmental approach to student needs and growth, "high academic achievement" (students averaging two to three years above grade level on standardized achievement tests), and a commitment to racial and socioeconomic diversity. The school has a minority population, almost all African American, of more than 25 percent; approximately one-fifth of the students, minority and nonminority receive need-based tuition assistance. New City has always had a commitment to aesthetic education, and prior to knowing about MI, had full-time teaching specialists in visual arts, performing arts, and physical education.

While New City is an independent school, many of the lessons learned there about implementing MI should prove applicable to public education. Children are children, and many of their needs—and areas of talent—are similar regardless of their race, ethnic background, or economic circumstances, and regardless of the kind of school that they attend. Similarly, many of the professional needs of teachers are similar regardless of where they work.

IMPLEMENTATION

During the 1988-89 school year, Director Thomas Hoerr read *Frames of Mind*. He was excited about the possible implications of the theory for student growth and how it could be used in identifying and nurturing students' various abilities. In the spring of 1989, Hoerr shared his interest in MI at a faculty meeting and convened a group of teachers who were interested in learning about the theory and investigating how it might be used at New City. Thirteen faculty members, one third of the staff, decided to participate in what was called "The Talent Committee." The Committee, which met regularly, began by reading *Frames of Mind*, and the Committee members, working in pairs, took responsibility for presenting portions of the book to the remainder of the Committee. In August, when the faculty returned to school, MI was given a prominent place in the in-service presentations. Other teachers were invited to join the Talent Committee and the expanded Committee continued to meet and discuss possible applications of MI ideas at New City.

Hoerr facilitated the inquiry by encouraging teachers to take risks in finding ways to implement MI, by supporting the model's use, and by sharing MI explorations with students' parents. MI was often a topic at faculty meetings as teachers shared which practices had been successful—and which unsuccessful. One teacher described having her children create and "act out" scenes from the books they had read, using their musical, bodily-kinesthetic, and spatial intelligences rather than submitting a written, narrative report. She found that this ploy encouraged reading among the students who found writing to be a chore. Another teacher, focusing on the personal intelligences, shared her experience of having children view videotapes of their performances in the classroom. Before witnessing themselves, the students were asked to speculate about their performances. After viewing the tapes, they were able to compare how they thought they were being perceived with how they were actually seen. But all was not rosy: teachers talked about the difficulties of incorporating an intelligence with which they were not comfortable—musical—in their classrooms. Using musical intelligence then became a topic of future staff meetings.

Throughout the process, Hoerr informed the parent body and the board of directors about the ongoing investigations and work. This step was important because both of these organizational entities make significant contributions to key decisions about the school. In the 1990-91 school year the school decided formally to implement MI. Perhaps because Hoerr began slowly and gradually expanded the group, all of the teachers were supportive and eager to participate. The staff saw the MI model as a tool which would enable them to identify and build upon students' strengths. Hoerr tried not to mandate how MI should be implemented, but rather allowed teachers to adapt it in their own ways. However, each teacher was expected to address all seven of a child's intelligences. In some classrooms, the MI presence is encompassing: MI terms and examples are on the walls everywhere. In other classrooms, there may be less obvious displays of MI. In all of the classrooms, however, teachers look at children differently because of MI theory.

Implementing MI means that teachers look for *many* areas of talent in their students, not just linguistic or logical-mathematical proficiency. Surely the abilities to use language and compute well are extraordinarily valuable; standardized tests, after all, remain the gatekeepers of educational institutions. But the MI model has shown the New City community that language and mathematics are not the only intelligences. Curriculum could—indeed, should—be designed to increase the chances for *all* students to succeed. Thanks to MI theory, for example, a sixth grade teacher reviews the seven intelligences and tries to ensure that her students have an opportunity to learn in each of them. She now offers ninety-minute language arts blocks with thirty minutes of direct instruction, thirty minutes with the class engaged in active learning and choosing where and with whom to work, and thirty minutes of youngsters sitting and working independently. The third grade teachers, in creating their year-long Native American theme, make sure that the information is available in many ways so that all of the students can learn in ways that best suit their intelligence profiles. As a result, the MI model has increased the likelihood that all children will have their talents identified and nurtured, not just those who are fortunate enough to have a teacher whose particular talents or interests happen to match their own.

The intelligences of greatest focus at New City have been the personal intelligences—interpersonal and intrapersonal. Teachers work at helping students understand how they are perceived by others with respect to their particular strengths and weaknesses. One fourth-grade boy, a good mathematics student, had always felt inferior to his older sister who was gifted linguistically. Each year she submitted innumerable book reports while he struggled with reading. One day he announced triumphantly to his teacher, "I've got it, she's talented linguistically, but I'm strong logically-mathematically!" Although he had known he liked mathematics, the MI model legitimized his strength for him, as well as the differences between him and his sister. The focus on the personal intelligences has made a positive difference in how New City students relate to each other.

The MI model has been catalytic with respect to issues of diversity. In talking with parents who are considering whether to enroll their children in the school, New City staff report that many of them find the school's use of MI attractive. Parents understand that the MI perspective increases the chances for their children to find success in school. Just as neither black nor white is "better," so, too, neither linguistic nor spatial-artistic intelligence is better. They are just different. (Again, this does not mean that the school abdicates its responsibility to teach all youngsters to read and write. It does mean that teachers try to recognize all of a child's potential and find the best way to help that child develop.)

CHALLENGES

For every answer found in the MI implementation, new questions arise. The staff is currently grappling with how to report student progress in the musical, spatial-artistic, and bodily-kinesthetic intelligences. Previously these areas have been the province of specialist teachers; but now the remaining members of the staff want to take some responsibility for developing and reporting on these intelligences as well. The staff is also working at integrating MI into thematic instruction and reviewing the entire parent communication process.

An implementation of this sort carries with it certain costs, of course. In the New City example, an enormous amount of energy has gone into ongoing staff training and development. How to incorporate MI in the classroom is the primary topic of the August in-service program each year, while in 1993-94, three other faculty committees are also tackling MI issues.

Finding the balance between traditional academic skills and implementing MI theory requires constant energies; despite much progress,

Hoerr and his colleagues are simply not "there" yet. Some teachers are comfortable with offering curricular options and opportunities in all of the intelligences, others with most, and a few with only several. Refining the implementation of MI theory continues to be a topic of faculty discussion and an opportunity for all, children and adults alike, to grow together.

Emerging Patterns

According to the mythology prevalent in scientific circles, researchers develop ideas in the pristine privacy of their labs and their studies; these ideas are then translated, with more or less ease, into useful form for practitioners. Whatever validity this view may hold in the biological or physical sciences, it has little credibility in the social or behavioral sciences. Not only are ideas from psychology or sociology rarely of sufficient precision to permit ready or unambiguous translation; more important, once these ideas are introduced into settings of practice, a far more complex interaction takes place between the world of the researcher and the world of the practitioner.

In this chapter, we have approached the general issue of the spread of an idea—in this case, the idea of multiple intelligences—in two contrasting cases: that of a university-based research program and that of a school-initiated attempt at reform. In each case, as we have seen, the way in which, and the extent to which, MI ideas have "taken" constitute a complex story. Moreover, from the many other "lab" and "field" experiences of MI that we have witnessed in the past few years, we can assert that these other stories would be as complex and in many ways as different from one another as the two accounts chronicled here.

Researchers and practitioners often have different missions and different concerns. Researchers are typically motivated by the desire to answer certain questions that arise in their discipline; and when they receive these answers, they are prone to publish and to move on to new questions and new sites. For their part, practitioners are concerned to do a good job in their schools. Unless both parties—researchers and practitioners—understand the different value structures, collaborative efforts will run into difficulties quite rapidly.

In reflecting on differences between the settings, a few points are worthy of mention. First, in the research context, tensions may arise between the demands and time line of a grant and the needs of the classroom. For teachers to feel a sense of ownership, ideally they should be involved in the creation or instantiation of materials and practice. However, grants (as well as top-down school administrations) often do not allow for this kind of time investment. Moreover, research that is classroom-based may not occasion the structural changes needed for released time. In the kind of innovations being advocated here, there can be no "package" or "kit" which can be ordered and implemented. Each teacher or school needs to devote time and energy to shape the approach in a way that makes sense for a given setting.

Also, research grants are often awarded for only brief periods of time; not only are processes rushed, but there is often little infrastructure that remains once the funding ceases.[10] While programs originating in the field typically have a person or group of people who spearhead the reform effort (for example, principal, assistant superintendent, or group of teachers and/or parents), the research team often serves this function in university-originated programs. Once a grant ends, school personnel rarely have the time or funding to oversee the transition to a school-based program.

Finally, in the case of classroom-based research, there is the risk of isolating or overwhelming the involved teachers if the demands of accountability and the larger school context conflict with the reform efforts. For example, the continued need to administer and report standardized test scores or to get all children reading and writing by the end of first grade may run counter to experimenting with alternative assessment and curriculum.

Our own work with MI has convinced us that there are also some general patterns that emerge, whether the primary energy comes from "lab" or "field" sources. To begin with, the core ideas of MI theory prove appealing to a wide variety of audiences. Most individuals know from their own experiences about the differences among youngsters and about the fact that there are many different forms of success and failure in our world. The categories and materials of MI provide a ready way to capture and communicate these ideas within a school community. As noted, MI theory is often a Rorschach test: individuals interpret it in different ways and perhaps even try to implement it in ways that are self-contradictory, or as part of an ensemble of programs that do not form a coherent whole. In the happiest case, MI provides teachers with ways to look more carefully at children and at their work, and to provide useful feedback to all those who are involved in the child's education. In a less happy case, MI becomes a new orthodoxy:

children are labeled as "linguistic" or "bodily-kinesthetic," but few efforts are made to go beyond the label and to try to devise more appropriate curricula or assessments on the basis of this personally configured knowledge.

There is also an intermediate case. In such an instance, some practices of MI theory are adapted and the school community feels good about them. However, in the absence of a continuing deepening process throughout the community—of the sort described in the New City School—the practices are either limited to one or two teachers, or they remain at a superficial level and eventually become invisible.

We have observed the course of MI adoption in places that have been reasonably successful. At first, a few individuals discover the theory and "buy into it." These individuals see MI theory as a way of promoting ideas and practices that were already congenial to them. However, in the absence of other converts to the position, MI is unlikely to have much effect. The kinds of careful and sensitive discussions and introductions undertaken at the New City School are necessary if MI is to bridge the gap between "another buzzword" and "a major organizing principle in a school."

Skeptics are most likely to be converted into enthusiasts if they can see the relevance of MI ideas for their own lives and/or if they can see how these ideas can help them to achieve greater success with their students. Theme-related curricula and cooperative learning are often useful vehicles for exploring the implications and limitations of an MI approach. Initially, there is little concern with issues like accountability, which often prove far more consequential to those remote from the daily lives of schools. Only after considerable immersion in the life of MI does an interest arise in the creation of instruments that allow one to assess different intelligences or to examine student work from the perspective of multiple intelligences.

In cases where MI has stimulated useful reform, it has been typically accompanied by a new and more sophisticated form of discourse among teachers and other stakeholders. However, as with other reform efforts, MI can be divisive as well. Sometimes "ingroups" and "outgroups" are created. And sometimes, despite good intentions, teachers find that it is too unsettling to speak to one another frankly about their goals, their strengths, their practices, their problems and fears.

In considering the educational fate of MI theory, we need to take into account two completely contrasting entities: an abstract theory conceived of in a scholarly community; and a set of daily practices taking place in a richly textured community organization. Ideas and institutions need one another, but they are very different kinds of "objects." The mission in which the three authors have been engaged in recent years has been to explore the ways in which a set of ideas can prove useful in an institutional setting, and the ways in which those ideas are themselves informed and sometimes transformed as a result of the lessons learned from practice in such settings.

We have given an "insiders' perspective" on the application of MI theory, drawing on two lines of work that have gone reasonably well and stressing the ways in which education can be enhanced as a result of the adoption of certain materials and practices. Yet it is important to apply critical lenses as well, and to ascertain whether these MI experiments measure up in terms of the more stringent standards articulated at the beginning of this chapter.

In the lines of work treated here, applications of MI theory have gone beyond the initial and most superficial phases, where old practices are simply relabeled in new ways, or when a reflexive effort is undertaken to approach every topic in seven ways, no matter how inappropriate these may be. Teachers are becoming acquainted with the limits as well as the powers of an approach grounded in the seven intelligences. However, with a few rare exceptions, it is probably fair to say that the MI approach has not been fully assimilated. That is, teachers are not yet in a position where as a matter of course they can draw naturally and readily on a range of approaches and materials so as to reach every child in an optimal way and to allow every child the best way in which to demonstrate what he or she understands. In all probability, it takes many years of regular practice, with ample support from parents, administrators, and the child before such a seamless "personalization via MI theory" can take place.

Turning to the issue of the breadth of MI influence, we see a somewhat different story in our two instances. In the case of the research-begun projects, there is often success at the particular site and program, but it is difficult to sustain once the funds have evaporated, individual teachers have moved, or the philosophy of a district or school has changed. Put succinctly, the necessary support mechanisms are absent.[11] In contrast, while the introduction of an MI approach may be far slower and more idiosyncratic in a field setting like the New City School, it seems probable that its integration with an entire community is more robust and is likely to last longer—perhaps even beyond the regime of a particular administration. We might say that efforts at changing school practices can properly begin with the kinds of lab experiments that we have undertaken, but that longer-term changes can only come about when a whole community becomes deeply immersed in examining, critiquing, and experimenting with new approaches.[12]

The fate of novel ideas in the classrooms of American schools is a long story and one that is not always optimistic. Many of the ideas that have most excited educators—for example, the ideas associated with John Dewey, Jean Piaget, and Jerome Bruner—never succeeded in affecting mass practice, though they flowered in certain more protected settings. Careful studies of these experiments have helped reformers to understand some of the obstacles that were not sufficiently appreciated before: institutional resistance, the need for considerable teacher development, lack of community "buy-in," the perceived lack of rigor and accountability, and the power of competing models that are more mechanistic and "efficiency-based."

Whether MI theory can avoid some of these problems and go on to achieve its educational potential is still an open question. An educational idea that revels in the individuality of all children and the idiosyncratic configurations of their individual minds is an appealing one, but one that soon runs into some of the forces that have daunted progressive ideas before. We place our hope in three factors: (1) the confluence of similar ideas, based on solid research, including ones described elsewhere in this volume; (2) the unprecedented need in our society to educate every child to the fullest; (3) the emergence of promising links between "lab" and "field" efforts that build on the strengths of these complementary perspectives.

The research reported in this chapter has been supported by the William T. Grant Foundation, the Rockefeller Brothers Fund, and the Spencer Foundation. We are grateful to Jie-Qi Chen and Julie Viens who gave many helpful comments on an earlier draft.

NOTES

1. Howard Gardner, *Frames of Mind: The Theory of Multiple Intelligences* (New York: Basic Books, 1983/1993).

2. David N. Perkins, Jack Lochhead, and John Bishop, *Thinking: The Second International Conference* (Hillsdale, NJ: Lawrence Erlbaum, 1987), pp. 77-101; Sandra Scarr, "Review of *Frames of Mind*," *New Ideas in Psychology* 3, no. 1 (1985): 95-100.

3. Howard Gardner, *Multiple Intelligences: The Theory in Practice* (New York: Basic Books, 1993).

4. Howard Gardner, " 'Choice Points' as Multiple Intelligences Enters the School," *Intelligence Connections* 3, no. 1 (1993): 1-8; Mindy Kornhaber and Mara Krechevsky, "Expanding Definitions of Learning and Teaching: Notes from the M.I. Underground," in *Creating School Policy: Trends, Dilemmas, and Prospects*, edited by Peter Cookson (New York: Garland Press, in press).

5. Thomas Hoerr, "How Our School Applied Multiple Intelligences Theory," *Educational Leadership* 50, no. 2 (1992): 67-68; Patricia Bolanos, "From Theory to Practice: Indianapolis Key School Applies Howard Gardner's Multiple Intelligences Theory to the Classroom," *School Administrator* 50, no. 1 (January 1994): 30-31.

6. David H. Feldman, *Beyond Universals in Cognitive Development* (Norwood, NJ: Ablex, 1994).

7. Mara Krechevsky, "Project Spectrum: An Innovative Assessment Alternative," *Educational Leadership* 48, no. 5 (1991): 43-48.

8. Mara Krechevsky and Howard Gardner, "The Emergence and Nurturance of Multiple Intelligences: The Project Spectrum Approach," in *Encouraging the Development of Exceptional Skills and Talents*, edited by Michael J. A. Howe (Leicester, U.K.: British Psychological Society, 1990).

9. For a full discussion, see Jie-Qi Chen, "Building on Children's Strengths: Examination of a Project Spectrum Intervention Program for Students At Risk for School Failure" (Paper presented at the Biennial Meeting of the Society for Research in Child Development, New Orleans, 1993).

10. Roland Tharp and Ronald Gallimore, "Inquiry Process in Program Development," *Journal of Community Psychology* 10 (1982): 103-118.

11. See Michael S. Smith and Jennifer A. O'Day, "Systemic School Reform," in *The Politics of Curriculum and Testing*, edited by Susan H. Fuhrman and Betty Malen (Bristol, PA: Falmer, 1991).

12. James Comer, *School Power* (New York: Free Press, 1980); Theodore Sizer, *Horace's School: Redesigning the American High School* (Boston: Houghton Mifflin, 1992).

CHAPTER XI

Democracy in a Multicultural School and Community

PAUL E. HECKMAN, CHRISTINE B. CONFER,
AND JEAN PEACOCK

Thirty elementary school children attend a city council study session. Unlike many field trips, this is not a tour of city hall, where children passively observe the workings of government. These children have placed themselves in the city council agenda and are active players in city politics.

"Mr. Mayor and members of the city council," says a student at the podium, "I came here to ask if you will donate a piece of land for education purposes. It would be used for planting and gardening and to do some research and school studies."[1]

In a series of speeches, some in Spanish and some in English, the students present a strong argument for why their school should be given a city-owned vacant lot to be developed into a pocket park and urban wildlife habitat for ongoing school studies. One child is poetic: "What is a park? It is a child and a family." Other children explain that the transformed lot could raise property values and "be a benefit to the community." In the end, the City Council votes unanimously to give the land to the school district.

The ongoing story of the vacant lot is one of many to evolve from a school reinvention project that embraces the democratic philosophy of decisions being made and action being taken by the people most involved. Reinvention centers on creating, within the context of the "real life" of the students and of the community, new concepts in school structure and curriculum that will encourage learning and

---

Paul E. Heckman, Associate Professor in the College of Education at the University of Arizona, is principal investigator for the Educational and Community Change (ECC) Project described in this chapter. Christine B. Confer is a Chapter 1 mathematics and science resource teacher at one of the schools in the project. Jean Peacock is the community program coordinator for the project.

diminish school dropout rates. The process consists of rethinking and reinventing all aspects of the educational environment.[2]

The Educational and Community Change (ECC) Project began in 1990 in one elementary school and expanded to a second school in 1992. Funded by national foundations for the purpose of identifying and demonstrating conditions that promote significant change, the project brings together a diverse group of participants with the common goal of reinventing curricula and structures in the two schools and their neighborhoods.

The Educational Community Change Project

Despite the current wave of school reform, democracy continues to struggle against the wide array of top-down policy initiatives that claim to be the cure for the ailing U.S. educational system. Much of the reform rhetoric offers little hope for change, and the system remains pervasively autocratic.[3] Consistent with a commitment to the democratic process, the ECC Project is grounded in the belief that school restructuring is most effective when it is created by those who understand best the needs and contexts of their own schools and communities.

The purpose of the project is to demonstrate the applicability and effectiveness of three propositions: (1) democratic norms will best promote reinvention in schools and communities; (2) when adults and children change conditions in their own schools and communities, they further their educational development, and (3) educational advancement is achieved and interconnections between school and community are best developed when all local learning resources work collectively as the axis for change. Within the ECC Project, the conglomerate of a community's educational, economic, societal, and all other resources is known as the "educational ecology."

The population of the area served by the two schools in the ECC Project is primarily Hispanic and Native American. Ninety-five percent of the students qualify for free or reduced-price school lunches. State and local demographic data indicate that students in these schools are more likely to drop out of school than to graduate.[4]

The project contends that all children can learn if provided equal opportunities in the educational system. It promotes the concept that these opportunities are more likely to materialize for those now underserved by the system if traditional teaching processes are changed to an understandable format that relates directly to the "real" world of the students. The best vehicle for such change is an ongoing united effort of school faculty, parents, and the community.

HOW ARE PROJECT PARTICIPANTS RESTRUCTURING THEIR SCHOOLS?

Maintaining that reflection by individuals and groups is vital to significant change, the project underwrites the cost of substitutes to enable teacher to attend weekly dialogue sessions with administrators, parents, community representatives, and ECC researchers, who serve as facilitators. In these sessions, teachers question their own practices and assumptions, share ideas, and explore alternatives. For example, during the project's first year, there were many questions raised about the traditional way that schools group children. Are fourth graders different from fifth graders in some significant way? Is the curriculum of fourth grade significantly different from fifth grade? During dialogue sessions, teachers discussed their theories and beliefs on this issue. They found that, for the most part, mathematics textbooks for fourth and fifth grades presented the same concepts and skills, although the calculations for fifth graders were a few digits longer. The teachers also questioned whether the textbooks furthered knowledge and skills that were essential for children's success in life. As a result of these discussions, the intermediate teachers implemented multi-age grouping of some classes, which in turn encouraged the development of new ideas about mathematics and new practices in mathematics for children to learn.

WHAT IS THE COMMUNITY'S ROLE?

An integral part of the ECC Project is a coalition and political advocacy group that engages parents, community residents, teachers, principals, school officials, business people, social service providers, city officials, church congregations, and other community representatives in a process of inquiry and action to improve the project's schools and neighborhoods. This coalition works closely with the countywide interfaith council of the Industrial Areas Foundation, which trains coalition members and staff in leadership development and community organization. The ECC Project provides one full-time and several part-time community workers to develop grassroots leadership in political advocacy and collective action aimed at transforming virtually all aspects of school and community.

Understandings of community and parent involvement in schools are being explored. Although parents are still encouraged to serve in traditional roles, the project found that when parents articulate their visions and concerns for their children, their interests extend far beyond what happens within the school building. During home visits and at community meetings, parents, children and residents have repeatedly raised their concerns about gangs, drugs, the proximity of liquor stores, vacant lots, abandoned houses, poverty, prostitution, unemployment, and the lack of after-school opportunities for children.

Based on the premise that learning happens—and schools become a more integral part of a child's learning experience—when parents and children join in efforts that directly impact their families and neighborhoods, the coalition seeks new opportunities that build on community leadership and resources. During its first two years, it worked with a state representative to draft legislation regarding liquor licensing. It engaged children and parents in organizing a summer school program and a Saturday environmental studies/fine arts program. Also, it brought adult education classes to both schools and obtained funding for an extended-day program that was designed by parents, students, and the YMCA.

Working with the interfaith council, the coalition organized more than 100 people to ask that the city clean up vacant lots and seal off abandoned houses in the school neighborhoods. More than 215 parents, students, teachers, and community members attended a jointly sponsored meeting and urged the city to collaborate in creating a comprehensive community development plan.

In summary, the coalition provides a forum for empowerment. It seeks ways to connect school and community so that children, teachers, and parents work together to realize their power to analyze a situation, develop strategies, make decisions, take action, and then evaluate and reflect on the results.

WHAT IS THE SCHOOL'S ROLE?

In the project schools, the weekly dialogue sessions build teacher confidence to try new ideas in the classrooms. One concept that emerged during these sessions was that of "real work"[5]: children learning essential skills and acquiring knowledge as they do work that is valued in their lives outside of school. Can children actually be scientists, mathematicians, and historians engaged in identifying key community problems, rather than just reading about those subjects?

Two teachers took their intermediate class on a neighborhood walk in search of "real" problems on which the children might focus. The children immediately identified the problem of trash—not just papers and food containers, but dirty diapers, an abandoned transient camp, empty liquor bottles, a cup of human urine, old clothes. One abandoned lot was singled out, and the children gathered data about the types and amounts of trash. They created graphs of their data and wrote about their concerns and feelings—the most prevalent of which was disillusionment. The garbage had always been there, they said, and always would be. One child announced: "Miss, you could clean it up tomorrow, and the next day it would be right back."

The teachers did not want that disillusionment to go unchallenged; they hoped to demonstrate that societal systems exist that are designed to change things, and that one has to learn how to access those systems. It sounded good, but the teachers themselves had little experience in this area and were unsure of how to begin. Then one of the teachers attended a meeting of the coalition and interfaith council, where parents and other members of the community were discussing neighborhood safety problems. The teacher saw the potential for children to participate in this real-life process for bringing about change. Subsequently, a community effort was organized in which the children, parents, school staff, and neighborhood residents elicited support and action from a city council member and the city staff. The action focused on sealing an abandoned house near the school and cleaning up vacant land, including the lot on which the students had gathered data. The children voiced the need for change, and parents spoke about their concerns over safety. Everyone involved began to see the power of people uniting for a cause.

The city had scheduled a special clean-up day the following week, and the children created leaflets and talked to their neighbors about it. Active participants in this event included people from neighborhood associations, three churches, a nearby soup kitchen, and even residents who did not have school-age children. The media became involved, and children, the school staff, and residents described the community problems on television. To elicit further support, an 11-year-old student and her teacher spoke before an audience of 900 at a countywide interfaith council meeting that was attended by members of the city council and the mayor.

The children were making the system of government work for them in solving problems that impacted their lives. They quantified real things to describe an unhealthy situation and to convince others of the magnitude of the problem.

Other community-wide projects, such as the clean-up effort, are ongoing in the schools' neighborhoods. These programs stimulate and build self-confidence in community residents, and consequently many residents are emerging as leaders in various community causes. And just as the adults are taking ownership of their community and becoming empowered to identify concerns, analyze power, plan solutions and create change, the children are seeing a vision of what can be and are participating in making it a reality. The school is functioning as an important part of the community, and the community is becoming a focal point for powerful transformation. As a result, important learning is occurring.

Three Propositions and Where They Fit

The ECC Project serves as a laboratory in which the three propositions of its democratic educational philosophy can be tested and evaluated.

PROPOSITION 1. *Democratic norms will best promote reinvention.*

While other systems may thwart change, democracy appears more able than some other systems of governance to cope with societal conditions of rapid technological, economic, political, and social change and to further social and organizational transformation.[6] However, current practices and innovative proposals in many public education systems often eschew democratic ideas in favor of more autocratic principles. In fact, many schools and their communities appear committed to retaining fairly traditional hierarchical and autocratic educational practices.[7] Failure to employ more democratic measures may partially explain why major structural and normative changes have not prevailed in many public schools and classrooms.[8]

In developing a plan to further educational change and promote reinvention, the ECC Project is committed to three democratic norms and activities: (1) equal and full participation; (2) expression of wants, wishes, and ideas; and (3) public inquiry.

Equal and full participation. Although some teachers and other adults choose not to participate, the ECC Project continues to urge everyone in the two schools and the communities to become involved in all project activities. It encourages them to examine what is happening in the schools and the neighborhoods, to determine what and how project work will be done, to make changes, and to judge the worth of these efforts.

Embracing diversity in opinions and perspectives adds important complexity to discussions. For example, it creates the dilemma of how to respect individual beliefs while arriving at new common understandings. Teachers who previously worked in the traditional isolated manner must now confront and resolve interpersonal and intellectual conflicts. Inevitably, tensions arise as participants make different decisions about change. Learning to respect and manage these differences has been a significant part of the process. An example of this was the earlier discussion of combining multi-age classrooms.

As parents more willingly express what they know and want, conflicts arise between their traditional views of education and newly invented practices. It is important to note that while the desire for change is keen among many parents and teachers, if change is to occur, that desire must be strong enough to deal with diversity in thought and theory.

The ECC Project assumes that in this kind of voluntary participation, project participants can take care of themselves throughout the change process. They know what they want and can make decisions, act on their own behalf, consider and explore new ideas, confront and resolve interpersonal and intellectual conflicts, and reinvent education in their own community.

Expressing wants, wishes, and ideas. Knowing and expressing wants, beliefs, and values are necessary for individuals to make good decisions and changes.[9] Dialogue about why certain things are wanted, valued, or believed can prod one to question the way things are.[10] Why is something believed to be important? What are the underlying assumptions of our beliefs? These types of exchanges serve as a basis for negotiating shared conceptions, decisions, norms, and ways of living in a community. In a community, self-knowledge brings with it a responsibility to reveal this knowledge and understanding to other community members.[11] These expressions serve as the basis for negotiating shared conceptions, decisions, and norms.

Public meetings that brought people together to discuss community concerns and desires generated common understandings of what needed to be changed, but the conversations were usually stymied when people expressed a belief that "nothing will change, no matter what we do." However, a few people would adamantly insist that "united, we can make a difference."

The quality of a decision depends on authentic expressions of people's perceptions, beliefs and desires.[12] Opportunities that provide people a forum for such authentic self-expression are crucial to this process. The fewer distortions in acknowledging what each individual wishes or believes, the greater the opportunities for authentic communication and negotiations that result in good decisions.[13] Public meetings allowed people to examine their beliefs about change. A process of inquiry ensued that led people to question their situation and to try something new.

Public inquiry. To acquire self-knowledge and negotiate good decisions, a norm of individual and public inquiry must exist. Examination of and reflection upon the thoughts, emotions, intentions, and actions of individuals and groups constitute public inquiry.[14] Community members who share in public inquiry increase the quality of shared beliefs, ideas, and actions that emerge.

At the school level, weekly dialogue sessions have been the principal forum for public inquiry, and over time the wondering and questioning in these sessions has carried over into the classrooms. One example is how the teachers questioned the way that adults have traditionally determined the curriculum for the children. They wondered what prior knowledge children brought with them to school. Through conversation, a first-grade teacher found that her students knew that plants grow from seeds, what plants need in order to grow, what kind of soil is best, and where in the neighborhood that kind of soil could be found—more than the first-grade science textbook told the children. The teachers concluded that children had much more extensive knowledge than the teachers had realized.[15]

What would children like to learn about? Again the teachers investigated and were surprised at the results: first graders wondered what makes the wind sing, why there is a "button" on the bottom of a pumpkin, and how seeds know it is a good time to germinate. The teachers concluded that children's interests and questions may be markedly different from their own. Many teachers found that focusing investigations on students' own questions substantially affected student ownership and interest in the activities. Over time, the school culture has changed to one in which children and teachers commonly negotiate decisions about curriculum.

Public inquiry is also an important part of the project's community meetings. Parents and students questioned the reasons for problems in their community and began to meet with city council members and to study the power dynamics of the city. They developed a shared understanding that citizens needed to hold politicians accountable to the concerns of the people. One parent described how her skepticism was challenged through this process: "Until this day, nobody asked questions. That's why things stayed the same. Now we are challenging the politicians and establishing working areas." This is one illustration of how new understandings are evolving out of a democratic process of full participation, sharing of wants and wishes and public inquiry. Of course, the process is never as clean as in this description. What is evident from these experiences, however, is a consensus that change is possible, especially when people are accountable to each other, express themselves authentically, and negotiate common understandings that support collective action.

PROPOSITION 2. *Educational development is furthered when adults and children make substantive changes in their schools and communities.*

Cremin contended that change efforts as well as outcomes of those efforts become educational when they seek to "transmit, evoke, or acquire knowledge, attitudes, values, skills, or sensibilities."[16] The ECC Project's change efforts become educational through the enlightenment of students and adults about access to resources and the successful results of group effort.

Identifying actual community problems and creating new conditions that resolve the problems further human development, according to Bronfenbrenner, Dewey, and Lewin.[17] In the ECC perspective, activities to change conditions in the educational system are closely aligned with changing conditions in the community. Education is advanced when the physical conditions of the community—housing, safety, education, and health-delivery systems—are addressed. These conditions become the texts for the kind of education on which the ECC Project focuses. Examining community from the viewpoints of scientists, mathematicians, and historians—and using knowledge gained in the process—is perceived by the participants in the project as both basic and good education. This basic education also joins social and citizenship development with intellectual development[18] as students learn how citizens in a democracy can change community structures.

A continuation of the story of the abandoned lot illustrates this point. The teachers suggested to the children that a wildlife habitat be created on the lot. They were surprised by the lukewarm reaction, as children made the following points: the lot is too small, they had no money for materials, transients would mess it up, and adults don't always follow through. The latter belief could be dealt with most effectively through a contrary experience, the teachers decided.

How big was the lot? The children learned about units of measure and how to use measuring devices. Where would they get the money? They learned about grants. As money was acquired, they created a system to manage it. What was a wildlife habitat anyway? What wildlife could exist in the desert? What plants could support that wildlife? Who and what were the resources in the community that could answer their questions? The children and teachers were busy trying to find the answers and keeping track of the acquired information. The students read books and pamphlets and learned to create and understand charts and diagrams. Builders, landscapers, and wildlife specialists were invited to talk to the children. Children went on field trips to a' desert nursery and museum. And always they had to record what they learned and communicate their findings to others.

The transformation of the lot into a wildlife habitat is expected to take many years. In this undertaking, children are not merely reading science books and being "taught" or told about science; instead, they function as scientists, working with soil samples and seeds, viewing insects under microscopes. They function as mathematicians by measuring fencing, estimating heights of trees and the shade they will provide; as artists by sketching plants and planning their color coordination; as writers by keeping journals of their work. And while developing intellectually and acquiring new knowledge, the children are actually changing their community.

PROPOSITION 3. *Educational advancement is achieved and interconnections between school and community are developed best when all local learning resources work collectively as the axis for change.*

Anthropologists have conceptualized education as consisting of formal, nonformal, and informal activities.[19] All learning resources (collectively, the educational ecology) are represented in these three dimensions.[20] Interconnections among schools (formal); club programs such as 4-H, Girl Scouts, Boy Scouts, and YMCA and YWCA youth activities (nonformal); and activities in families and neighborhoods (informal) will determine the power of (and can enhance the well-being of) the ecology.

With regard to reinventing the educational process for elementary school children, the ECC Project seeks to alter the structures, practices, and activities of the nonformal and formal dimensions of the context. An attempt is being made to connect what children do in school to their nonformal experiences in the community. The city council member who worked with the children to acquire the land has come to understand the importance of making these school/community connections:

Lots of times, knowledge in a classroom is sort of abstract, detached, disembodied, but this ground [the lot] will be used to create a habitat . . . a field classroom that will do more to make knowledge relevant to students' lives than what goes on, unfortunately, in classrooms most of the week.[21]

School work can become less "abstract and detached" when it is connected to the context that children know best: their own environment. As one student stated in his speech to the city council: "Some kids don't like science, but if they could get to see what they are studying about, they might get more enthusiastic."[22]

The ECC Project is joining with parents, children, and teachers to create nonformal activities, such as after-school programs and Saturday programs, that provide greater continuity between what they learn at school and what they do after school. The project has not sought to change directly the informal education that occurs through children's interactions with their families and neighborhoods. Instead, it seeks to change what the formal and nonformal contexts expect from or assume about informal education. In particular, acceptance of the view that families and the neighborhood create and maintain funds of knowledge[23] is being urged. The vacant lot project is one example of how relationships can be restructured to incorporate the children's work with the community's existing knowledge and skills. A Native American parent in the community explained how the work of the habitat will allow "us, as parents, to pass on to our children the uses of saguaro cactus fruit, cholla buds, and other desert plants. Children need to know that these natural resources exist in our surroundings."

Building on this foundation, the ECC Project seeks to promote parents' and other community members' knowledge and skills in finding and solving community problems. As parents use their knowledge and gain skills to make changes in community structures, children are further advantaged in their informal educational activities. They also benefit when formal and nonformal learning builds on knowledge and skills acquired in informal education. As connections across these dimensions are strengthened, the vitality of all learning resources increases.

The Project in Perspective

These propositions do not offer a blueprint or model as much as they suggest guidelines for context-based action. Invention of new community structures, programs, norms, and activities suggests creating anew what has existed before. Given the democratic norms discussed earlier, invention then is to be done by all of the participants from their own knowledge and needs. Results of the ECC Project during the first four years are encouraging. By using the educational ecology as it exists to create it anew, children and adults are acquiring new knowledge and skills. While the project has had good fortune in securing funds for extending its five-year effort to explore conditions for reinventing the educational ecology, there exists a sense of urgency to find answers to the many questions that continue to arise. Although it will be several years before comprehensive responses can be advanced, just noting the questions will signify the first step in responding:

1. Participants are acquiring knowledge and skills to think like scientists, mathematicians, and historians, for instance, in finding and solving significant community problems. This knowledge and these skills are the type that an educational ecology should evoke and transmit; however, yet to be determined is the degree of knowledge and skills necessary. While others are attempting to develop new standards for teaching basic school subjects in a decontextualized, structured manner, the ECC Project asks: What knowledge and which skills are necessary and how can they be learned in a contextualized, unstructured environment?

2. The school curriculum has existed in its general form for the past one hundred years[24] and appears to persist today across societies in the Americas, Europe, and Asia.[25] While efforts such as the ECC Project are under way to develop more contextualized knowledge and skills and activities, how far can schools and communities go in contextualizing their educational efforts in this democratic fashion? Is it possible to sustain, day after day and year after year, a curriculum based on finding and solving community problems through a democratic process?

3. A technology to perpetuate efforts of projects such as ECC is nonexistent or at the very least underdeveloped, and both physical and mental tools are necessary to develop this technology. Computers, rulers, calculators, and chart paper are typical and easily accessible material tools, but the necessary mental tools—such as creativity and abilities to identify, analyze, and solve problems—are not yet fully defined.

However, the importance of mental tools in teaching and learning is being addressed. For instance, Brown, Collins, and Duguid suggest that the mental tools in mathematics require an understanding of the world in which the tools will be used as well as an understanding of the tools themselves.[26] They also point out that "the understanding, both of the world and of the tool, continually changes as a result of their interaction. Learning and acting are interestingly indistinct, learning being a continuous, lifelong process resulting from acting in situations."

If, as Resnick pointed out, much problem identification and solution in today's complex world is ill-structured,[27] another question arises. Are different mental tools needed to solve problems today than were needed in solving well-structured problems that schools have dealt with during the past century? Children and adults have figured out ways to find patterns and sense problems and solutions, but to what degree can these mental tools be developed and incorporated in a technology that is feasible on a daily basis?

4. Very early efforts of the project to change structures and practices have been applauded by outsiders, but what happens if significant community problems are identified that threaten the vested interests of powerful individuals and groups? Will those vested interests seek to mute or degrade the educational effort and declare its benefits inferior or inadequate? Counts urged that the schools create a new social order;[28] clearly the schools did not. The ECC Project seeks something more modest, but no doubt its goals in both the schools and the community can be threatening to some. What kinds of changes can be successfully undertaken, and when do changes seem excessive or too revolutionary?

5. Will the efforts of the ECC Project be seen as promoting significant knowledge and skills that are utilized in the real world of mathematics, science, the arts, and other subjects, and will this real-world concept of learning meet the goals established for public education? The project participants sense that good things are happening for children and adults, and alternative learning experiences are being created to demonstrate the effectiveness of the project's work. But it is too early to determine if the project's efforts will be seen by a larger community as consequential, if children will be advantaged in middle and senior high school and, more important, when they are adults. Answers must be found to questions about the consequences of such work and what and how others will view these efforts.

As educational and community changes occur, new conditions will call for further change. Although on an uncharted course, the ECC

Project is dedicated to equipping all children and adults with the will, skills, and knowledge to bring about changes through a democratic process, as the needs for change emerge.

NOTES

1. Transcribed record of Tucson City Council meeting, Tucson, AZ, February 8, 1993 from a recording made by Tucson Cable, Channel 12.

2. Paul E. Heckman and Francine Peterman, "Indigenous Invention," Education and Community Change Project Paper (Tucson: University of Arizona, 1993).

3. Jack Frymier, "Bureaucracy and the Neutering of Teachers," *Phi Delta Kappan* 69, no. 1 (1987): 9-16; Paul E. Heckman, "School Restructuring in Practice: Reckoning With the Culture of the School," *International Journal of Educational Reform* 2, no. 3 (1993): 263-272; Gene Maeroff, "A Blueprint for Empowering Teachers," *Phi Delta Kappan* 69, no. 7 (1988): 473-477; Alan Odden and David Marsh, "How Comprehensive Reform Legislation Can Improve Secondary Schools," *Phi Delta Kappan* 69, no. 8 (1988): 593-598; Seymour B. Sarason, *The Predictable Failure of Educational Reform* (San Francisco: Jossey-Bass, 1990).

4. Arizona State Data Center, Population Statistics Unit, "Census of Population and Housing Summary," Tape file 3 (Phoenix, AZ: Department of Economic Security, 1992).

5. Howard Gardner, *The Unschooled Mind: How Children Think and How Schools Should Teach* (New York: Basic Books, 1991); Jean Lave, *Cognition in Practice: Mind, Mathematics, and the Culture of Everyday Life* (New York: Cambridge University Press, 1988).

6. Warren G. Bennis, *Why Leaders Can't Lead: The Unconscious Conspiracy Continues* (San Francisco: Jossey-Bass, 1990); Philip Slater and Warren G. Bennis, "Democracy Is Inevitable," *Harvard Business Review* 42, no. 2 (1964): 51-59; Robert A. Dahl, *Democracy and Its Critics* (New Haven, CT: Yale University Press, 1990); Philip Slater, *A Dream Deferred: America's Discontent and the Search for a New Democratic Ideal* (Boston: Beacon Press, 1991).

7. Michael W. Apple, "Do the Standards Go Far Enough? Power, Policy, and Practice in Mathematics Education," *Journal for Research in Mathematics Education* 23, no. 5 (1992): 412-431; Michael S. Smith and Jennifer O'Day, "Systemic School Reform," in *The Politics of Curriculum and Testing*, 1990 Yearbook of the Politics of Education Association, edited by Susan H. Fuhrman and Betty Malen (New York: Falmer Press, 1990), pp. 233-267.

8. Sarason, *The Predictable Failure of Educational Reform*.

9. James G. March, *Decisions and Organizations* (London: Basil Blackwell, 1988); Lee S. Sproul, "Beliefs in Organizations" in *Handbook of Organizational Design*, vol. 2, *Remodeling Organizations and Their Environments*, edited by Paul C. Nystrom and William H. Starbuck (New York: Oxford University Press, 1981).

10. David Cohen and Michael S. Garet, "Reforming Educational Policy with Applied Social Research," *Harvard Educational Review* 45, no. 1 (1975): 15-43.

11. Bennis, *Why Leaders Can't Lead*; Gerry D. Ewert, "Habermas and Education: A Comprehensive Overview of the Influence of Habermas in Educational Literature," *Review of Educational Research* 61, no. 3 (1991): 345-378; Slater, *A Dream Deferred*; Charles Lindbloom, *Inquiry and Change: The Troubled Attempt to Understand and Shape Society* (New Haven, CT: Yale University Press, 1990).

12. Paul Siljander, "Education as a Communicative Action: Aspects of Critical-Emancipatoric Pedagogy," *Scandinavian Journal of Educational Research* 33, no. 2 (1989): 111-121.

13. Jürgen Habermas, "Interpretive Social Science vs. Hermeneuticism" in *Social Science as Moral Inquiry*, edited by Norma Haan, Robert N. Bellah, Paul Rabinow, and William Sullivan (New York: Columbia University Press, 1983), pp. 251-269; Robert N. Bellah, Richard Madsen, William M. Sullivan, Ann Swidler, and Steven M. Tipton, *The Good Society* (New York: Alfred Knopf, 1991).

14. John Dewey, *The Public and Its Problems: An Essay in Political Inquiry* (Chicago: Gateway Books, 1946); Peter M. Gollwitzer, Heinz Heckhausen, and Heike Ratazczak, "From Weighing to Willing: Approaching a Change Decision through Pre- or Postdecisional Mentation," *Organizational Behavior and Human Decision Processes* 45 (1990): 41-65; Joseph R. Gusfield, *Drinking-Driving and the Symbolic Order* (Chicago and London: The University of Chicago Press, 1981); Lindbloom, *Inquiry and Change*; Robert B. Reich, "Policy Making in a Democracy" in *The Power of Public Ideas*, edited by Robert B. Reich (Cambridge, MA: Ballinger, 1988).

15. Paul E. Heckman, Christine B. Confer, and Delia C. Hakim, "Planting Seeds: Understanding through Investigation," *Educational Leadership* 51 (February, 1994): 36-39.

16. Lawrence E. Cremin, *The Genius of American Education* (New York: Vintage Books, 1966), p. viii.

17. Urie Bronfenbrenner, *The Ecology of Human Development: Experiments by Nature and Design* (Cambridge, MA: Harvard University Press, 1979); Dewey, *The Public and Its Problems*; Kurt Lewin, *Resolving Social Conflicts* (New York: Harper and Row, 1948).

18. John I. Goodlad, *What Schools Are For* (Bloomington, IN: Phi Delta Kappa Foundation, 1979).

19. Thomas J. LaBelle, "Formal, Nonformal, and Informal Education: A Holistic Perspective on Lifelong Learning," *International Review of Education* 28 (1982): 159-75; Sylvia Scribner and Michael Cole, "Cognitive Consequences of Formal and Informal Education," *Science* 182 (1990): 553-559.

20. Urie Bronfenbrenner, *The Ecology of Human Development*; Lawrence E. Cremin, "Family-Community Linkages in American Education: Some Comments on the Recent Historiography," *Teachers College Record* 79, no. 4 (1978): 683-704; John I. Goodlad, "Education, Schools, and a Sense of Community" in *Communities and Their Schools*, edited by Don Davies (New York: McGraw-Hill, 1981), pp. 331-53.

21. Council member Steve Leal, transcribed from Tucson Cable, Channel 12, recording of the Tucson City Council meeting, Tucson, AZ, Feb. 8, 1993.

22. Quote transcribed from Tucson Cable, Channel 12, recording of Tucson City Council meeting, Tucson, AZ, Feb. 8, 1993.

23. Luis C. Moll, *Vygotsky and Education: Instructional Implications and Applications of Sociohistorical Psychology* (New York: Cambridge University Press, 1991).

24. Larry Cuban, *How Teachers Taught: Constancy and Change in American Classrooms, 1890-1980* (New York: Longman, 1984).

25. John W. Meyer, David H. Kamens, and Aaron Benavot, *School Knowledge for the Masses* (Washington, D.C.: Falmer Press, 1992).

26. John W. Brown, Alan Collins, and Paul Duguid, "Situated Cognition and the Culture of Learning," *Educational Researcher* 18, no. 1 (1989): 32-42.

27. Lauren B. Resnick, "Treating Mathematics as an Ill-Structured Discipline" in *The Teaching and Assessing of Mathematical Problem Solving*, edited by Randall I. Charles and Edward A. Silver (Englewood Cliffs, NJ: Lawrence Erlbaum Associates, 1988), pp. 32-60.

28. George Counts, *Education and American Civilization* (New York: Bureau of Publications, Teachers College, 1952).

CHAPTER XII

Creating Coalition Schools through Collaborative Inquiry

PATRICIA A. WASLEY, SHERRY P. KING
AND CHRISTINE LOUTH

At the Coalition for Essential Schools we have been working to build the kinds of schools where all students can learn to use their minds well. To this end, the small staff of the Coalition at Brown University and the much larger faculty of partners who work in schools across the country have combined efforts to support school change through a series of collaborative, interactive projects. Through these projects we work steadily to build a more effective dialogue about school change and to increase our understanding about how progress is made and maintained.

Not unexpectedly, the work of combining effort and expertise has not yet generated a foolproof formula for highly engaging schools. And yet, while the going seems terrifically slow, we have learned a great deal: (1) school change is exceedingly difficult and takes far more time than anyone imagined; (2) few traditional high schools have been able to move from a small group of supporters to whole-school change; and (3) faculty in reforming schools spend more time planning change strategies than assessing existing practices to uncover basic beliefs, attitudes, and assumptions that drive their work. Their reticence to engage in serious analysis seems to emerge from norms which suggest that planning for tomorrow is much more powerful than examining historically what happened today and yesterday. Because that analysis does not take place, the changes made in many cases merely tinker rather than build significant possibilities for students.[1]

Patricia A. Wasley is Senior Researcher at the Coalition of Essential Schools at Brown University. Sherry P. King, formerly the principal of the school where the work described in this chapter was carried on, is currently Superintendent of Schools for the Croton-Harmon Schools in Croton-on-Hudson, New York. Christine Louth, a teacher in the Croton-Harmon Schools, is a Fellow and a member of the National Faculty of the Coalition of Essential Schools.

As we have better understood these findings we have learned that to achieve our most important ends, those in schools and in universities must extend all effort and all resources to the task of breaking through the barriers to school change. This means that the traditional roles of each must change, that the interplay must be reconceived.

We describe here a project underway at the Coalition which attempts to do that. We are nearing the end of a three-year study of school change which translates collaborative inquiry into a research process to build a school's capacity for change while simultaneously contributing to our understanding of the nature of change and how it is encouraged and supported.[2] What follows is a brief description of collaborative inquiry and a brief history of such inquiry at the Coalition. Then we describe our current research project and we include statements from the perspectives of a principal, a teacher, and a researcher who together are engaged in the process of creating better schools. Our intention is to suggest that the actual process of research can and should be redesigned to contribute to the goals of reform; our experience helps to make clear both the advantages and the difficulties of doing so.

Setting the Stage: The Researcher's Perspective

Collaborative inquiry takes its roots from many sources. For years Seymour Sarason has been writing about the need for change in schools.[3] He has long advocated that the system as we know it is too bureaucratized, too isolating—each role group unto its own world— and that this contributes greatly to the intractability of the regularities in schools. Things like schedules, bells, end-of-year exams are regular features in schools, but they do not necessarily contribute to powerful learning for students. Over and over again Sarason has advocated a system which allows each member greater access to those whose roles are different. He makes a central point that change cannot be done by insiders alone, or by outsiders alone, but that people from different places in the system must work together. And he suggests that what we want for students we must also want for the adults. He notes that despite these quite simple and clear understandings, the formula for shared understandings about different roles and for collaborative problem solving remains elusive.

Years ago Ann Lieberman, now co-director of the National Center for Restructuring Education, Schools, and Teaching at Teachers College, Columbia University, worked on a project in the League of

Cooperating Schools at the University of California (Los Angeles). Her task was to give feedback to a group of principals about the research she and colleagues were conducting. Stomach churning, she agonized trying to figure out how to give tough feedback while maintaining their trust and interest in working together. Much to her surprise, they were receptive. Since then she has been encouraging closer collaboration between universities and schools as a means of generating more accurate and more powerful understandings about teaching, learning, and schools.[4] She has long advocated closer collaboration between researchers and practitioners to promote greater depth and accuracy for all. In spite of this early work, many questions remain about the delivery of feedback and its utility.[5]

John Goodlad and his colleagues at the Center for School Renewal at the University of Washington have worked for years to build stronger school/university partnerships to strengthen both institutions. To create an ecology for the continuous renewal of both, Goodlad suggests that projects of mutual interest must be generated and responsibility shared.[6] Again, traditional roles—university professors as teachers and school practitioners as students—make the development of this collaborative culture challenging.

Another contributing argument for collaborative inquiry emerges from recent discussions about critical inquiry, its nature and processes.[7] At its best, critical inquiry describes a process to foster social change through the involvement of those most in need of new structures and practices. More recently, school reformers have described critical inquiry as central to serious reform in schools. The characteristics of a praxis for critical inquiry have been outlined by Sirotnik (1991) and by Sirotnik and Oakes (1986).[8] Groups must be challenged to think together about their own underlying interests and ideologies in hopes of creating better worlds and more effective systems. The current dilemma lies in negotiating a kind of balance between top-down and bottom-up change in schools, so that those who work in schools have a very real opportunity to influence the changes they believe should be made.

All of these scholars suggest that to build better schools we need to collaborate across roles and organizations. They also suggest that collaborative work requires dialectics, argumentation and mutual investigation, dialogues, clear communication between the collaborating partners, and shared purposes. Collaborative inquiry is, then, the process of engaging in inquiry on a topic of mutual interest, negotiating the conditions of the partnership, and, once underway, communicating about the subject of inquiry. In theory, it makes sense; in practice, like new roses, it sometimes results in more thorns than flowers.

COMMON PRINCIPLES OF THE COALITION OF ESSENTIAL SCHOOLS

Since its inception in 1984 by Theodore Sizer and a small number of practitioner colleagues, the Coalition has been a loosely structured partnership based on the premises of collaborative inquiry. All parties involved agree to translate the Nine Common Principles (9CPs) into action in schools. (See pages 221-222 at the end of this chapter for a full statement of the Nine Common Principles.) These principles are a set of commonsense ideas, many of which have been well debated for centuries by educational theorists. In this case, however, they emerged from A Study of High Schools.[9] Put in place, the 9CPs should produce schools from which all students graduate more confident about their own ability to learn and to contribute to our society.

A school that is working with the principles necessarily finds itself grappling with a variety of issues—tracking, for example. Can all students learn to use their minds well in a school where the tracks suggest that teachers hold predetermined beliefs about individual student capacity, have different goals for the students, and use different strategies for the talented and the confused? Teachers find themselves grappling with the question of which instructional strategies, curriculum, and assessments best foster important intellectual activity. Does performance on an objective test demonstrate that a student can apply the concepts of economic theory? Does notetaking during a lecture make it possible for students to interact with the material in a way that enables them to connect what they are learning to what they already know? Are they able to dispel long-held misconceptions? Do science laboratories and classes in home economics, agriculture, and shop, long the centers of hands-on work in schools, require that students do more with their minds than follow a series of simple directions? The school community finds itself engaged in a discussion about how teachers know when their children use their minds well. Does the number of classes taken and passed with As, Bs, Cs, or Ds constitute a satisfactory demonstration? How might complaining employers be convinced of a student's ability to read and to comprehend, to work in a group, to generate solutions to complicated problems? A high school mathematics department, whose members are trained to be subject area specialists, challenges many of its assumptions about learning as it strives to determine whether it is more important for their students to cover all the activities contained in algebra 1 or geometry than to be able to apply a few essential mathematical thinking skills in a variety of circumstances.

In the beginning, partnership in the Coalition suggested that member schools embraced the 9CPs and interpreted them individually according to the values, beliefs, and customs of their local contexts. A common refrain has been that just as no two good students are alike, so are no two good schools alike. By suggesting that schools interpret the principles in their own contexts, the Coalition holds that the intellectual and analytic work of determining what to change and how to change is the central responsibility of those in the school. Involvement of teachers, administrators, parents, and students in constructing the course of reform and in doing the analytical and imaginative work of reshaping their local schools has been a constant recommendation in the reform literature as well as a central tenet in critical inquiry.[10]

Over the years, the dialogue has continued between the schools and the central staff of the Coalition. As a result of school requests, new partnerships entitled "Re:Learning" were formed in 1987— between the Coalition and the Education Commission of the States, between the Coalition and states, and between the Coalition and schools in each of these states—to build systems better able to support changing schools.[11] In order to help schools gain better dialogic and analytic support, the Coalition conducts year-long seminars in the management of change. It trains teachers and principals in the facilitation of change and develops processes to help schools move from desired student outcomes to daily practices and programs to achieve those outcomes. Requests from schools turn into books like Sizer's *Horace's School* where the lessons learned and the obstacles that remain are discussed.

While these manifestations of the Coalition's commitment to collaborative inquiry continued to grow I began to think about its potential application in research. In order to ensure greater accuracy in our reports we have been negotiating with individuals in the schools about the meaning of what we have written. But we have needed more rigorous dialogue between whole schools and researchers, both to help the schools achieve their ends and to ensure the accuracy of the research. We designed a study which we believed would do just that by returning a series of "snapshots" to the school during the course of data gathering.

When we designed the study, we knew of no one who had attempted this kind of research. It is not action research, but it is interactive, designed to affect the behavior of those studied. It consciously attempts to use research as a tool to build reflective practice, the value of which Schön and his colleagues have convinced us.[12] We cast aside pretenses of distance (the classic uninvolved objective stance of the researcher) since we wanted to affect the context as we went along. We wanted to look in schools and at the surrounding system at the same time. We wanted another set of "outsiders" to watch the process to help us understand the benefits and the tensions. For those of us at the Coalition this uncommon type of research was worth doing because, as a partnership organization, we are bound by mutual obligation to find new and ever more powerful ways to work together while honing our mutual understandings of the benefits of and barriers to change.

The project, currently midway through the third of three years, translates collaborative inquiry into a research process. A description of the basic design follows, after which we briefly describe our first critical incident from the perspectives of three of the stakeholders at one of the sites in our collaborative inquiry project. David Tripp describes how the examination of single incidents reveals the benefits, tensions, and dilemmas inherent in a larger whole.[13] We agree. Multiple perspectives gathered around one critical incident help us to illustrate the difficult terrain of collaborative inquiry cum research.

THE SCHOOL CHANGE STUDY

The School Change Study was designed to answer two broad questions we felt previous research left uncovered: (1) What is the experience of high school students like in schools that are undergoing change? (2) What is the interplay between a changing school and its surrounding context? To find answers to these questions, we are working in five schools in four states, following some 200 students through three of their high school years. The schools were selected because each belonged to the Coalition for several years and demonstrated serious commitment to continue working on the implementation of the 9CPs. They also represent a cross section of the most common American high schools—urban, suburban, small town. Ten researchers are divided into five teams of three members, with several team members working at two sites. We spend two weeks a year in each of three schools and six to eight days in the other two schools. We shadow students through their classes, interview them and a small sample of parents, teachers, school board members, and administrators. Another team of researchers tracks the policy arena, interviewing in state departments, governor's offices, and district offices so that we can place the schools' efforts to change within their proper context. Students and teachers at each site are writing weekly journals, and a colleague and students at Brown University have read local newspapers to better understand what kind of information community members get about their local schools.

While the broader questions mentioned above guide the study, the substance of our mutual inquiry is more specific. We are investigating three themes in particular. We are interested in understanding how the 9CPs are interpreted in each school, how each of the schools maintains the momentum for change over an extended period of time, and whether or not the work in these schools suggests change throughout the school.

The process of collaborative inquiry becomes apparent when, after each site visit, we return a written snapshot to the school which describes what the researchers saw and heard. This is our way of communicating with the school, and it is the tool we use to foster dialogue and to encourage analysis of existing practices and conditions in the school. We chose the term *snapshot* deliberately to acknowledge that we are capturing the school at work at a particular point in time.[14] Over the duration of the study each school will get six of these snapshots which can be arranged into a kind of photo album. We wanted to provide schools with information about themselves which they do not ordinarily get—a mirror or an action photo at which they glance to see whether they are really doing what they say they want to do. Because schools generally lack the norms of reflective practice, and the time for it, we hoped that the snapshots might provide a reflective tool to get them started, and one with which they could build their analytic skill over the three-year period.

Each snapshot includes information from various perspectives: students, parents, school faculty, and in the spring, from the surrounding context. Each captures some component of classroom work, and each gives a brief analysis of the dominant emerging themes from our perspective. While all names are changed and students are generally composite fictionalized characters, anonymity is not possible for the adults inside the school. There is, after all, only one principal and, say, one English teacher who teaches American literature. However, all those featured in the snapshot are given an advance draft to critique and proofread. (At the outset of the study, faculty agreed to participate on condition that inside their own school community no one outside the faculty and administration would read the sections about classroom practice and about faculty discussions. Parents and students agreed to this condition as well.) Early respondents either write comments or call us with revisions. Meanings are negotiated between the research team leader and individuals participating in the study when necessary.

At the outset, the schools and researchers forged an agreement about the negotiation of meaning. We wanted to ensure that what we wrote was what we really saw. At the same time, school faculty needed the ability to point out oversimplifications, erroneous assumptions, and material which they felt was insulting. We agreed to chew on troublesome material until we developed mutually acceptable work. When we could not reach agreement we agreed to include minority opinions. Just in case we might find ourselves truly stalemated, we established a mutually acceptable committee to function as arbitrators. While the study is in progress, study participants and researchers have agreed to negotiate differences in the meaning of any written material. At the conclusion of the study, however, the researchers will use the entire data corpus in an attempt to answer our broader questions and to pursue themes. All parties agreed in advance that what we write at the conclusion of the study will represent the perspective of the researchers.

From the outset we hoped that the school would use the information contained in the snapshot to further their own work; they agreed to participate based on their own beliefs that it should prove useful. We also made it clear that after the school approved the final draft, the snapshots would be used as analytic tools in many of the Coalition's professional development activities involving other member schools and states. (The snapshots are available through the Coalition of Essential Schools at Brown University).

Furthermore, we wanted to balance the normal distribution of power in a research study so that both those researched and the researchers were equal partners in this venture. To understand better the effects of the snapshots on the schools and on the study itself, and to provide a feedback loop to the research team, Ann Lieberman Arthur Powell, and Seymour Sarason agreed to function as an advisory committee to study the project. Once a year, between the first and second snapshot, advisory team members each make a two-day visit to one of the schools, each visiting a different school each year. They interview staff and students about their reactions to the snapshot and the research process. In an open session with the faculty they then summarize the staff's response to the snapshots. When the information they have obtained has been verified the committee members then convey that same information back to the researchers. In essence, they function as critical friends to the researchers just as the researchers are functioning as critical friends to the schools. This attempt to equalize power across the study participants was designed to ensure that a real dialogue could take place.

When we set out to do this we all understood that it would be tough going along the way. We did ask everyone to agree that no one would quit no matter how bad it got. Agreements made, puffed with the confidence of novices, we prepared for the first site visit and snapshot.

Reactions to the First Snapshot

The principal's reaction. Preparation for the School Change Study really began in July 1981. As Pat explained the study, as I began to understand how different it was, and as we explored the relationships embedded in such research, I was filled with misgivings. The study itself seemed highly complex and almost too scientific for a qualitative piece. I knew that Pat and Ann Lieberman had historically supported teacher empowerment.[15] I was particularly anxious about whether researchers with this bias could possibly understand or favorably convey the role of a principal who exerted strong leadership in a changing school. Nonetheless, I left the meeting having decided that our school could only gain if the faculty agreed to participate, which they did. My concerns about the portrayal of the principal were no different than the concerns the faculty would have about the representation of their roles as teachers.

The week of the site visit was an intensely emotional roller coaster: elaborate color-coded schedules of activities, lap-top computers, and tape recorders everywhere. By midweek I began to see nothing but the blemishes in the school and believed that the visiting researchers would find us imposters.

The time after the first site visit was one of enormous letdown. I do believe that the intense scrutiny and self-reflection that the week's visit engendered subconsciously took a toll. Nonetheless, we asked that the research team "give it to us straight!" After a preparatory activity in which we asked the staff to read a problematic case Pat had written for another school, the snapshot arrived.

My anxious anticipation seemed misguided when I actually read the first draft of the snapshot. It was twenty-eight pages long and was crafted into a kind of story in which a number of role-group conversations and classroom observations were reported. It contained a somewhat idealized picture of our village; a section of conversation between freshmen, sophomores, and juniors; a sound byte of faculty-room talk; a conversation among thirty-six parents; an interview with the principal and other administrators; descriptions from twenty-two class visits; and an analysis of how the nine common principles are being implemented.

Even the less flattering descriptions appeared to be accurate. I believed that the writing would provide the source of incredible professional development. Unfortunately, the faculty reacted quite differently. A few very vocal members of the staff voiced all kinds of objections. They found the snapshot judgmental, unfair, and in some cases inaccurate. Quotations like "In science, our teacher gives us assignments, . . . every couple of weeks we do a report, . . . he doesn't teach us anything" left people reeling. Quickly, we developed a process which enabled us to clarify our concerns and convey those to the researchers.

A teacher's reaction. Enthusiastic anticipation gave way to a gnawing anxiety when I first heard about the chance to participate in the School Change Study. My enthusiasm stemmed from a sense that this study had the possibility to model for our faculty the same sort of practice/feedback/revision process that drives my own theories and practices of teaching and learning. In my own classroom, I try to structure learning so that students get feedback on their "practice" (a writing, for instance) in a way that gives them the opportunity to act on that feedback by revising a writing in progress, or maybe by changing the way they approach the next writing. At the same time, I ask students for feedback as well, about how the class is and is not supporting their learning. Together we continue to construct how we learn together. I saw in the methods in the School Change Study a structure which had the potential to give us information about student learning in our school that might move us beyond tinkering with change to deep revision of our learning community—in other words, real systemic reform.

However, to be frank, my anxiety ran a little deeper than my anticipation. I also knew well the discomfort that inevitably comes from feedback. I knew we would hear things both individually and collectively that would not sit well. We could not avoid some disagreement, some conflict. I was anxious about whether, collectively, we would respond simply by shoring up our individual defenses or whether we really would forge a new and mutually sustaining working relationship.

When I first read the snapshot, I saw it as primarily accurate but not particularly explosive. Students do make negative comments about their school experiences and I knew—from countless discussions in faculty rooms—that too often teachers brush off what students tell us. While there were comments in the snapshot which were hard to digest, I felt it would be helpful. Others reacted quite differently, feeling quite attacked.

Just at this point, Art Powell came for his initial visit and helped us to recognize that what seemed like consensus was not; there were multiple reactions to the snapshot. He also pointed out a major problem: no one felt we received adequate recognition for the changes made to date. He helped us to inch toward the more distanced perspective required to actually participate in this study in the spirit in which it was designed. In the following weeks, we read the second draft of the snapshot and realized that our feedback was, in fact, being taken seriously. When we met with Pat to negotiate the content for the second snapshot, it seemed to me that we were beginning to take the first visible steps toward not merely accepting as accurate a reflection of life and learning in our school, but also toward using that mirror image to actually construct a better school.

A researcher's reaction. I worried the whole time I wrote the first snapshot. While I felt that we had been as clear as we could be about the fact that the faculty were going to get a snapshot that would show problems as well as gains, I knew that some of the information contained would be tough for the staff to take. While we saw pockets of excellent teaching, we saw much of what we had read about in Sizer's *Horace's Compromise* and in Goodlad's *A Place Called School*: passive and disengaged students, fragmented curriculum geared toward coverage as opposed to understanding, and teachers who talked and talked and talked.

While we wanted to acknowledge the teachers' accumulated expertise, we also wanted to provide a glimpse of what a broader repertoire of instructional, curricular, and assessment techniques might do for their students. We believed that part of our responsibility in this collaborative inquiry was to ask tough questions and to pose alternatives, knowing full well that alternative images of teaching are difficult for teachers and principals to generate in the face of careers of constancy.

In an advanced reading, the principal thought that while the snapshot contained tough information, it was accurate and the faculty would recognize that. Several days later, she called back to say that the faculty reaction had turned into a virtual maelstrom of negativity. After a very short and terse conversation, I was left to wait for feedback from the staff and from Art.

The students agreed with their section of the report more because their comments were actually there, I think, than because of their careful analysis of the accuracy of the report. Several parents felt that they had had a much richer conversation and that collapsing an evening into a couple of pages did not do them justice; others thought it was a good encapsulation. Every faculty member responded, and in addition to the comments on cards that they wrote, I got letters from eight teachers. Their reactions ranged from finding the snapshot an inaccurate, poorly written mess to finding it a fair assessment and an indicator of work they must address.

When comparing their comments with the actual snapshot I began to see that some of the comments were legitimate. I revised the snapshot. I understood that the staff needed to understand the analytic processes I used which led me to a particular organizational format for the snapshot, and perhaps most important, we realized that we had made a critical error in the translation of collaborative inquiry. While we had negotiated the project carefully, we forgot to involve the faculty in generating the actual research protocols; they had less interest in our questions than in questions they might have asked. Finally, in the snapshot I had not adequately acknowledged the very difficult progress they had made so far—the changed schedule, a new governance structure which involved students, faculty-based decision making, interdisciplinary work. Each of these had been hard-won changes and deserved significant attention.

In the long run, I felt that I was able to send off a second draft which did not sacrifice what the researchers believed to be an accurate picture of the school. The staff responded favorably and we negotiated the next round of work together. Interestingly enough, they asked us to investigate a point which had emerged in the first snapshot. They also questioned whether we would be able to give them an accurate picture in the future, given the force of their reaction. We believed that we would.

After the First Snapshot

Since then, we have done three more snapshots, and are preparing the fifth. With each new snapshot we have learned how to make the process serve the schools better, but it has been slow going. The faculty generated their agenda for the year's faculty meetings from issues in the snapshots, but have spent little time discussing them collectively or with much specificity. Attempting a new tack, we mailed the fourth snapshot out just before school started in the fall, and the staff used it during their fall activities to clarify their direction for the year. The staff continue to ask us to pursue issues introduced to them in previous snapshots.

We have been able to chart steady, quiet progress. They have begun to shift their confidence in standardized tests and are experimenting with various alternative assessments. They redesigned the schedule again for longer blocks of time. They have managed to maintain their work in the midst of several key turnovers: the principal became the superintendent, the vice principal retired, and a new principal and vice principal came on board. The mathematics department has moved from creating another track as a means to help students having trouble in mathematics to removing the coverage exam at the end of the first year of mathematics so that they are able to reduce the curriculum. More teachers are teaming and the staff determined to spend the next year assessing the quality of the work they are doing by examining student work.

At each of the other schools in the School Change Study the issues, the relationships, the context, and their approach to Coalition work are different. Not surprisingly, their reactions to their own snapshots have been different. One high school, heavily researched, experienced more difficulty switching from research done for researchers to research which they might use. Another high school used the snapshot initially to foster what they already did quite well without our help— pointing fingers at each other: the faculty blame the principal, the administrators blame the teachers and the central office. Over time in these schools, we have seen shifts in their use of the snapshots and in their programs for students.

During the summer of 1993, the researchers gathered to look across the snapshots. Some of the tentative cross-case themes are:

1. The building of shared values is much more complicated than we expected and much more central to a significant change effort. The culture of autonomy is much stronger than the culture of collaboration and the incentives are not necessarily in place which would move people to change.

2. People are caught in the web of their individual conceptions of teaching and learning. Teachers' beliefs about teaching and learning are similar, however, and remain perhaps the strongest cross-cultural, cross-site characteristic. These beliefs undergird every decision they make as well as their own professional actions. For instance, tracking is based on people's beliefs about how learning takes place, and it is difficult to undo tracking until these beliefs are revised.

3. Curriculum, pedagogy, and assessment are interrelated and must be considered as a single piece rather than separately. This is contrary to most conventional practices in schools which suggest a more linear approach.

4. Pedagogy is the least considered topic in changing schools. Much more consideration is given to assessment, to curriculum, to schedules, to decision making than to actual teaching practices. Teachers are unaccustomed to discussion about instructional strategies, and do not acknowledge the need for an ever-expanding repertoire.

5. Unpredictable change is perhaps more certain than planned change and often confounds faculty attempts to move forward. Teachers and principals move; students enter and leave the school. The state changes its requirements; the district changes its focus. In the midst of so much unpredictable movement, planned change frequently sounds more like cacophony than a symphony.

6. Holding a focus over time in schools is a very unfamiliar activity. For those raised on an ever-increasing menu of possible tactics for reform and on the notion that implementation means accomplishment, sticking with a particular approach over time seems counterintuitive to real productive change and not supportive of the conventional political exigencies of leadership. Superintendents, state department personnel, and administrators make their reputations on the new approaches they introduce.

In addition to learning about school change, we are learning about the conduct of this kind of research and the likelihood that it too can contribute to reshaping schools into places where all students learn to use their minds well.

Benefits and Problems of Collaborative Inquiry

While we recognize that we are not yet finished, we here share several emerging themes that are helping us to understand the benefits and the problems of research as collaborative inquiry.

COLLABORATIVE INQUIRY TO FOSTER WHOLE-SCHOOL CHANGE:
INSIGHTS FROM A TEACHER

I said earlier that the School Change Study had the potential to move our school beyond tinkering with change to real systemic reform. I believed that because built into the study were the continuous collaboration and reflection that are so foreign to life in most schools, and so much a part of what I see as the key to authentic teaching and learning. Based on my previous experience with a writing process seminar prior to the beginning of the School Change Study, I had viewed such a collaborative change process as the domain of small teams of teachers and their students. The School Change Study has the potential to bring similar feedback, reflection, and revision to the entire institution.

Looking back now to when we received the first snapshot, I see it as a critical turning point for the whole faculty toward *real collaborative inquiry*. I emphasize *real* because I suspect that we—like most school communities—were not equipped originally to collaborate with Pat. We had no community framework for dealing with feedback, much less any sort of institutionalized practice to act on it. In fact, it is possible that the most important element in that first process was that our feedback to Art and subsequently to Pat was seriously attended to; they modeled for us the sort of thoughtful "revision" that we ourselves might consider after reading a snapshot.

What had happened since that time shows clear signs of an emerging learning community. As a result of information in the second snapshot—information about staff interpretations of the 9 Common Principles that we specifically asked the researchers to focus on—we used faculty meetings and in-service time revisiting the 9CPs. More significantly, in my mind, during one of those faculty meetings we asked whether or not current institutional practice in the school prompted students to use their minds well. The resulting faculty survey indicated few institutional practices that did. As a result, we now have a schedule that fosters more "in-depth" learning, and we have agreed that we need to decide together what specific learning outcomes must serve to focus all our work, regardless of discipline. Since this chapter was originally drafted, two teams of English and social studies teachers have finally gained mutual planning time and have begun to integrate and team teach. This move was fostered by continuous reference in the snapshots to the need for mutual planning time, and a discussion about the distinction between interdisciplinary and integrated work. In addition, the snapshots have continuously pointed out the isolation of the staff. It would seem that while small pockets of reflection and collaboration were present in the school when the study began, the study made such activities more visible, encouraged more faculty to become involved, and required that more people analyze the steps taken thus far.

Clearly, we are just beginning to think and act as a group that has shared values and common purposes, and so we have a great distance to go. However, at the moment hope is bright: resistant strains against collaborative inquiry are weakening. Individual teachers have begun to ask the researchers for more feedback on their classrooms. We are looking into the snapshots to retrieve useful information about ourselves as we try to envision a school where both time and collaborative practice result in an institution where all students can be smart.

Still, as we near the end of the study, new difficulties become manifest. The researchers noted during their most recent site visit that the divisions between the staff are clearer than they ever have been. As we move closer to whole community change, those who have been quiet in hopes that they would be left undisturbed are now becoming more vocal. Breaking down isolation to create professional communities which place a student's long-term learning first in their consideration will ultimately require much more than reflection on information received. Thus a central question about the value of this kind of research remains: Can research which takes collaborative inquiry to heart be a key in a transformative model—where both students and teachers come to see learning as a continually constructive act? If research like this fosters the faculty's realization that ongoing feedback and reflection are elements that must be continually sustained so that they maintain it after the study is over, the answer will be clearly affirmative.

CREATING CRITICAL FRIENDSHIPS: INSIGHTS FROM A PRINCIPAL

Hindsight has provided me with several important insights. My chief regret about the first year of the study is that we were so naive. We had ample reason to know that critical reflection is easier said than done. The School Change Study was intimidating since it opened classroom practice not just to invited individuals but to the whole faculty. We should have known that the portraits of individual practice contained in the snapshot would be explosive and that our inclination would be to protect one another.

Then I learned that we must remember that whole-school change is daunting. Teachers who do not necessarily share a common philosophy cannot hide behind the privacy of their classrooms when the snapshot comes out. Students who come to the neighborhood school do not necessarily want to be held to higher standards; they may prefer the less taxing requirements their older siblings enjoyed. Parents whose children excelled under a more traditional system want assurances. While the School Change Study did not create these issues, it continues to illuminate them.

Finally, I am reminded by this incident that one can never tell when or why people are able to look carefully at their own practice. Today more teachers in our school talk about pedagogy than was the case a year ago. We also accept more responsibility for our part of the research process, asking for information from the researchers which we need to enhance our practice. Some of our staff insisted that we keep the tough descriptions—even of a student falling asleep in class— and their insistence helped generate self-reflection. Others listened to the voices of students in the snapshots. Some individuals have benefited not so much from the snapshots themselves but from the activities the faculty generates as a result of the written pieces. Still others have not gained from the study itself, but from other experiences like going to conferences and talking to faculty from other Coalition schools. For a few the need to consider and then act on the need for change has not come. I am increasingly aware that any single strategy, whether it is participation in a critical inquiry study, or the act of joining an organization, or peer observation is not enough to move an entire community. We need multiple strategies.

I do believe, however, that the study has pushed us harder as a group and that it has contributed significantly to our capacity for change. The mathematics department three years ago thought that a strategy for improving support for students was to add another tracked class. Directly as a result of the continuous discussion in the snapshots about the difficulty students have with mathematics, the whole department is now willing to move away from coverage of the curriculum, to build a course around essential concepts and skills, and to build their own end-of-year performance assessment. I have now become the superintendent. From that vantage point I view the questions raised by the study as the essence of educational reform. We knew three years ago that instruction, faculty collaboration, and decision making were issues and that students' voices should be listened to, but today the staff are actually willing to tackle these issues. The fact that the researchers continue to force us to press hard and that we continue to ask for such honest feedback gives me cautious optimism.

I have come to understand that the researchers and our faculty are building critical friendships—critical in that the researchers give tough feedback and critical also in that they are essential to helping us see ourselves.

The issue that keeps me awake these nights is how we will sustain the mirrors of our practice when the study is over. Can we translate focus groups into study groups? Will we be able to become critical friends in our own family? Despite the many gains, classroom practice is still uneven. Will we have the ability to ask the necessary hard questions of each other when there are no researchers to record our conversations and track our practice?

MATCHING AIMS TO OUTCOMES: INSIGHTS FROM A RESEARCHER

One of the central aims of the study was to assist schools in the process of building practices which help all students to be smart. We believed that the research process would involve teachers in using their minds well by asking them to think about conventional practices as well as innovative strategies. We hoped that the process itself would mirror for them the kind of interesting and engaging intellectual activity which we hoped to see in their classrooms. We take quite literally Sarason's point that teachers' professional lives must change in order to foster more engaging academic lives for their students.

Now, in the final year of the study, we have asked ourselves what evidence we see that this research strategy has the ability to contribute to the strengthening of school reform. I can cite three examples which affect a number of teachers and their students. These suggest to me that the strategy has been compelling. Each example, however, also points out the insufficiency of this strategy alone.

1. The whole school is more engaged in the discussion about how to help students. When we arrived, some were engaged but many were silent. While more are now engaged, there is more conflict, as the various beliefs and attitudes between the various stakeholders in the group are revealed.

2. Individual groups, some interdepartmental, others cross-departmental, are more inquiring of their own work in ways that have direct results for students. The mathematics department is a good example, as Sherry indicated. Still, while they are rethinking basic practices, their classroom instruction remains much the same.

3. More teachers are voluntarily reducing the isolation in which they work. Two teachers of French, teaming for the first time, describe the substance of their debate. One believes that they should cover a great deal, read three stories in a given unit, have four different activities in a given class period. The other teacher favors a slower pace, deeper immersion, more comparison of the stories they are reading in French to stories they have read in English. The two of them suggest they are in constant negotiation, and believe that as a result they have achieved a stronger middle ground. On other teams, however, the negotiations are wearing, and in one case, one teacher simply gives in to the will of the other.

As a strategy designed to strengthen the intellectual life of the adults, the study has promise. Its flaws lie in the brevity of its duration, and in the complexity of building ongoing relationships like this over time.

Concluding Thoughts

Several questions remain to be thoroughly investigated at the end of the study. All of us wonder whether the study will have any carry-over effects in the schools. Currently, the staff are engaged in building a process which would allow them to work as a whole faculty, reviewing videos of classes, looking at student work together. Will such activities build the kind of analytic capacity schools need?

The second question is a broader one. The study assumes that the analytic process which researchers find productive would be equally valuable to those in schools who have very different daily responsibilities. Is it? This assumption in itself may be either naive, arrogant, or both.

Regardless of the answers to these questions, both researchers and practitioners have learned a great deal about engaging in difficult but mutually sustaining collaborative work. Clearly, changes are necessary for both; meaningful partnerships demand that this is so. We do agree at this point that it is valuable to blend the purposes of research and of securing change in schools and that all the resources we can muster must be brought to bear if we are to create whole systems where all students can be smart.

The Nine Common Principles
of the Coalition of Essential Schools

1. The school should focus on helping adolescents learn to use their minds well. Schools should not attempt to be "comprehensive" if such a claim is made at the expense of the school's central intellectual purpose.

2. The school's goals should be simple: that each student master a limited number of essential skills and areas of knowledge. While these skills and areas will, to varying degrees, reflect the traditional academic disciplines, the program's design should be shaped by the intellectual and imaginative powers and competencies that students need, rather than necessarily by "subjects" as conventionally defined. The aphorism "Less Is More" should dominate: curricular decisions should be guided by the aim of thorough student mastery and achievement rather than by an effort merely to cover content.

3. The school's goals should apply to all students, while the means to these goals will vary as those students themselves vary. School practice should be tailormade to meet the needs of every group or class of adolescents.

4. Teaching and learning should be personalized to the maximum feasible extent. Efforts should be directed toward a goal that no teacher should have direct responsibility for more than eighty students. To capitalize on this personalization, decisions about the details of the course of study, the use of students' and teachers' time, and the choice of teaching materials and specific pedagogies must be unreservedly placed in the hands of the principal and staff.

5. The governing practical metaphor of the school should be student-as-worker rather than the more familiar metaphor of teacher-as-deliverer-of-instructional services. Accordingly, a prominent pedagogy will be coaching, to provoke students to learn how to learn and thus to teach themselves.

6. Students entering secondary school studies are those who can show competence in language and elementary mathematics. Students of traditional high school age but not yet at appropriate levels of competence to enter secondary school studies will be provided intensive remedial work to assist them quickly to meet these standards. The diploma should be awarded upon a successful final demonstration of mastery for graduation—an "Exhibition." This Exhibition by the student of his or her grasp of the central skills and knowledge of the school's program may be jointly administered by the faculty and by

higher authorities. As the diploma is awarded when earned, the school's program proceeds with no strict age grading and with no system of "credits earned" by "time spent" in class. The emphasis is on the students' demonstration that they can do important things.

7. The tone of the school should explicitly and self-consciously stress values of unanxious expectation ("I won't threaten you but I expect much of you"), of trust (until abused), and of decency (the values of fairness, generosity, and tolerance). Incentives appropriate to the school's particular students and teachers should be emphasized, and parents should be treated as essential collaborators.

8. The principal and teachers should perceive themselves as generalists first (teachers and scholars in general education) and specialists second (experts in but one particular discipline). Staff should expect multiple obligations (teacher-counselor-manager) and a sense of commitment to the entire school.

9. Ultimate administrative and budget targets should include, in addition to total student loads per teacher of eighty or fewer pupils, substantial time for collective planning by teachers, competitive salaries for staff, and an ultimate per pupil cost not to exceed that at traditional schools by more than 10 percent. To accomplish this, administrative plans may have to show the phased reduction or elimination of some services now provided students in many traditional comprehensive secondary schools.

NOTES

1. Stephen M. Corey, *Helping Other People Change* (Columbus, Ohio: Ohio State University Press, 1963); Seymour Sarason, *The Culture of the School and the Problem of Change* (Boston: Allyn and Bacon, 1971); idem, *The Predictable Failure of Educational Reform: Can We Change Course before It's Too Late?* (San Francisco: Jossey-Bass, 1991); Larry Cuban, *How Teachers Taught: Constancy and Change in American Classrooms, 1890-1980* (New York: Longman, 1984, 1993); idem, "Reforming Again, Again, and Again," *Educational Researcher* 19, no. 2 (1990): 3-13; David Cohen, "Teaching Practice: Plus Que ça Change . . .," in *Contributing to Educational Change: Perspectives on Research and Practice*, edited by Philip W. Jackson, pp. 27-84 (Berkeley, CA: McCutchan Publishing Corp., 1988); Michael Fullan, with Suzanne Stiegelbauer, *The New Meaning of Educational Change* (New York: Teachers College Press, 1991); Theodore Sizer, *Horace's School: Redesigning the American High School* (Boston: Houghton Mifflin, 1992); Donna Muncey and Patrick McQuillan, "Preliminary Findings from a Five-Year Study of the Coalition of Essential Schools," *Phi Delta Kappan* 74, no. 6 (1993): 486-489; idem, "The Dangers of Assuming Consensus for Change: Some Examples from the Coalition of Essential Schools," in *Empowering Teachers and Parents: School Restructuring through the Eyes of Anthropologists*, edited by Alfred Hess, Jr., pp. 47-69 (Westport, CT: Greenwood Publishing Group, 1992); Patricia Wasley, *Stirring the Chalkdust* (New York: Teachers College Press, forthcoming).

2. The School Change Study is generously funded by Exxon Education Foundation, DeWitt Wallace Reader's Digest Fund, and The Pew Charitable Trusts.

3. Sarason, *The Culture of the School and the Problem of Change*; idem, *The Predictable Failure of Educational Reform*.

4. Ann Lieberman, "Problems in Making Feedback Useful to School Staff" (Paper presented at the Annual Meeting of the American Educational Research Association, New York, 1971).

5. Ann Lieberman, "Collaborative Research: Working With, Not Working On . . .," *Educational Leadership* 43, no. 5 (1986): 28-32; idem, "Collaborative Work," *Educational Leadership* 43, no. 5 (1986): 4-8.

6. John I. Goodlad, ed., *The Ecology of School Renewal*, 86th Yearbook of the National Society for the Study of Education, Part 1 (Chicago: University of Chicago Press, 1987).

7. Paulo Freire, *Pedagogy of the Oppressed* (New York: Continuum, 1970, 1982); Jürgen Habermas, *Theory and Practice*, tr. by John Viertel (Boston: Beacon Press, 1973); Ira Shor, *Critical Teaching and Everyday Life* (Boston: South End Press, 1980); Kenneth Sirotnik and Jeannie Oakes, *Critical Inquiry and School Renewal: A Liberation of Method within a Critical Theoretical Perspective*, Occasional Paper no. 4 (Los Angeles: Laboratory in School and Community Relations, University of California, 1983).

8. Kenneth Sirotnik, "Critical Inquiry: A Paradigm for Praxis," in *Forms of Curriculum Inquiry*, edited by Edmund Short (Albany, NY: State University of New York Press, 1991), pp. 243-258; Kenneth Sirotnik and Jeannie Oakes, "Critical Inquiry for School Renewal: Liberating Theory and Practice," in *Critical Perspectives on the Organization and Improvement of Schooling*, edited by Kenneth Sirotnik and Jeannie Oakes (Boston: Kluwer-Nijhoff, 1986), pp. 3-93.

9. The findings from A Study of High Schools are reported in the following three volumes: Theodore Sizer, *Horace's Compromise: The Dilemma of the American School* (Boston: Houghton Mifflin, 1984); Arthur G. Powell, Eleanor Farrar, and David K. Cohen, *The Shopping Mall High School: Winners and Losers in the Educational Marketplace* (Boston: Houghton Mifflin, 1985); and Robert M. Hampel, *The Last Little Citadel: American High Schools Since 1940* (Boston: Houghton Mifflin, 1986).

10. Sarason, *The Culture of the School and the Problem of Change*; idem, *The Predictable Failure of Educational Reform*; John I. Goodlad, *A Place Called School* (New York: McGraw-Hill, 1984); Sizer, *Horace's Compromise*; Larry Cuban, "A Fundamental Puzzle of School Reform," *Phi Delta Kappan* 69, no. 5 (1988): 340-344; Cohen, "Teaching Practice: Plus Que ça Change . . ."; Ann Lieberman and Lynn Miller, "School Improvement in the United States: Nuance and Numbers," *Qualitative Studies in Education* 1, no. 1 (1988): 3-19.

11. Presently ten states are involved: New Mexico, Rhode Island, Illinois, Pennsylvania, Delaware, Colorado, Arkansas, South Carolina, Maine, and Indiana. In addition, some states or regions have formalized agreements for the same purpose—to build better systemic support for changing schools. They are: Southern California, the Bay Area in California, New York, Florida, and Louisville, Kentucky.

12. Donald Schön, *The Reflective Practitioner: How Professionals Think in Action* (New York: Basic Books, 1983); idem, *Educating the Reflective Practitioner* (San Francisco: Jossey-Bass, 1987).

13. David Tripp, *Critical Incidents in Teaching: Developing Professional Judgment* (London: Routledge, forthcoming).

14. We acknowledge an important debt to Sarah Lawrence Lightfoot's methodology of portraiture. Her work freed us to think about the metaphor that might best describe what we were trying to accomplish.

15. Lieberman and Miller, "School Improvement in the United States"; Patricia Wasley, *Teachers Who Lead* (New York: Teachers College Press, 1991).

Section Three
IMPLICATIONS FOR RESEARCH
AND POLICY

CHAPTER XIII

Creating New Educational Communities:
Implications for Policy

KATI HAYCOCK

This volume contains accounts of school success and insights into the process of achieving success. Rather than simply viewing the finished photo, we are allowed to watch the process by which film becomes print.

From a policy point of view, what is so striking about this montage is that it portrays not successful programs but successful schools: schools that succeed with poor and minority students. Striking because both these children and the schools that serve them struggle under the dual weight of social blight and inadequate resources. Striking because government policy has never sought good schools for poor children, only good programs.

In fact, my own experience over the past fifteen years suggests that the schools described in this book and others like them succeed *in spite of* government policy rather than because of it. In this chapter I describe the current policy framework and analyze its effects and then I suggest an alternative approach.

Government Policy in the Education of Poor and Minority Children

With the exception of a half-hearted effort to reduce segregation in some cities, for more than twenty-five years both federal and state

---

Kati Haycock is Director of the Education Trust of the American Association for Higher Education in Washington, D.C.

governments have used a single strategy to improve the education of poor and minority children: categorical programs. By now, the tendency is clear. Whenever policymakers identify a new population with a new problem, their answer is to create a new *program* to fix it.

Increasing numbers of poor children? The response is Chapter 1 and state-level compensatory education programs. Increasing numbers of "limited English-proficient" children? The response is bilingual education programs. Increasing drop-out rates? The response is drop-out prevention programs (as if, somehow, students drop out of school because of the lack of such programs). And the list goes on and on.

THE ADVANTAGES OF CATEGORICAL PROGRAMS

The advantages of such an approach have been obvious for some time. First, categorical programs are a reasonably "safe" way to increase spending on particular kinds of students. By creating discrete programs, policymakers can be relatively sure that the dollars they allocate will be spent on the youngsters about whom they are worried. At the very least, *somebody* within the educational system will be paying attention to those students.

Second, categorical programs build strong, activist constituencies—stronger, perhaps, than those around less focused streams of money. These constituencies rally around their programs in the annual budget process, helping to drive appropriations ever higher.

Third, most of the evaluations of the major programs for poor and minority students suggest positive outcomes for students. Though the advantage is not large, students who attend schools that provide these extras tend to perform somewhat higher than their peers in other schools. In combination with the effects of other changes in schools and society at large, these advantages seem to add up. Over the past sixteen years, for example, the achievement gap between white and African-American students has declined by about one half and the gap between white and Latino students by about one third. The gap between poor and rich students has also declined, again by about one half.

THE LIMITS OF CATEGORICAL PROGRAMS

There are, however, clear limits to what is attainable with such an approach. Indeed, these limits begin to be suggested by available data on student performance. For starters, as is clear both in reports of the National Assessment of Educational Progress and in state data on student achievement, almost all the gains in student achievement over the past two decades have occurred at very low skill levels. In the past sixteen years, we have made almost no progress in enabling poor and minority youngsters to master higher-level knowledge and skills.

Moreover, though the gap that separates poor and minority students from other students certainly has declined, it remains significant. By third or fourth grade, the average poor or minority student is already about six months behind other students. By sixth grade, such students are about a year behind. By eighth grade, they are about two years behind other students. And by twelfth grade, if they reach twelfth grade at all, poor and minority students average more than three years behind other students.

Indeed, according to the most recent data available from the National Assessment of Educational Progress, the skills of the average black or Latino 17-year-old in English, mathematics and science are about the same as for the average white 13-year-old. This is particularly worrisome given findings from recent international assessments, where even performance among white students in the United States lags considerably behind the performance of students in other industrialized nations.

WHY DOES THE GAP PERSIST?

Why, after so many years and so many dollars, does this gap persist? Most people, of course, think they know the answer: "The problems of poor and minority people are intractable; they cannot be overcome." "We teach all kids the same thing, but some—especially minorities and the poor—just can't learn as much as others."

The truth, of course, is quite different. Into the education of minority and poor children we put less of everything that makes a difference. These children get:

- less in the way of experienced and well-trained teachers;
- less in the way of a rich and well-balanced curriculum;
- less actual instructional time;
- less well-equipped laboratories and libraries; and,
- less of what makes the biggest difference of all: a belief that they can really learn.

It is hardly surprising, then, that these students perform less well on any test of achievement: we systematically teach them less.

That some children get less than others is not unusual in American education, for we have constructed our elementary and secondary system on a local rather than on a state or a national foundation. Governed by locally elected boards and nested within the norms and values of their communities, American school districts differ considerably in the quality of the education they provide.

The differences, however, do not occur willy-nilly. Rather, there is a clear pattern: affluent communities, especially those with substantial property values, tend to invest the most and can therefore offer the most to their students; poor communities, by contrast, can provide much less to their children. Even though many poor communities tax themselves at much higher rates than rich communities, their lower property tax bases tend to yield inadequate revenue. The net effect is that poor and minority children, who often have less at home, also get less at school because they are concentrated in poorer communities.

IS A LEVEL PLAYING FIELD LIKELY IN THE IMMEDIATE FUTURE?

Over time, governors and state legislatures in a few states have chipped away at these differences in per-student expenditures, typically in response to court orders to equalize the education provided to students in poor and rich communities. But even in states under legal mandate, progress has been slow and limited. Indeed, for every step forward it seems as though there is a step backward. The experience of Governor James Florio, who lost in a bid for reelection in New Jersey, has convinced all but the very bravest of politicians that funding formulas which take away from affluent districts to give to poor districts are sheer political suicide.

So, rather than address the fundamental inequalities in resources that contribute mightily to inequalities in instruction and, consequently, to the achievement gap, policymakers attach categorical bandaids onto the outside of poor schools. One after another after another.

The effect of this categorical pile-on on urban schools and districts is stunning. Principals of schools in big cities report that their schools participate in countless special programs—some initiated by government, some by the private sector, some by higher education. Each of these programs has its own rules and bureaucracy; each makes its own demands on school leaders. I shall never forget the response from an Oakland (California) high school principal to a question about how she spent her time. "Look," she said, "my school participates in ninety-three special programs. Most of my time is spent filling out forms and otherwise trying to stay on top of those programs." The proliferation of categorical programs has also caused dramatic expansion of school district bureaucracies. A recent report on categorical spending from the Philadelphia School District suggests why: the "Table of Contents" listing of state and federal categorical programs administered by the district is four single-spaced pages long.[1] It takes little imagination to conjure up the number of employees required simply to produce financial reports on these programs, much less to ride herd on schools to make sure that their expenditures and practices are in line with program requirements. This may be one of the reasons why poor districts and poor schools spend a smaller fraction of their budgets on the classroom—and a larger fraction on administration—than more affluent schools and districts spend on those categories.

What do most of these program administrators do? In my experience, almost everything except focus on teaching and learning. Rather, the focus is entirely on process and expenditures. The way schools and districts keep out of trouble is to document, in extraordinary detail, that they spent program dollars only on program-eligible students. When representatives from federal or state agencies visit, they look only at expenditures. What one San Francisco principal told me is common: "I've been a principal in a compensatory education school for fifteen years, and never once—in all their visits—did any representative of the state or federal government inquire whether my students actually were learning anything. They only wanted to see the books." To make matters worse, some of these programs—including Chapter 1, the largest of them all—are actually designed in a way that takes money away from schools that improve students' achievement!

Most damaging of all, though, are the effects of categorical pile-on on *students*. One day in an urban elementary school is all it takes to see what happens. Children "ping pong" from program to program. They may begin in the classroom with the regular teacher, then go down the hall to read with the compensatory education aide, then back to the classroom, then to the bilingual teacher, and so on. It often seems as though more time is spent in transit than in anything else. This bouncing around fragments the education of the most disadvantaged of students, robbing them of coherence and absolving their regular teachers of any sense of responsibility for their achievement. "Who is responsible? The instructional aides."

In sum, then, this analysis of the limits of categorical programs suggests, among other things, that:

- they can fragment the education of students who most need coherence;
- they usually focus only on remediation and very low-level skills;
- they tend to focus attention and energy on process and accounting rather than results;
- they often lead to bloated bureaucracies;
- they frequently distract educators from a much-needed focus on teaching and learning;
- they tend to absolve regular teachers and administrators of a sense of responsibility for the achievement of poor and minority students.

SOME EXAMPLES FROM CALIFORNIA

My own experiences heading up the Achievement Council, a California organization that works with low-performing, predominantly minority schools, provide some examples of these phenomena.

The first such experience occurred in an elementary school in San Jose. When I arrived at the school for my first meeting with the principal, she said, "I'm so glad you've come at 10 A.M. That is when our new Chapter 1 reading program takes place, and we're so proud of it that I want you to see what we do."

What I saw in the next hour was chilling. First, we went to the library, where a group of about thirteen poor Latino children were "reading" with an instructional aide. The aide, who could barely read English herself, read aloud to the students from a ditto, stumbling over every other word and mispronouncing many. Then the children "read" back to her, mispronouncing the same words. Next, we went to the audiovisual room, where I saw the same thing: thirteen poor Latino children learning to read with assistance from a poorly educated instructional aide.

Meanwhile, what was going on back in the regular classrooms? The more affluent, higher-achieving students were reading books, discussing ideas, and writing about what they were reading. They were doing this with the undivided attention of their well educated, fully certified classroom teacher.

This was the first time that I asked myself, "Who really benefits from this program?" But it was by no means the last. In fact, only a few months later, I had another worrisome experience, this one in Southern California.

My staff and I had been asked to spend the day with the faculty at one of California's lowest-performing high schools. The school was in

terrible shape, literally hemorrhaging students, and the principal
thought we might be able to help him enlist the teachers in a drive to
overhaul the school and raise student achievement. At the end of the
day, a group of teachers approached and asked if they could talk with
me for a moment. "We could probably do what you are suggesting,"
said their spokesman. "We could change the school and raise student
achievement. But do you know what would happen if we were successful?"

"What?" I asked.

"We would lose money," he said. "We get about a million dollars a
year in categorical aid and we would lose some of that if we improved
our test scores."

"But wouldn't you be proud?" I asked in response.

"Well," he said, "The students would probably be better off. And
their parents would probably be happier. But for us it means jobs. And
we'd have to think about that."

THE VIEW FROM WASHINGTON

These and other experiences like them caused me to wonder, early
on, if categorical programs were not part of the problem, rather than
the solution. But that thinking was not uncommon in California,
where "minorities" had become the majority, thus calling into question the entire proposition that special programs had to be created to
serve "special" populations. If the system itself did not work for what
was now the *majority* of its students, for whom did it work?

Though the need to make the system work for poor and minority
students had become ever more apparent in California, such was not
the case in Washington, D.C. when I arrived in 1989. Indeed, the
reader can imagine my horror when, on my first day at work as Vice
President of the Children's Defense Fund, I heard my new boss say to
an audience of several hundred policy leaders, "The best thing to do
to improve the education of poor children is to fully fund the Chapter
1 program."

Washington, D.C. is filled with people whose lives are wrapped up
in the defense of categorical programs, either for the programs' sake
or as a vehicle to drive more dollars into education budgets. Their
objective, always, is to get the program "fully funded," as if anyone
really understood what that means. That most of these programs
make too little difference in the lives of children is not important.

Better Strategies for Improving the Education
of Poor and Minority Children

If fully funding categorical programs is *not* the best way to improve the education of poor and minority youngsters, what *is*? What should policymakers concerned about these children actually do?

As is obvious in the accounts found elsewhere in this book, the answer is to shift the focus from *creating more programs* to *improving whole schools*. Policymakers must understand that their favorite tool of educational policy—the categorical program—is fatally flawed. No matter how well crafted the law, how faithful the implementation, or how dedicated the staff, it is not possible to compensate in a few minutes a day for the effects of watered-down instruction the rest of the school day and year. Like additions to a house built on a crumbling foundation, these extras can never achieve their purpose. Instead, policymakers must drive their policies toward supporting the new educational communities described so well in earlier chapters of this volume.

Weaning policymakers away from their favored approach will not be easy, though. As is demonstrated elsewhere in this book, bringing about change in education is very difficult. And that would seem to apply regardless of whether we are talking about changing practice *inside* of schools or about changing practice in the making of educational policy.

The 103rd Congress provided numerous examples of just how difficult such changes are. With leadership from the White House and the Governors' Association, the leaders in this Congress worked at embracing "systemic reform." They even learned the language of standards and assessments, and incorporated it into their legislative initiatives, including "Goals: 2000," the "School-to-Work Act," and the "Improving America's Schools Act." But in the end they not only left the existing categorical programs and structures in place, but added new categorical programs, as well. Each is aimed at a particular purpose or student population; each will have its own regulatory structure; and each will lead inevitably to yet another layer of bureaucracy in participating school districts.

Along the way, many of us involved in the reauthorization of the Elementary and Secondary Education Act (called the "Improving America's Schools Act") pushed hard for different strategies. Among other things, we pressed lawmakers to earmark for professional and organizational development a substantial portion of dollars from

Chapter 1, the large federal education program that provides supplemental dollars to schools serving poor children. This recommendation drew enthusiastic support from teachers and administrators across the country. They said, almost with one voice, "If you want us to teach students to new high standards, you need to invest in improving *our* knowledge and skills."

But the recommendation fell on deaf ears in the House, where members opposed such a "set-aside" because it would "take away services from poor kids." And to the rejoinder that well-educated teachers with up-to-date skills were the best possible "service" for poor students, there was only silence.

So, too, was the reaction to proposals that schools with concentrations of poor children should be able to use Chapter 1 funds to finance schoolwide improvements, rather than simply to provide add-on services. Both the educational community and the civil rights community strongly supported this change. But, in the end, lawmakers voted to extend the option to only a small number of schools. Most Chapter 1 schools will continue to be prevented from using their resources in the only way likely to significantly improve the achievement of poor children, that is, *by improving teaching and learning in the school as a whole.*

APPROPRIATE ROLES FOR POLICYMAKERS IN REFORM

If policymakers are to abandon these old categorical controls, clearly they will need new ones that meet their own rules of accountability. It hardly seems likely that they will simply turn dollars over to local educators with no sense of how they will be spent. How, then, should reform-minded policymakers exercise responsible leadership?

My own sense, shared by an increasing number of others, is that reform-minded government leaders must strip policy to the bare essentials. Rather than multiple messages for multiple purposes, new policy initiatives must concentrate on six key levers for institutional change. In so doing, policymakers can simultaneously empower school-level educators to create new educational communities, reinvent schooling, and eliminate the need for vast educational bureaucracies that get in the way of improved teaching and learning.

The six key levers are:

- establishing clear and high *goals* for what all students should know and be able to do and *assessments* for measuring progress toward those goals;

- turning over to *school-level* educators *decision-making authority* over how to get their students to the goals, including staff selection, curriculum, instruction, textbooks, and use of time;
- assuring that all schools have a share of the *resources* proportionate to their need in order to help their students reach the goals;
- assuring the availability to all schools of high-quality *staff development programs for teachers and administrators*;
- creating a system of *incentives* that rewards progress toward the goals and intervenes where progress is insufficient; and
- monitoring and reporting publicly on progress, or lack thereof, toward the goals, including both progress of students in general and progress of historically underachieving groups.

Let us take each of these levers separately, beginning with the establishment of goals.

ESTABLISHING GOALS

Unlike education elsewhere, American education has long suffered from a lack of clarity on goals for student learning. Most other industrialized nations have a single set of well-articulated goals for what they want their students to learn at various grade levels. By contrast, we leave this matter of goals largely to local school boards—more than 15,000 of them. Some standardization is, of course, achieved through the influence of widely used textbooks or standardized tests. But there are wide differences. And these are especially evident when one compares expectations in wealthy school districts with those in poor school districts.

Many of those who support the development of a set of national goals or standards for student performance do so because of the changing nature of the marketplace and increasing rates of family mobility. However, in my judgment two reasons are more powerful than these.

First, clear goals have the power to focus the energy of a system— and even those around it. In my own work with low-performing schools, I have often worried about the number of staffs that spend enormous energy trying to "improve" student achievement without any clear sense of where they are headed. Typically, they know only that they suffer by comparison with other schools. They do not know what students *should* know, nor what their own students actually *do* and *do not* know. Parents know even less. Needless to say, this makes focused, concerted effort involving both schools and families pretty difficult. It also begins to explain why there is so much blind flailing around in efforts to increase students' achievement.

Clear goals for all students could also help to counter one of the thorniest features of our current system of local control: higher expectations in school districts serving affluent families than in districts serving the poor. This unevenness has had awful consequences for poor and minority children. When held only to low standards of performance they inevitably learn less than other students for whom expectations are higher.

A reasonably small set of clear goals—Denmark's, for example, are all contained in a very small pamphlet[2]—could help to change all this. They could help focus the efforts of school people. They could help focus the efforts of parents. And they could help to put an end to the widespread practice of expecting less of poor and minority children.

This, of course, could be true only if the goals were assessable and if assessments were developed to record student progress toward the goals. Current tests, which mostly consist of multiple-choice questions on which students are compared to each other, rather than to common standards, clearly will not do. Fortunately, however, work underway in a variety of states to develop new, performance-based assessment systems seems quite promising. Several states, including Kentucky, Vermont, and Maryland, have new assessment systems up and running; all told, nearly forty states are working toward this end.

EMPOWERING SCHOOL-LEVEL EDUCATORS

Experience in the private sector suggests that most decisions are best made by those closest to the product. That experience suggests, further, that even workers whose minds have been dulled by endless years of mindless work can—with support—make good decisions.

We know, of course, that the minds of many teachers and administrators have been dulled by a bureaucracy that strangles creativity and expects blind obedience. That they can come alive again has been amply demonstrated in the work of Theodore Sizer, Robert Slavin, Henry Levin, and many others. Whether their energies and intellects can be rekindled on the necessary scale, though, is still unclear. But there is encouraging evidence—in the small schools of New York City, in Philadelphia's Charters, and in newly chartered schools across the country—suggesting that this can be so. Clearly, too much authority now rests in the hands of central bureaucracies, in the state and in

school districts. Some of that authority has recently been transferred
to the building level. Districts refer to the new management relationships as "site based" or "shared" decision making.

My own sense, however, is that the shifts to date—with the notable
exception of Chicago, Kentucky, and the new small schools in New
York City—have not been radical enough. It takes more to reenergize
school faculties and administrators than a gradual shifting in the locus
of decision making. If teachers and administrators are to feel a new
sense of responsibility for student outcomes, they must *control* the
means of getting there.

Among the matters that should be decided at the building level
are: curriculum; instructional strategies, including class size and
schedule; hiring, firing, and evaluation of personnel; use of time;
choice of professional development and other outside assistance; texts
and other instructional materials; and use of funds. These decisions
should be subject to two "higher authorities": (1) civil rights laws, and
(2) health and safety laws. In addition, professionals in the school
would be required to articulate the basis for their practices, to predi-
cate their practices on research or other evidence of effectiveness, and
to conduct regular evaluations so that practices that prove ineffective
are replaced.

RESOURCES PROPORTIONATE TO NEED

As noted earlier, the current funding base for schools is uneven. If
anything, schools serving students who get the *most* at home get the
most in the way of resources, too. Those serving children of the poor
get the least.

Kozol decries this situation as unfair and morally wrong. Others
argue that it constitutes social and economic suicide. Both analyses are
correct and are alone sufficient grounds to remedy current inequities.
But there is a third effect that, in the end, may be the most pernicious:
it robs both teachers and students of the *will* to strive, to perform.

Architects of outcomes-based accountability systems seem to
believe that school people will strive to improve student outcomes if
the incentives are right. They see reform as a kind of competition,
each school competing against its own record in past years, as well as
against the standards themselves. What they do not seem to understand is what will happen if the players see the game as rigged.

In much the same way that assembly line workers in an automobile
plant with antiquated equipment and no employee training—or, for

that matter, soldiers in a ragtag army—would *expect* to be beaten by their better equipped counterparts, so, too, will teachers and students in poor school districts *expect* to be beaten by those in affluent school districts. This expectation will drive teachers to expect less of themselves and their students, and to attribute underachievement to inadequate investment. Similarly, students will come to expect less of themselves and their teachers. Individual and group *effort* will be replaced by *excuse making*—hardly the stuff of high performance.

If we are to get maximum effort out of all students and educators, we need to invest according to need. What does this mean? Not merely that resources should be equalized across districts, so that all schools have their fair share of the resources—like high-quality teachers, rich curricula, and up-to-date instructional materials—they need to get their students to high standards. In the end, to achieve maximum results, these resources need to be disproportionately generous in schools with the poorest students. These students, and in some cases their families, may well need extra time and extra supports to reach the standards.

PROFESSIONAL DEVELOPMENT FOR TEACHERS AND ADMINISTRATORS

If educators are to get their students to standards higher than ever before, they will need a good deal of help. Many teachers, for example, will need to deepen their own knowledge of the content areas they teach; others will need help in learning how to engage students more effectively with that content. Similarly, principals will need to learn how to manage their schools in very different ways. And teams of educators will have to learn how to work *together* to improve student achievement. For these reasons and others, many reform leaders, especially those whose work is described in this volume, have concluded that high quality professional development is the *core* of school reform.

We have seen policy leaders take important strides in beginning to understand the need for investing in professional development. Yet a concern about the quality of most existing professional development opportunities, as well as the worry about taking services away from children, has dimmed enthusiasm for making investments of sufficient size to make a real difference.

In *Making Schools Work for Children in Poverty*, the Commission on Chapter 1 proposed what I think is a good way to handle this issue, given supply problems. The Commission urged a two-pronged funding strategy.³ The first prong would set aside dollars at the state and/or regional level to build the supply of high-quality providers, in effect, to "front load" the system. The second prong would place dollars in the hands of school people, which they could use to purchase and/or develop expertise. Funds for the first prong would start high and decline to almost zero over time, while funds for the second prong would grow. Eventually, then, you would have a pure market-based system.

These set-asides would make it possible for far more high poverty schools to participate in some of the reforms described elsewhere in this book, including Success for All, Accelerated Schools, and the Coalition of Essential Schools. Current limits on dollars available to support the kind of high-quality professional development provided by these networks limit their penetration in most urban districts.

INCENTIVES FOR IMPROVED PERFORMANCE

At the moment, there are no real incentives for school people to struggle hard to improve student performance. Indeed, there are countless disincentives for high performance. Teachers, for example, who work especially hard and draw outside attention are often isolated and dismissed by their colleagues as "trying to make the rest of us look bad." Principals, too, whose schools are recognized for usually high performance frequently become suspect among their own peers. Think about it: we take funds away from Chapter 1 schools if their students' achievement improves!

The current system of incentives sends the wrong message. We need to replace it with an incentive system that sends the right messages.

The state of Kentucky has gone further than any other state in changing its incentive structure. Beginning in 1990, the Kentucky Education Reform Act (KERA) put in place a complex system of rewards and sanctions. At one end, schools that improve student performance the most (in comparison to the school's own performance in past years), get substantial financial rewards. These big gainers get an amount calculated at *40 percent of payroll.* The funds can be used for faculty bonuses, for school improvement, or both. At the other end, schools that make no gains over prior years or that fall backwards first receive a lot of help. If that does not work, the school is eventually closed.

While no other state or local school district has yet gone as far as Kentucky, many are now rethinking their incentive structures. Some are thinking along financial lines, others around more "psychic" rewards. These efforts will likely be pushed even further ahead with passage of the "Improving America's Schools Act," which requires of all states and most districts new plans that include incentives for progress and concrete consequences for stagnation.

There is also the matter of incentives for students. What reason will they have to work hard to meet new higher standards? Too little thought is being given to this subject. Albert Shanker, president of the American Federation of Teachers, is pressing the higher education community to align admissions requirements with the new standards. Pressure for change is also coming from leaders in the Coalition of Essential Schools, whose reform efforts are being impeded by mechanistic admissions processes in many universities. But so far those pleas are falling mostly on deaf ears. And those who are pressing employers to require high school transcripts and to give preference to prospective employees who have worked hard in high school are having similar experiences.

But, here again, there are some promising developments. In Oregon, for example, the higher education system is shifting to performance-based admissions standards. There is movement in this direction, too, in Wisconsin, Minnesota, and in the State University of New York (SUNY) system. To move ahead on this issue, though, we need more vehicles for cross-sector action about incentives.

MONITORING AND REPORTING ON PROGRESS

With the exception of annual reporting of test scores, we educators do not talk often with our publics about how we are doing. Not only are we not clear about our learning goals, but we are even fuzzier about current performance. Here are some typical responses to the question, "How are we doing?"

- "Oh, about where urban schools generally perform." (And where is that?)
- "Our percentile ranking increased from 36 to 37." (Compared to whom?)
- "Our SAT average is 650." (On a scale of what? Verbal, Math, or Combined?)

We are often vague, also, about the performance of individual students. Parents want to know whether their children are learning what they need to learn. But instead, they are told what "stanine" their child is in or, perhaps, what percentile. Needless to say, responses of this sort are not particularly helpful to parents who wish to focus their energies on areas of need.

So, policy needs not only to provide for the establishment of clear learning goals for all students but also for clear communication on progress toward those goals. And that reporting should be done for the state and nation as a whole and also for individual schools and districts.

Professional educators need to know *in clear language* how they are doing compared to the goals, and in particular, where their students are falling short. Even more important, though, parents and communities need to know. For their oversight and their advocacy can accomplish what government never can.

MAKING A DEAL

Each of these six levers is important and potentially quite powerful. However, it is critically important to understand that they are likely to be immensely more powerful—simultaneously more liberating and more demanding—if pulled *together* and all at once.

What I propose here is, perhaps, best expressed in the form of a "deal" between policymakers and schools. In effect, that deal trades control over the means of education for outcome-based accountability with real consequences.

Specifically, policymakers would provide for the establishment of goals, fair and need-based distribution of resources, high-quality staff development programs for teachers and administrators, a system of consequences, and would require regular reports on progress toward goals.

Schools would make all decisions about how to use resources to help students reach goals, including control over staff selection, instruction, curriculum, professional development, and time. Schools would be held accountable for results.

Will this approach work? Obviously, there is no way to tell. But it could hardly be less successful than government's current favorite: the categorical program.

NOTES

1. Elliott Alexander, ed., *1992-1993 Compendium of Projects* (Philadelphia: Office of Categorical Programs and Governmental Relations, School District of Philadelphia, n.d.).

2. *The Subjects in the Danish Gymnasium* (Copenhagen: Ministry of Education and Research, 1992).

3. Commision on Chapter 1, *Making Schools Work for Children in Poverty* (Washington, DC: American Association for Higher Education, December 1992).

CHAPTER XIV

Sustaining New Educational Communities: Toward a New Culture of School Reform

KAREN HUNTER QUARTZ

What do people in schools expect to happen when the banner of reform is waved? Some are quite hopeful, expecting teaching and learning to be significantly altered, roles reconceptualized, and daily school life changed. Others are cynical as they wait for the current wave to just pass over as they duck, trying not to get wet. The vast majority, however, seem to receive and interpret change efforts in a much more tempered light, expecting to pick up a few helpful hints or techniques and maybe some new materials—all toward an incremental betterment of their professional lives. This last set of expectations expresses what I will call the dominant culture of stabilizing reform. Changes within this network of norms and assumptions are not supposed to alter existing practice radically. Instead, they are first-order reforms, refining existing modes of teaching and learning. That is why the cynic can easily avoid reform; it does not challenge the basic core of his or her practice.

Breaking out of the cycle of stabilizing reform, proponents of restructuring expect their agenda to change schools radically by encouraging people to relearn or rethink fundamental beliefs about education. Significantly, the reform-minded researchers and practitioners in this volume venture beyond the usual rhetoric to articulate what such deep, normative change means on a local level. What and how do local school members expect to change as a result of participating in one of these restructuring projects? In this chapter, I look across authors' reflections on their efforts to explore this question. For the key to sustaining these new educational communities depends, I believe, on fostering a new culture of school reform—one in which it makes most sense to local school members to alter current practice fundamentally, not merely refine it.

Karen Hunter Quartz is a Research Associate in the Graduate School of Education, University of California, Los Angeles.

Studying Reform from a Cultural Perspective

Let me first explain why I think it is fruitful to look at reform from a cultural perspective. On one level, the whole concept may seem paradoxical: Can change be described in terms of the enduring and stable norms that define a culture? But this, of course, is exactly the point. The business of change in schools and elsewhere is laden with regularity.[1] As my opening paragraph suggests, people have knee-jerk responses to reform; they know just how to behave. On a basic level, these shared expectations or norms about what to believe and how to act within specific contexts constitute what social theorists call "culture."

From a research perspective, cultural analysis differs from other forms of social analysis insofar as it investigates the nature of collective behavior in terms of its meaning to participants—how they make sense of social situations. Analyzing collective sense making amounts to understanding the patterns of beliefs and expectations—the norms—that people use to negotiate their interactions with others. In the case of this chapter, those interactions revolve around school reform. Understanding the culture of school reform, therefore, involves understanding the norms that structure school members' approach to change.

Given this explanation, however, why might it be useful to stand above the phenomenon of reform to study its regularities? First, this cultural perspective follows a fruitful line of recent research that ventures beyond the classroom door to study what reform means at a local level.[2] As opposed to past efforts that understood reform as a centralized imposition of new policies, rules, and techniques, this cultural perspective looks from the bottom up to understand how teachers, who are ultimately responsible for change, make sense of reform efforts. What, for example, does the seasoned veteran expect to happen when his or her principal announces the onset of another new program? To understand the veteran's probable lack of interest or resistance, we need to delve into the network of assumptions and beliefs that fuel his or her reaction. Studies of reform that focus narrowly on compliance and resistance as indicators of success bypass this level of analysis, resulting in relatively meager insights into why planned changes typically fail.

A second reason to look at the culture of school reform, then, is not only to understand what reform means locally, but to gain insight into how these meanings can be challenged to sustain, not defeat, efforts to change. Prior to understanding the details of any reform effort, the intricate set of norms surrounding change itself must be understood, challenged, and eventually replaced. Let us look, then, at the culture of reform that currently exists, turning afterwards to its proposed successor—a new culture of transformative reform as articulated throughout this volume.

The Dominant Culture of Stabilizing Reform

All schools share common reform experiences that may have heightened the quality of education, but not substantially altered the nature of schooling. Indeed, schools are quite expert at adding on and assimilating new programs, curricula, and teaching strategies to fit their usual daily routine.[3] In this way, they are all caught up in what I refer to here as the dominant culture of stabilizing reform. Cuban offers a thorough review of research concerning stability and change in schools.[4] Focusing on external and internal factors that work both to maintain and reform the intended and taught curricula, he argues that constancy and change coexist in schools. At the same time, however, he maintains that changes are rarely fundamental or second order in nature; typically, they are incremental or first order, seeking to refine, not challenge, the status quo. Examples include adopting new textbooks, increasing teacher salaries, and requiring more "time on task." Schools respond to these usually imposed incremental changes in ways that preserve their stability. Cuban reviews a variety of explanations for this pervasive stability in schools, ranging from the conservative culture of teaching to constraining school and classroom structures.

Efforts to inspire fundamental change through restructuring, then, must be viewed in relation to schools' general tendency to remain stable—the dominant culture of stabilizing reform—and the way these norms about change affect how the reform is likely to be received, interpreted, and acted upon locally. The authors in this volume recognize the force of this dominant reform culture and propose ways to challenge deep-seated norms around change. Beyond the usual rhetoric, these researchers and practitioners combine their wisdom to relate theoretically grounded experiences about the difficult process of fundamental change. In this way, they substantiate or flesh out what may be termed a new culture of transformative reform.

The New Culture of Transformative Reform

TRANSFORMING, NOT TINKERING

Affecting fundamental change is clearly the mission of the reform efforts chronicled throughout this volume. As Chasin and Levin put it in chapter 6, "An Accelerated School is not just a conventional school with new principles or special programs grafted onto it. It is a dynamic environment in which the entire school and its operations are transformed" (p. 134). This point is made repeatedly as authors talk of deep changes, reinventing education, turning schools on their heads. Cuban and others refer to this type of change as "second order":

Second-order, or fundamental, changes seek to alter the essential ways that organizations are put together because of major dissatisfaction with present arrangements. Fundamental changes introduce new goals, structures, and roles that transform familiar ways of performing duties into novel solutions to persistent problems.[5]

Sustaining such new goals, structures, and roles requires that these changes become part of the school's culture—the norms or regularities that people use to make sense of daily practice.[6] Reforms only stick, in other words, because people come to see them as *normal* practice.

Though the process of coming to see second-order changes as normal is extremely complex, it seems to hinge on people's expectations for reform itself. Going into a reform process carrying the one-shot, helpful-hint approach to change is sure to sabotage the depth of the effort. Rather, school members must go in believing that this reform is not business as usual, and that it really does make sense to rethink and challenge their core beliefs about schooling. With Sarason, I believe that most reform efforts have focused too much energy on disseminating and applying new ideas in the absence of adequately engaging school members in "unlearning what custom, tradition, and even research had told [them] is right, natural, and proper."[7] The authors in this volume all speak to this concern, suggesting new norms to structure this unlearning or rethinking process—new norms that together define a radically different culture of school reform.

NEW REFORM CULTURE EMBEDDED IN NEW CLASSROOMS

The norms of this new reform culture are readily at hand, themselves embedded in the restructuring agenda. Put simply, the reformed learning environment for children is the same one proposed as a guideline for implementation and on-going professional development. The new classrooms, advocates of restructuring advise, should resemble new workplaces for teachers—more inquiry-based, cooperative, and empowering. In struggling to reform their students' academic lives, then, teachers are also struggling to change the way they approach their own practice, learning, and development.

This point is made repeatedly by contributors to this volume. Wasley, King, and Louth, for example, write in chapter 12 of their collaborative inquiry among researchers and school staff as mirroring what should happen within classrooms. Lieberman, Falk, and Alexander make a similar point in chapter 7 in relation to leadership: "Directors facilitate and support teacher growth in much the same way that teachers are expected to do with children" (p. 120). In chapter 3 Gutierrez and Meyer echo this idea relative to a teacher's development: "She became an apprentice as she simultaneously constructed apprenticeship opportunities for her students" (p. 33). The argument runs throughout the volume: What we know about facilitating learning and change should be applied to all learners, that is, to *all* members of a school's community.

ANALYZING NEW NORMS OF REFORM

What do we know about facilitating learning and change for all school members? Based on the chapters in section two, I have grouped this knowledge under three new sets of expectations for student as well as for teacher and school development. Importantly, these new norms prescribe shifts away from current practice. Change, therefore, is best thought of along a continuum which harbors an ever-present tension between the old and the new.

First, and most broadly, the restructuring efforts described in this volume prescribe new pedagogical norms, challenging deep-seated beliefs about the nature of knowledge and the process of learning. Moving away from "mimetic"[8] models of learning based on a teacher-centered transmission of objective facts, these reforms are based on constructivist theories of learning that espouse student-centered, inquiry-based teaching toward the social construction of knowledge. The second normative shift challenges the way school members relate to one another. Moving away from individualistic and competitive modes of interaction toward norms of care, trust, and common purpose, good school practice is based on new relational norms. Finally, the norms governing how power is distributed among all school members (distributive norms) are being challenged, moving away from hierarchical, centralized bases for authority to structures that are decentralized, inclusive, and more democratic.

Together, then, these three normative tensions capture the nature of the struggle facing schools engaged in fundamental change. To be sure, these norms and tensions overlap, particularly in the case of pedagogical norms which might be interpreted as encompassing relational and distributive norms as well. On a conceptual level, however, these three norm types are useful for carving up authors' experiences and reflections on challenging the dominant culture of stabilizing reform and thus ensuring the staying power of their innovations.

Pedagogical norms. Shifting norms around teaching and learning has been an age-old concern of school reformers. Cuban examines historical trends in teaching along a continuum from teacher-centered to student-centered instruction, noting that despite vigorous reform efforts by progressive educators in the 1920s and 1930s and more recently between 1965 and 1975, teacher-centered pedagogical norms have, to a large extent, persisted.[9] Restructuring in the 1990s brings yet another rekindling of the progressive flame, but this time the push toward new pedagogical norms is bolstered by advances in cognitive and social psychology. This research base adds concepts such as situated learning and multiple intelligences to the student-centered approach.

If new learning and instructional methods are to change for students, surpassing the track record of one hundred years of reform, they must also change for teachers. As it stands, "schools neglect teachers' learning and undermine their professional development."[10] Learning opportunities such as district-sponsored in-service training are sporadic and usually superficial; if teachers pick up a few helpful hints, the enterprise is considered a success. As Johnson further explains, teachers' learning and growth occur "largely at the margins of their work."[11] Is it any wonder, then, that reform follows suit? How could superficial and marginal learning opportunities create fundamental change?

The authors in this volume all speak to this point in their calls for new pedagogical norms to structure staff development around restructuring. As Steinberg and Rosenstock put it in chapter 9, "Teachers, like students, are not empty vessels into which the current wisdom can be poured" (p. 158). Rather, as Lieberman, Falk, and Alexander explain, teachers need to be "continually engaged in talk about work, values, processes, ideas, and concerns. These conversations, facilitated by the directors, are the cornerstone of professional development through which staff members develop a powerful sense of collegiality, collaboration, and community" (pp. 122-23). Provided with continual growth opportunities, then, teachers in learner-centered schools meet formally and informally, from after-school meetings to semiannual all-school retreats. Far from sporadic and superficial, these learning experiences "deepen understandings of children, of teaching, and of [teachers'] own personal/professional growth" (p. 117).

Challenging teachers' understandings of children's ability and learning is at the heart of the Program for Complex Instruction and Project Zero, described in chapters 2 and 10 respectively. Both sets of authors view this challenge as involving a fundamental shift in perception. From her perspective as a teacher, Patricia Swanson reflects in chapter 2 on her own learning process.

It is not a simple matter for a teacher to treat status problems in the classroom, even when she intellectually understands and philosophically embraces the concepts. Putting that knowledge into practice requires a series of changes in perceptions that can be difficult to achieve and may take considerable time to acquire (p. 26).

Part of this perceptual shift involves learning to use a sociological lens to focus on groups rather than individuals and this requires "confronting our cultural predisposition to regard all behavior as the result of individual motivation or capacity" (p. 127). As Krechevsky et al. point out in chapter 10, another shift in teachers' perception is required to "look for *many* areas of talent in their students, not just linguistic or logical-mathematical" (p. 179).

Plainly, these are complex learning tasks, requiring intensive development opportunities to master; they are far from the one-shot in-service workshop after school. To facilitate this learning process, both sets of authors mention the importance of adopting a new language and set of concepts. Having the words to express a phenomenon may be the first step in seeing it. As Krechevsky et al. report, successful implementation of MI theory is "typically accompanied by a new and more sophisticated form of discourse among teachers and other stakeholders" (p. 183). For example, "Labeling ability in music, movement, and art an 'intelligence' is an important linguistic shift, one which elevates the traditional 'nonacademic' subjects to a higher status both in and outside the classroom" (p. 176). To facilitate this type of linguistic shift, Cohen et al. prescribe intensive classroom observation and feedback framed as "an open-ended exchange of information and expertise designed to enable teachers to translate the theoretical concepts they have learned into classroom practice" (p. 28).

Another new pedagogical norm for teachers centers on the role that context plays in shaping learning and knowledge. Creating communities of effective practice, as Gutierrez and Meyer maintain in chapter 3, requires recognizing "how the contexts for learning influence what is learned" (p. 50). For teachers' development, this necessitates a shift away from reform packages and kits and toward locally constructed knowledge. Gutierrez and Meyer explain their approach: "It is a situated model and, therefore, must be reconstructed across contexts and communities; it cannot simply be imposed. This process model is culturally sensitive and accounts for the multiple ways participants co-construct contexts and activities and use language" (p. 34). The Educational and Community Change Project is guided by very similar principles. In chapter 11, Heckman et al. explain what they mean by transforming an ecology of education: "The school is functioning as an important part of the community. The community context is becoming a focal point for powerful transformation. As a result, important learning is occurring" (p. 192).

Together, then, the authors in this volume provide much substance for the idea of reforming teachers' learning. From specifics on the importance of intensive opportunities for growth through meetings, retreats, observation, and feedback to more general concerns regarding changing discourse and situating knowledge, new pedagogical norms clearly emerge to tackle the problem of creating and sustaining new educational communities.

Relational norms. Teaching is traditionally a very isolating profession. Well documented is the almost sacred privacy that school structures create for teachers.[12] Breaking down these structures to reduce teacher isolation and promote collegial interaction is one of the pillars of restructuring and an integral part of each reform project described in this volume. At the roots of this recommendation are a number of sources, from the learning theories alluded to above to organization theories that espouse new management strategies to current debates among communitarian ethicists. As Little notes, however, "the term collegiality has remained conceptually amorphous and ideologically sanguine."[13] As researchers have recently demonstrated, teacher collaboration has many meanings, some of which carry few or even negative consequences. In typical first-order reform fashion, collaboration may be

mandated from above, forcing teachers to work together in adminis-
tratively designed structures, such as teaching teams and formal meetings. Hargreaves and Wignall call this "contrived collegiality."[14] Moreover, on the issue of change itself, Little also warns that teachers can
collaborate effectively to achieve a variety of ends, including blocking
reform efforts to preserve the status quo.[15]

What does it mean, then, to move beyond incremental, contrived,
or even combative collaboration toward meaningful new relationships
among school members that promote change? What does it mean, in
other words, to build a collaborative culture of school reform? Again,
the authors in this volume give substance to this question and the
prevalent policy talk around teacher collaboration.

Wasley, King, and Louth's collaborative experience among Coalition researchers and school staff, reported in chapter 12, is particularly
telling. Describing a reform process that is designed to give insights to
both researchers and school members, the authors recount the hurdles
encountered as they negotiated and unraveled the meaning of change.
Their snapshots of the intricacies of school life—both good and bad—
made public the private worlds of classrooms. As Sherry King explains:
"Teachers who do not necessarily share a common philosophy cannot
hide behind the privacy of their classroom when the snapshot comes
out" (p. 218). Making public traditionally protected beliefs and turf,
then, was the first step in "beginning to think and act as a group that
has shared values and common purposes" (p. 217). The process of
change itself, therefore, became a collective and public enterprise rather
than something one could discreetly sidestep while no one was looking.

In chapter 9 Steinberg and Rosenstock describe another essential
facet of changing relational norms to facilitate restructuring. Working
from within a strong competitive ethic where vocational teachers vied
for students' interest and fought to preserve craft specialization, City-
Works faced quite a challenge in moving toward meaningful collaboration. Breaking down norms of noninterference was an essential step
in this process. Teachers needed to get beyond invoking disclaimers
such as "I would never say what's right for anyone else" or "this is just
the way I do things" or "I know that everyone has their own way of
doing things and that's fine" (p. 161).

After two years of team meetings, the authors report, teachers have
developed a sense of broader responsibility for students and the school.
The project carved out crucial time and space for meetings, giving
teachers "both informal and formal opportunities to work together"

(p. 159). Moreover, as facilitators, the authors ensured that meetings were more than just gripe sessions, and involved a "broader conversation about teaching and learning" (p. 159). As a result of these opportunities for collaboration, relational norms have shifted dramatically:

Now teachers approach the task of restructuring with a kind of rolling up of the collective sleeve. There is noticeably greater tolerance for ambiguity. People are more willing to bring issues to the team for group problem solving and have found ways to deal constructively with disagreements. Teachers are evolving a shared language for talking about how they work together and for getting through the inevitable crises. Perhaps more importantly, we now have a picture of what we could and should become: a high performance workplace where staff members are highly interdependent yet each is an active participant, focusing energy on the tasks at hand (p. 162).

Breaking down norms of noninterference to foster collective responsibility for students and teaching was also a crucial step in securing the legitimacy of the AVID program among school staff. As Mary Catherine Swanson recalls in chapter 4: "Not infrequently I received notes from colleagues such as 'this student is your responsibility; he does not belong in this school much less in my college preparatory class' " (p. 55). Symbolizing teachers' distrust of the program, one teacher even wrongfully accused AVID students of cheating on her biology midterm. Getting the whole school staff to recognize the abilities of AVID students and collectively participate in reform efforts to facilitate their learning was, to say the least, a major challenge.

In an effort to conquer this faculty distrust of her efforts, Swanson explained her students' goals to the faculty and welcomed them to visit the AVID class. But to really bolster acceptance of the program, its philosophy had to enter their classrooms. Acting in an almost subversive fashion, AVID staff worked with teachers in ways that did not overtly threaten their beliefs or turf. Tutors were sent into teachers' classrooms to work specifically with AVID students as part of a strategy to make teachers conscious that an expert was observing their lessons, thereby encouraging more effective teaching. As the relationship between tutors and teachers progressed, Swanson and the tutors developed mini-lessons that modeled AVID's philosophy but could be easily slipped into a class period. Before long, and after twenty-five years of stagnation, the school staff as a whole was "discussing student learning and implementing the writing process, inquiry methods, and collaborative groups" (p. 58).

As these three experiences demonstrate, there are many ways to foster new relational norms among school members. Importantly, the reform process plays out differently in different settings. Essential to all three collaborative experiences, however, was an effort to make public what is private and encourage norms of constructive interference and collective responsibility.

Distributive norms. Many deem inequities in power relations the largest culprit of failed reform efforts.[16] For reforms have been traditionally imposed from above with little regard for the interests of those below. Not surprisingly, then, teachers, who are most often "those below," feel no compunction in either sidestepping imposed reforms or taking only the bits that seem useful. In attempting to reverse this trend, reformers now call for teacher empowerment to manage change. Again, the authors in this volume add important substance to this often vague buzzword.

The Accelerated Schools Project is grounded in the concept of site responsibility for education. Moreover, the project has established a detailed structure and process to translate this concept into practice. Speaking of their goal to localize responsibility, Chasin and Levin write in chapter 8:

To make this a reality, there must be an appropriate decision structure built around the school's unity of purpose, and there must be a functional process to develop the capacity of the school to identify challenges, create an inquiry process to understand the challenges and potential solutions, and to implement and evaluate solutions (p. 135).

The decision structure consists of three levels of participation: the School as a Whole, the Steering Committee, and the Cadres.

New distributive norms also encompass the content of decisions: power to do what? Essential to both the Accelerated Schools Project and Success for All is the power to choose whether or not to change, a radical departure from the era of top-down mandates. For a school to become an Accelerated School, "90 percent of the entire school staff and student and parent representatives must support the commitment to move forward" (pp. 137-38). Similarly, school staffs considering the Success for All program must, after an initial process of discussion and debate, vote 80 percent in favor of changing. As Slavin and Madden explain in chapter 5: "By this point the great majority of school staffs vote in excess of 80 percent positive, but the exercise is essential in letting teachers know that they had a free choice to participate from the outset" (p. 78).

Flattening hierarchies does not remove the fact that different people carry different responsibilities and interests. And this can be a great source of strain. As the process of reform becomes decentralized, hierarchies can reproduce themselves locally. In Success for All, for example, a school-level facilitator is responsible for overseeing the project and training the staff. Anticipating problematic power relations, the project staff recommends "an experienced, respected teacher, usually from the school's own staff. We try to impress upon schools the importance of having a facilitator who will be seen as a friend and helper to teachers, not an evaluator or supervisor" (pp. 78-79).

Finally, in chapter 11 Heckman et al. offer the sage advice to embrace the diversity in school members' opinions and perspectives. Though "it creates the dilemma of how to respect individual beliefs while arriving at new common understandings" (p. 193) the ultimate end makes this tension-filled process worthwhile. According to the authors,

The quality of a decision depends on authentic expressions of people's perceptions, beliefs and desires. Opportunities that provide people a forum for such authentic self-expression are crucial to this process. The fewer distortions in acknowledging what each individual wishes or believes, the greater the opportunities for authentic communication and negotiations that result in good decisions (pp. 193-194).

These authors demonstrate that redistributing power more equitably among all school members requires careful attention to many factors, from creating a functional decision structure to ensuring a meaningful process of empowerment. Keeping in mind how traditional distributive norms are likely to affect a process of empowerment seems crucial. Through strategies such as choosing whether or not to reform, ensuring facilitative leadership, and recognizing the legitimacy of diverse interests, these projects demonstrate their commitment to a fundamental shift away from calculated and imposed change.

Reviewing innovative restructuring experiences relative to their new pedagogical, relational, and distributive norms has provided substance to the call for fundamental change. Clearly, none of the authors in this volume approaches reform carrying the incremental, helpful-hint guide to change; each expects core conceptions of schooling to be relearned.

As I have argued, sustaining these ambitious change efforts hinges on establishing a new culture of transformative reform in local schools. Embedded within this culture is the belief that all members understand why it is good to become learners who constantly challenge the core of their practice, collaborators who work together toward a common end, and equals who participate in a democratic process of reinventing their school.

NOTES

1. Michael G. Fullan, *The New Meaning of Educational Change* (New York: Teachers College Press, 1991).

2. Seymour B. Sarason, *The Culture of the School and the Problem of Change* (Boston: Allyn and Bacon, 1982); Fullan, *The New Meaning of Educational Change*; Jeannie Oakes, Karen Hunter Quartz, Jennifer Gong, Gretchen Guiton, and Martin Lipton, "Creating Middle Schools: Technical, Normative, and Political Considerations," *Elementary School Journal* 93, no. 5 (1993): 461-480.

3. David K. Cohen, "Origins," in *The Shopping Mall High School*, edited by Arthur G. Powell, Eleanor Farrar, and David K. Cohen (Boston: Houghton Mifflin, 1986); Fullan, *The New Meaning of Educational Change*.

4. Larry Cuban, "Curriculum Stability and Change," in *Handbook of Research on Curriculum*, edited by Philip W. Jackson (New York: Macmillan, 1992).

5. Ibid., p. 218. See also, Paul Watzlawick, John H. Weakland, and Richard Fisch, *Change: Principles of Problem Formation and Problem Resolution* (New York: W. W. Norton, 1974).

6. Sarason, *The Culture of the School and the Problem of Change*.

7. Seymour B. Sarason, *The Predictable Failure of Educational Reform* (San Francisco: Jossey-Bass, 1991).

8. Philip W. Jackson, *Life in Classrooms* (New York: Holt, Rinehart and Winston, 1986).

9. Larry Cuban, *How Teachers Taught: Constancy and Change in American Classrooms 1890-1980* (New York: Longman, 1984).

10. Susan Moore Johnson, *Teachers at Work: Achieving Success in Our Schools* (New York: Basic Books, 1990), p. 252.

11. Ibid., p. 249.

12. Dan Lortie, *Schoolteacher* (Chicago: University of Chicago Press, 1975); John I. Goodlad, *A Place Called School* (New York: McGraw-Hill, 1984); Judith Warren Little, "The Persistence of Privacy: Autonomy and Initiative in Teachers' Professional Relations," *Teachers College Record* 91, no. 4 (1990): 509-535.

13. Little, "The Persistence of Privacy."

14. Andrew Hargreaves and R. Wignall, *Time for the Teacher: A Study of Collegial Relations among Elementary School Teachers* (Toronto: Ontario Institute for Studies in Education, 1989).

15. Little, "The Persistence of Privacy," p. 527.

16. Sarason, *The Predictable Failure of Educational Reform*.

Questions for Further Study

Since its founding in 1901, the Society has had as one of its purposes the encouragement of the "study of education." Its publications are intended to provide a background as well as a stimulus for such study.

To give further emphasis to this purpose the Board of Directors has requested the editors of the two volumes of the 94th Yearbook to prepare sample questions that individuals and study groups can use to guide further inquiry into issues raised by the books. Accordingly, the editors have prepared the following list of questions which they hope will encourage readers to probe more deeply into the important problems with which this volume deals.

1. The chapters in this volume have much to say about norms or "regularities" of school culture that need to be challenged if meaningful reforms are to be implemented and sustained in schools. In your own school setting, are there particular norms that you see as impeding reform?

2. What strategies would be useful for changing the ways in which the expectations for and the abilities of students in heterogeneous classes are judged by their peers? By their teachers? By themselves?

3. Some of the programs reported in this volume describe innovations or reforms that are taking place in a single school. Does this suggest that efforts to achieve systemwide school reform are unrealistic? Are there any of these reforms that you think could be profitably undertaken on a systemwide basis in your school district?

4. In some of the projects or programs described in this volume there are various "players" involved: students, teachers, administrators, researchers, parents, outside consultants. What conditions must obtain if these various players are to participate effectively in establishing "new learning communities"?

5. Select a particular change initiative in the school or district with which you work. What are the normative, technical, and political dimensions of that particular change? Do not worry about overlapping, since individual elements may not fall clearly into a single category.

6. Discuss the salience of race in your community and school. Begin with the obvious, overt signs of racism and continue to explore

more subtle expressions. How does race matter as you consider your school or district, a particular chapter in this volume, and other dimensions of the salience of race in society and schools? You may want to contrast the discussions of race in other, more general social commentaries, such as Cornel West's *Race Matters* and Richard Hernstein and Charles Murray's *The Bell Curve*.

7. Why would it be fun and gratifying to work in or with a school that is basing its reform on democratic, egalitarian principles? In addition to such a school being good for students, why would it be good for you? Provide specific reasons.

8. What would constitute evidence for you that the reforms described in this volume really work? How might schools document the democratic impact of these reforms as well as their effects on students' cognitive learning? Why might it be important for schools to demonstrate both?

Name Index

Subject Index

INFORMATION ABOUT MEMBERSHIP IN THE SOCIETY

Membership in the National Society for the Study of Education is open to all individuals who desire to receive its publications.

There are presently two categories of membership: Regular and Comprehensive. The Regular Membership (annual dues in 1995, $30) entitles the member to receive both volumes of the Yearbook. The Comprehensive Membership (annual dues in 1995, $55) entitles the member to receive the two volume Yearbook and the two current volumes in the Series on Contemporary Educational Issues.

The Series on Contemporary Educational Issues is to be discontinued after 1995. The Comprehensive Membership will therefore not be available after the end of calendar year 1995 (December 31, 1995).

For calendar year 1995 reduced dues are available for retired NSSE members and for full-time graduate students *in their first year of membership*. These reduced dues are $25 for the Regular Membership and $50 for the Comprehensive Membership.

Membership in the Society is for the calendar year. Dues are payable on or before January 1 of each year.

New members are required to pay an entrance fee of $1, in addition to annual dues for the year in which they join.

Members of the Society include professors, researchers, graduate students, and administrators in colleges and universities; teachers, supervisors, curriculum specialists, and administrators in elementary and secondary schools; and a considerable number of persons not formally connected with educational institutions.

All members participate in the election of the six-member Board of Directors, which is responsible for managing the affairs of the Society, including the authorization of volumes to appear in the yearbook series. All members whose dues are paid for the current year are eligible for election to the Board of Directors.

Each year the Society arranges for meetings to be held in conjunction with the annual conferences of one or more of the major national educational organizations. All members are urged to attend these sessions. Members are also encouraged to submit proposals for future yearbooks.

Further information about the Society may be secured by writing to the Secretary-Treasurer, NSSE, 5835 Kimbark Avenue, Chicago, IL 60637.

RECENT PUBLICATIONS OF THE NATIONAL SOCIETY FOR THE STUDY OF EDUCATION

1. The Yearbooks

Ninety-fourth Yearbook (1995)
Part 1. *Creating New Educational Communities.* Jeannie Oakes and Karen Hunter Quartz, editors. Cloth.
Part 2. *Changing Populations/Changing Schools.* Erwin Flaxman and A. Harry Passow, editors. Cloth.

Ninety-third Yearbook (1994)
Part 1. *Teacher Research and Educational Reform.* Sandra Hollingsworth and Hugh Sockett, editors. Cloth.
Part 2. *Bloom's Taxonomy: A Forty-year Retrospective.* Lorin W. Anderson and Lauren A. Sosniak, editors. Cloth.

Ninety-second Yearbook (1993)
Part 1. *Gender and Education.* Sari Knopp Biklen and Diane Pollard, editors. Cloth.
Part 2. *Bilingual Education: Politics, Practice, and Research.* M. Beatriz Arias and Ursula Casanova, editors. Cloth.

Ninety-first Yearbook (1992)
Part 1. *The Changing Contexts of Teaching.* Ann Lieberman, editor. Cloth.
Part 2. *The Arts, Education, and Aesthetic Knowing.* Bennett Reimer and Ralph A. Smith, editors. Cloth.

Ninetieth Yearbook (1991)
Part 1. *The Care and Education of America's Young Children: Obstacles and Opportunities.* Sharon L. Kagan, editor. Cloth.
Part 2. *Evaluation and Education: At Quarter Century.* Milbrey W. McLaughlin and D. C. Phillips, editors. Paper.

Eighty-ninth Yearbook (1990)
Part 1. *Textbooks and Schooling in the United States.* David L. Elliott and Arthur Woodward, editors. Cloth.
Part 2. *Educational Leadership and Changing Contexts of Families, Communities, and Schools.* Brad Mitchell and Luvern L. Cunningham, editors. Paper.

Eighty-eighth Yearbook (1989)
Part 1. *From Socrates to Software: The Teacher as Text and the Text as Teacher.* Philip W. Jackson and Sophie Haroutunian-Gordon, editors. Cloth.
Part 2. *Schooling and Disability.* Douglas Biklen, Dianne Ferguson, and Alison Ford, editors. Cloth.

Eighty-seventh Yearbook (1988)
Part 1. *Critical Issues in Curriculum.* Laurel N. Tanner, editor. Cloth.
Part 2. *Cultural Literacy and the Idea of General Education.* Ian Westbury and Alan C. Purves, editors. Cloth.

Eighty-sixth Yearbook (1987)

Part 1. *The Ecology of School Renewal.* John I. Goodlad, editor. Paper.

Part 2. *Society as Educator in an Age of Transition.* Kenneth D. Benne and Steven Tozer, editors. Cloth.

Eighty-fifth Yearbook (1986)

Part 1. *Microcomputers and Education.* Jack A. Culbertson and Luvern L. Cunningham, editors. Cloth.

Part 2. *The Teaching of Writing.* Anthony R. Petrosky and David Bartholomae, editors. Paper.

Eighty-fourth Yearbook (1985)

Part 1. *Education in School and Nonschool Settings.* Mario D. Fantini and Robert Sinclair, editors. Cloth.

Part 2. *Learning and Teaching the Ways of Knowing.* Elliot Eisner, editor. Paper.

Eighty-third Yearbook (1984)

Part 1. *Becoming Readers in a Complex Society.* Alan C. Purves and Olive S. Niles, editors. Cloth.

Part 2. *The Humanities in Precollegiate Education.* Benjamin Ladner, editor. Paper.

Eighty-second Yearbook (1983)

Part 1. *Individual Differences and the Common Curriculum.* Gary D Fenstermacher and John I. Goodlad, editors. Paper.

Eighty-first Yearbook (1982)

Part 1. *Policy Making in Education.* Ann Lieberman and Milbrey W. McLaughlin, editors. Cloth.

Part 2. *Education and Work.* Harry F. Silberman, editor. Cloth.

Eightieth Yearbook (1981)

Part 1. *Philosophy and Education.* Jonas P. Soltis, editor. Cloth.

Part 2. *The Social Studies.* Howard D. Mehlinger and O. L. Davis, Jr., editors. Cloth.

Seventy-ninth Yearbook (1980)

Part 1. *Toward Adolescence: The Middle School Years.* Mauritz Johnson, editor. Paper.

Seventy-eighth Yearbook (1979)

Part 1. *The Gifted and the Talented: Their Education and Development.* A. Harry Passow, editor. Paper.

Part 2. *Classroom Management.* Daniel L. Duke, editor. Paper.

The above titles in the Society's Yearbook series may be ordered from the University of Chicago Press, Book Order Department, 11030 Langley Ave., Chicago, IL 60628. For a list of earlier titles in the yearbook series still available, write to the Secretary, NSSE, 5835 Kimbark Ave., Chicago, IL 60637.

2. The Series on Contemporary Educational Issues

This series is to be discontinued after 1995.

The following previous volumes in the series may be ordered from the McCutchan Publishing Corporation, P.O. Box 774, Berkeley, CA 94702-0774. Phone: 510-841-8616; Fax: 510-841-7787.

Academic Work and Educational Excellence: Raising Student Productivity (1986). Edited by Tommy M. Tomlinson and Herbert J. Walberg.

Adapting Instruction to Student Differences (1985). Edited by Margaret C. Wang and Herbert J. Walberg.

Choice in Education (1990). Edited by William Lowe Boyd and Herbert J. Walberg.

Colleges of Education: Perspectives on Their Future (1985). Edited by Charles W. Case and William A. Matthes.

Contributing to Educational Change: Perspectives on Research and Practice (1988). Edited by Philip W. Jackson.

Educational Leadership and School Culture (1993). Edited by Marshall Sashkin and Herbert J. Walberg.

Effective School Leadership: Policy and Prospects (1987). Edited by John J. Lane and Herbert J. Walberg.

Effective Teaching: Current Research (1991). Edited by Hersholt C. Waxman and Herbert J. Walberg.

Improving Educational Standards and Productivity: The Research Basis for Policy (1982). Edited by Herbert J. Walberg.

Moral Development and Character Education (1989). Edited by Larry P. Nucci.

Motivating Students to Learn: Overcoming Barriers to High Achievement (1993). Edited by Tommy M. Tomlinson.

Radical Proposals for Educational Change (1994). Edited by Chester E. Finn, Jr. and Herbert J. Walberg.

Reaching Marginal Students: A Prime Concern for School Renewal (1987). Edited by Robert L. Sinclair and Ward Ghory.

Research on Teaching: Concepts, Findings, and Implications (1979). Edited by Penelope L. Peterson and Herbert J. Walberg.

Restructuring the Schools: Problems and Prospects (1992). Edited by John J. Lane and Edgar G. Epps.

Rethinking Policy for At-risk Students (1994). Edited by Kenneth K. Wong and Margaret C. Wang.

School Boards: Changing Local Control (1992). Edited by Patricia F. First and Herbert J. Walberg.

The two final volumes in this series are:

Improving Science Education (1995). Edited by Barry J. Fraser and Herbert J. Walberg.

Ferment in Education: A Look Abroad (1995). Edited by John J. Lane.

These two volumes may be ordered from the Book Order Department, University of Chicago Press, 11030 S. Langley Ave., Chicago, IL 60628. Phone: 312-669-2215; Fax: 312-660-2235.